Red State

Number Forty-Two
Jack and Doris Smothers Series in Texas History, Life, and Culture

Red State

An Insider's Story of How the GOP
Came to Dominate Texas Politics

WAYNE THORBURN

To Bill Phelps,
With gratitude for
all your efforts

Best Wishes,

University of Texas Press ◆ *Austin*

Publication of this work was made possible in part by support from the J. E. Smothers, Sr., Memorial Foundation and the National Endowment for the Humanities.

Library of Congress Cataloging-in-Publication Data
Thorburn, Wayne J. (Wayne Jacob), 1944–
    Red state : an insider's story of how the GOP came to dominate Texas politics / Wayne Thorburn. — First edition.
        pages   cm. — (Jack and Doris Smothers series in Texas history, life, and culture ; Number Forty-Two)
    Includes bibliographical references and index.
    ISBN 978-0-292-75920-6 (cloth : alk. paper)
    1. Texas—Politics and government—1951–   2. Republican Party (Tex.)—History.
3. Democratic Party (Tex.)—History.   4. Political parties—Texas—History.
5. Party affiliation—Texas—History.   6. Political culture—Texas.   I. Title.
    JK4816.T56   2014
    324.09764′09045—dc23   2013046760

doi:10.7560/759206

Contents

Preface and Acknowledgments

On the morning of Wednesday, November 9, 1960, Democrats across Texas woke up, and all was well. Their party had wrested back the White House, occupied by the opposition for the last eight years, and the new vice president of the United States was one of their own. Texas had returned to its traditional roots, and the state had been carried by the Democratic presidential candidate once again, albeit in a too-close election. Beyond that one contest, there was little concern. All thirty statewide elective positions, from governor to court of criminal appeals, were in the hands of Democrats. The same picture would be drawn in the Texas legislature: 181 Democrats and no Republicans or anyone else. One lone Republican would sit, however, among the twenty-four Members of Congress representing Texas. Clearly, after a little aberration in the Eisenhower elections, Texas was once again a one-party Democratic state.

Fast-forward fifty years to November 3, 2010, once again the day after an election, and the picture is dramatically different. There was again a Democrat in the White House, but he had achieved election without the support of Texas, a state that had not voted for a Democratic presidential candidate in thirty-four years. Moreover, every statewide elective office was now held by Republicans; no Democratic candidate had won a single statewide position in sixteen years. Representing Texas in Washington was a congressional delegation of twenty-five Republicans and nine Democrats. Republicans controlled the Texas Senate by a margin of nineteen to twelve and had elected ninety-nine of their party to the 150-seat Texas House of Representatives, a number soon to be enhanced by the switch of three Democratic state representatives to the GOP. What had been for more than a century a one-party Democratic state was now clearly a predominantly Republican state.

How did this transformation of Texas politics take place, and what do the recent changes imply for the future? That is the story to be told on the following pages, beginning with a brief overview and background information on Texas itself, followed by a description of the four categories of counties in the state. Attention is then drawn to the extent of political competition in Texas during the 112 years of statehood prior to the election of 1960. It's a story of various factions and forces attempting to compete as a political party against the dominant Democratic Party, with only sporadic and localized success. More recently, however, it is also the story of conflict among ideological groupings within the dominant party, conflict that provided a modicum of choice for Texas voters and that ultimately facilitated the development of a viable alternative political party.

From the end of the Reconstruction era in Texas and the return of the ex-Confederates to the electorate in 1873 until the 1960s, Texas political competition took place within a one-party system. As was true in other states of the Confederacy, that one political force was the Democratic Party. With few exceptions in isolated parts of the state, especially the German-settled Hill Country, Democrats won all elections for public office, Republican candidates rarely appeared, and the actual selection of public officials took place in the Democratic primary.

The first movement away from a one-party system began to appear with the emergence of presidential Republicans, individuals whose opposition to many policies of the New Deal and the national Democratic Party led them to support a Republican candidate for president. At the same time, these individuals continued to view themselves as Democrats and continued to vote in the Democratic primary. By the 1960s and 1970s, cracks were beginning to appear in the Democratic dominance of the state's politics, first with the election of John Tower to the United States Senate in 1961 and then several years later the election of Bill Clements as governor. Competition developed first in the state's major urban areas, for top-of-the-ticket candidates. As these metropolitan areas expanded geographically, a Republican base began to develop in their suburban counties. At the same time, competition spread to the smaller, outlying metropolitan statistical areas where race, ethnicity, economic base, and extent of union membership had an impact on the degree of competition that developed. It would be much later before partisan change would occur in many of the state's rural counties.

By the 1980s Texas had entered into a brief period of true two-party competition, with both major parties able to elect a number of candidates, fewer contests that were settled in the party primary, and growing competition expanding to down-ballot candidates. During the period from 1978 to 1998 the office of governor alternated between the two parties every four years, and for most of this period the state was represented by one Democrat and one Republican in the United States Senate. Beginning with the election of 1996, however, the Republican Party has won every statewide election, eventually acquiring a majority in both chambers of the Texas legislature as well as the congressional delegation. As the twenty-first century began, Texas appeared to have entered a period of one-party politics once again, albeit not to the overwhelming extent of Democratic domination in the previous era.

As the geographical spread of party competition was taking place, so too was it moving down the ballot, limited at first by the visibility of the office. Thus, party competition first took hold in federal elections, followed by gubernatorial elections and then those for the state legislature, bypassing the lower-profile statewide executive and judicial offices. For the individual Texan, changes in voting behavior preceded changes in party identification, which, in turn, preceded changes in primary election participation. Yet, to a large extent, individual conversions have been less significant than the inclusion of new voters in the electorate, comprising both new residents and younger voters. In the following pages, the changes in party competition will be viewed using a number of measures, including perceived party identification, actual affiliation with a political party by participating in its primary, the performance of candidates for statewide elective offices, representation in the U.S. House of Representatives and the state legislature, elections for county offices, and the extent and nature of straight-ticket voting.

Without question, this fifty-year period witnessed a phenomenal change in Texas population numbers, composition, and location. The state has undergone a transition from a predominantly rural to an overwhelmingly urban society, witnessed the influx of new residents from other states and nations, and experienced the diversification of its economy. The economic base of the state has broadened to include new industries not even known fifty years ago, from semiconductors to biomedical research. As the state has changed, so too has the electorate, and these changes opened up the opportunity for alternative political forces to develop. Eventually, the longstanding practice of contesting ideological positions and elections within one single political party seemed a less viable path to follow.

This book focuses on the period from 1960 to 2010, but the story of the transformation of Texas politics will continue into the future as Texas meets the challenges of the twenty-first century. The Texas of 1960 is not the Texas of 2014, nor is it the Texas in which our children and grandchildren will make their lives. As the state and society change, so too will our political parties and the choices they provide to Texas citizens. To predict where we are going is much more difficult than to describe where we have been. At the same time, understanding the past is an important component to being prepared for the future. In this spirit, the pages that follow describe the political changes in Texas politics since 1960, closing with some predictions regarding changes still to come. My hope is that this work will in some way contribute to an understanding of the significant modifications in party competition that have taken place in Texas in the past fifty years.

Acknowledgments

In attempting to present an overview of the changes and continuities that have occurred in political competition since 1960, I am indebted to the efforts of many previous authors and researchers on various aspects of Texas political history. Too many to mention here, their publications have been cited in the endnotes. Without these contributions, and those of the authors of several unpublished works, the current manuscript would not have been possible.

Additionally helpful to my research were the archival materials at the Dolph Briscoe Center for American History, the University of Texas at Austin; the Lorenzo de Zavala State Archives and Library, Austin; the Perry-Castañeda Library, the University of Texas at Austin; Southwestern University Special Collections, Georgetown, Texas; and the University of Texas at San Antonio Libraries Special Collections. My thanks go to the archivists and staff at these valuable collections of historical records.

Many individuals have contributed suggestions for this work, and I am especially grateful for those who read and critiqued parts or all of the manuscript: Ernest Angelo Jr., Paul Burka, David O'Donald Cullen, Gregory Davidson, John Knaggs, Steven Munisteri, and Peck Young. While their recommendations have improved this manuscript immeasurably, the final product and the conclusions herein are solely mine.

This work would not have been possible without the interest and support of Casey Kittrell, my acquisitions editor; Theresa J. May, editor-in-chief; and the entire staff at the University of Texas Press. Working with them has been a most pleasant experience. In the end, however, my greatest appreciation is given to Judith Abramov Thorburn, my proofreader extraordinaire, computer expert, best friend, and wife. Without her support, I could not have completed this effort.

A Note on Sources

In the following tables and text, population totals and characteristics are from the U.S. Census Bureau unless otherwise indicated. Estimates for the 1960 Hispanic population are from Alice Eichholz, ed., *Red Book: American State, County, and Town Sources* (Provo, UT: Ancestry, 2004).

Election-related data comes from a variety of sources. Voter registration totals are from *Texas Almanac, 1961–1962* (Dallas: A. H. Belo Company, 1961) for 1960; *Texas Almanac, 1992–93* (Dallas: Dallas Morning News, 1991) for 1990; and from the Elections Division of the Texas Secretary of State for 2010.

County-level returns for presidential (1848–1988), U.S. senatorial (1912–1990), and gubernatorial (1845–1990) elections can be found in Mike Kingston, Sam Attlesey, and Mary G. Crawford, eds., *The Texas Almanac's Political History of Texas* (Austin: Eakin Press, 1992). Election returns for these offices from 1992 to the present were obtained from the Elections Division of the Texas Secretary of State.

The partisan affiliation of members of the Texas legislature was obtained from the Legislative Reference Library of Texas. Information on the partisan affiliation of county elective officials is not readily available. While the *Texas State Directory* (Austin: Texas State Directory, various years) has been published since 1935 as a reference guide and currently lists the party affiliation of most state elective officials, it does not indicate party for county officeholders. A number of documents prepared by the Republican Party of Texas and in author's possession list the names of Republican county elected officials for various years. Data on party affiliation for county judges, commissioners, and sheriffs as of 2013 was obtained by the author directly from county sources.

While some earlier Republican primary data is available from the Texas

State Archives, returns for several years were among the author's personal papers or were included in the John G. Tower Papers. Both Republican and Democratic primary returns for state offices beginning with 1992 can be found at the Elections Division of the Texas Secretary of State. Democratic primary data for selected offices from 1908 to 1990 is included in Kingston, Attlesey, and Crawford, eds., *The Texas Almanac's Political History of Texas*.

Public opinion survey data on party identification was obtained from several sources, including the John G. Tower Papers, the *Texas Poll Report*, and the author's personal files.

Some of the data on straight-ticket voting for 1988 to 2010 is available in "Studies of Political Statistics: Straight Ticket Voting in Texas, 1998–2012," Report no. 8, Center for Public Policy and Political Studies, Austin Community College, Austin, Texas, December 2012. This data was augmented by information collected by the author directly from the 112 counties surveyed.

Red State

CHAPTER 1

Understanding Texas

In order to better understand the politics of Texas it is helpful to start with an overview of the state—by outlining what Texas is today, what makes it the state that it is, and how Texas is different from the other forty-nine states. To do this one can look back to an observation originally made more than sixty years ago by a political scientist who was a native Texan. In many ways, this one brief quote still sums up much of what Texas is all about: "The Lone Star State is concerned about money and how to make it, about oil and sulphur and gas, about cattle and dust storms and irrigation, about cotton and banking and Mexicans."[1]

Much has changed in Texas since these words were written but much also remains the same. In any attempt to describe Texas today one would add several elements to the list, including technology and entertainment, air travel, and international trade. Nevertheless, the concerns cited over a half-century ago remain essential elements of present-day Texas. Thus, while it is important to look at the changes that have occurred in Texas, one cannot overlook those elements that have long been present and constitute the essence of the Lone Star State.

Pride and Patriotism

To understand Texas today one must begin with its uniqueness. During its history Texas has been under six different sovereign governments: Spain, France, and Mexico all ruled this area prior to the Texans' successful battle for independence in 1836. Nine years later, Texas became part of the United States of America, but then seceded and joined the Confederate States of America in 1861.[2]

Texas won its independence from Mexico in 1836 and existed as an independent nation, the Republic of Texas, for the next nine years. It is the only nation to petition to join the United States of America, freely give up its sovereignty, and be admitted as a state of the Union. The uniqueness of this situation was evident in the congressional action admitting Texas as a state. Congress provided that Texas could subsequently divide into five states. As the Joint Congressional Resolution of 1845 stated, "New States of convenient size, not exceeding four in number, in addition to the said State of Texas, and having sufficient population, may hereafter, by consent of said State, be formed out of the territory thereof, which shall be entitled to admission under the provisions of the Federal Constitution."[3]

While some in Texas periodically talk of dividing the area into five separate states, especially when they are at odds with the federal government, the actual likelihood is less than that of a ten-inch snowfall in June in the Rio Grande Valley. Weighing against any such effort is the fact that Texans have less regional than state loyalty; people think of themselves first and foremost as Texans. Any effort to subdivide the state today would be greeted with little enthusiasm and a feared loss of common identity.[4]

Perhaps it is from the uniqueness of Texas history that its people have developed a pride and patriotism unsurpassed by any other state. An individual's identity as a Texan is much more fully incorporated within his or her self-awareness than any similar identification for the residents of other states. "Proud to be a Texan" has an acceptance and a legitimacy not normally granted to other states: "Proud to be a North Dakotan" or "Proud to be New Jerseyan." Likewise, "Don't Mess with Texas" hits home more than "Keep New York Clean" could ever convey. As *New York Times* columnist Gail Collins noted, "I come from Ohio, a fine state which once prided itself on being an incubator of presidents. . . . We certainly didn't pledge allegiance to the Ohio flag—Ohio didn't have a flag back then, and we wouldn't have recognized the state flag if you'd dropped it on our heads. And try envisioning a bunch of Cincinnatians or Clevelanders running around in 'Don't Mess with Ohio' sweatshirts."[5]

While many concerned about the impact of illegal immigration have supported building a wall along the Rio Grande, only in Texas would someone even humorously propose building "the Great Wall of Texas" to force out what was described as "the riffraff." Several years before the discussion of building a wall along the southern border, Kenny Bob Parsons solicited financial support for his announced goal of building a brick wall some forty feet high and forty feet wide along all 3,816 miles of the state's border. As Parsons lamented, "Our forefathers fought hardily, risking life and limb to protect and preserve from the exploitationists, this Edenesque land we call Texas . . . we have banded together for the purpose of constructing a wall around the Great Republic of Texas." Parsons estimated at the time that it would take 9 million bricks just to build one mile of the wall. His plans were to start on the Texas-Oklahoma border, claiming that "we may have been worrying about the wrong border all these years."[6]

Infusing all these manifestations of pride is a sense that life can be better in Texas if one applies oneself and takes charge of one's own destiny. As one writer concluded, "If there's a theme to life in Texas, it's hope. When Stephen F. Austin brought his settlers to this then-Mexican territory, he was selling hope—hope for a new start in a new land." The writer went on to add, "In a way, being Texan is like being a Marine, or a Rockefeller, or a Harvard graduate. The name evokes something both visceral and subliminal, a whole construct of images and ideas, myths and realities."[7]

Whether native born or "born again," millions of Texans take great pride in their state and closely identify with Texas. To them, Texas means much more than a state or a geographical area, more than merely an artificial political unit in which they live. Texas is much more closely bound up in its residents' self-identification; it is a part of who they are. As one familiar advertising campaign by the Texas travel bureau proclaims, "It's like a whole other country."[8]

Political Culture

While the term "political culture" is a concept that was first employed by political scientists in the comparative study of nations, it can also be used to discuss the underlying attitudes, beliefs, assumptions, and expectations held by individuals within one country or state. In this way, to describe the political culture of an area is to describe how people view politics, what they expect from government, whether they become active in deciding government policies, and the way government and politics are carried out.

When viewing different countries, one can recognize distinctive views of government and politics. To the south, in Mexico, the "mordida," or bribe, was for long an accepted common practice for dealing with the police, and while several political parties competed in elections, for seventy-one years in the twentieth century only one party won the presidency. To the north, in Canada, it is relatively common and accepted that one's national legislator (Member of Parliament) not live in or come from the district he or she represents and that federal taxation is expected to pay 100 percent of every citizen's medical bills.[9]

Just as there are differences across countries in the way people view politics and government, so too there are differences among the fifty states and even within a state. The most important early effort to apply the concept of political culture to measuring differences among the states was a work by Daniel Elazar published in 1966.[10] As different types of people settled in the various areas of the nation they brought with them distinctive values, perspectives, and outlooks on government, society, and life. Elazar outlined three general types of poltical culture in the United States that he labeled moralistic, individualistic, and traditionalistic. One or more of these differing outlooks was then viewed as dominant in each of the fifty states. Elazar's picture of the dominant political cultures in the United States was drawn in the middle of the twentieth century, and much has changed since that time, with the migration of individuals to other states and the increased influence of a national media and culture. Yet, there remain key differences among the fifty states that are reflective of differences in political cultures.

Elazar characterized Minnesota as having a moralistic political culture. In this political culture, most people have a positive view of government as a force for good in society with a responsibility for promoting the general welfare. Citizens have a duty and obligation to participate in government and issues are hotly debated. Government should be strong and active, government service is viewed as a moral duty, and there is little acceptance of any form of corruption. Perhaps the various Garrison Keillor stories from public radio's *Prairie Home Companion* reinforce this association in the public mind.[11]

Elazar characterized Nevada, home to legalized prostitution and hundreds of casinos, as a state where the individualistic political culture has been dominant. Politics is viewed as just another business, neither inherently good nor bad, and government exists merely to provide what people want and demand, not to promote some elusive "common good." Getting involved in government is done to give out favors and rewards to one's supporters. Corruption is simply a cost of government and can never be eliminated. The range of government activities and involvement should be limited so that individual citizens can exercise more freedom in how they live their lives.

Finally, Elazar cited Arkansas as an example of the traditionalistic political culture. Government is designed to preserve and maintain the status quo and the existing social order. Few voters participate in politics, and a small group of decision makers runs government. Social and family ties (personality politics) are important in selecting government officials, and one political party wins virtually all elections. In sum, politics is in the hands of a small elite who wish to keep things as they are.

Elazar viewed Texas as having significant numbers of people who hold to both the individualistic and traditionalistic political cultures. As in other states, these general beliefs about government can be seen in the types of people who settled in Texas and the attitudes they brought with them.

Many of the attitudes associated with the traditionalistic political culture, with its emphasis on family, culture, and religion, were initially brought to Texas by the Spanish and Mexican settlers. Over time, the distinct and different language added to the traditionalistic political culture. Just as important, however, was the contribution of Anglo settlers, who brought with them what can be called the "culture of the Old South." This influence has been felt most especially in East Texas; new settlers brought with them a cotton economy based on slavery and an emphasis on Southern agrarian values.

When the Civil War broke out, Texas quickly went with the other Southern states into the Confederate States of America, although some of its most prominent leaders, including Governor Sam Houston, were opposed to secession. Ever since its admission as a state up to the present, much of Texas has identified itself with the South—politically, culturally, religiously, and socially. Thus, while slavery was abolished, discrimination against Blacks continued through most of the twentieth century and took many of the same forms as in other Southern states. This included segregation in housing, schools, and public facilities as well as a poll tax and "white primary" to minimize Black influence on public policy.

Reflective of the traditionalist culture is the importance of religion in the lives of many Texans as well as the nature of the most dominant religious traditions. According to an in-depth study of religious membership compiled by the Roper Center for Public Opinion Research, the various Baptist groups in Texas had a combined membership of 4.5 million in 2000, the overwhelming percentage of whom were affiliated with the Southern Baptist Convention. Closely following Baptists were members of the Roman Catholic faith, another religious influence emphasizing traditionalist values (table 1.1).

Of the so-called Mainline Protestant denominations, only three had more than 100,000 members (Lutheran, 301,518; Presbyterian, 204,804; Episcopal, 177,910), and together they had fewer adherents than the vari-

Table 1.1. Predominant religious groups in Texas, 2000

Denomination	Adherents	Percentage of population
Baptist (various groups)	4,537,918	21.8
Roman Catholic	4,368,969	21.0
Methodist (various groups)	1,219,533	5.9
Pentecostal/charismatic	763,070	3.7
Churches of Christ	377,264	1.8

Source: Data from Texas Almanac, 2004-2005, 525-528.

ous pentecostal and charismatic churches. More liberal Protestant denominations, such as the United Church of Christ, American Baptist Churches in the U.S.A., and the Unitarian-Universalist Association, had much fewer members in Texas.[12]

Presently Texas is home to more Southern Baptists than any other state and today more Texans call themselves Baptist than any other religious identification. Testimony to the importance of the Southern heritage can be seen most clearly in the name of this denomination, which still calls itself "Southern" nearly 150 years after the Civil War division occurred among Baptists and long after its churches spread to all fifty states. While it is no longer geographically Southern in its membership, it is still very much culturally Southern in its attitudes and modes of worship.

As in the remainder of the "solid South," once the period of Reconstruction was over, throughout the latter part of the nineteenth century and the first half of the twentieth century, the Democratic Party was totally dominant in Texas. Until very recently, Democrats remained the stronger party locally in the rural areas of the state, where the traditionalist political culture remains the dominant outlook. It is from this culture of the Old South that Texans obtain much of their emphasis on tradition ("That's how we do things here," "If it ain't broke, don't fix it!"), community (a greater concern with upholding community standards than with individual rights), and family (the importance of the extended family as well as "old family" names and reputations).

Much has changed over the last fifty years, but perhaps the clearest example of the influence of this culture can be found in small-town Texas. In Texas small towns, most of one's relatives still live in the town; and Sunday is spent going to the First Baptist Church in the morning, having fried chicken dinner at Wyatt's Cafeteria after church, and visiting at a relative's home in the afternoon. In this environment, nearly everyone was a Democrat when he or she voted and nearly all the local officeholders were Democrats of the conservative variety. On his 1984 television series *A Walk through the Twentieth Century*, Bill Moyers went back to his hometown of Marshall, Texas, a city he described as having "more Baptists than people." In Marshall, according to Moyers, one always felt "the powerful presence of the past." As one high school friend who moved away also put it, in Marshall one had a sense of belonging: "They knew when you were sick and cared when you died." The downside to life in small-town East Texas was that most who remained were locked into a certain role in town and lived in a tightly structured community. The limits were even greater for those who were not Anglo.[13]

While Texas has become much more urban and millions of residents have moved away from their rural roots, the views and attitudes dominant in these communities have often gone with these Texans to the larger cities and suburbs. Thus, it would be wrong to view the culture of the Old South as being present only in small-town Texas. Indeed, it can be found in the attitudes of some Texans in all areas of the state.

The Mexican cultural influence also made a major contribution to this traditionalist political culture. Especially in South Texas, this influence supported many of the same values and attitudes toward society, family, and traditions handed down from one generation to the next. While the East Texas Southern influence and the South Texas Mexican influence were quite different, they both resulted in a traditionalistic outlook on politics and the role of government in society.[14]

Yet another distinct trait has also been present in Texas. For thousands of people seeking a new start in life, Texas has been viewed as the frontier—a place waiting to be settled, where new beginnings could occur. The frontier was both an outlook on life and a reality. In the nineteenth century, those who settled in much of Texas battled nature, Indian tribes, and each other. This was a very different way of life from that of East Texas, where tradition, community, and family were valued above all else. Life on the frontier in the nineteenth century often meant life alone, without family, where no real community existed for miles, and with no traditional ways of dealing with many everyday problems.

To survive and succeed on the real frontier of Texas meant emphasizing different values from those dominant in the more settled areas of the state. Survival on the frontier placed a great emphasis on self-reliance (living alone on the frontier meant one needed to solve one's own problems), individualism (one is responsible for one's own fate because life is what you make of it), and innovation and experimentation (with few resources at hand, one must try new ways of doing things and make do with what is available). Living on the frontier depended almost totally on the individual's own efforts. There was little order and little social fabric holding individuals together. Judge Roy Bean may well have been the only "Law west of the Pecos," as most disputes were settled in one fashion or another among individuals. In such an environment it is natural that the values of the individualist political culture would become dominant. The individual was truly responsible for his or her own fate and, left alone, would succeed or fail depending on his or her own efforts.

This individualist trait can also be seen in Texas religious movements. The emphasis on personal commitment and decision, the existence of hundreds if not thousands of independent Baptist and nondenominational churches, the loosely structured and nonhierarchical alliances such as those among the Churches of Christ—all exemplify the individualistic spirit. Perhaps no one institution typifies this individualistic and entrepreneurial approach to religion better than the Lakewood Church in Houston, led by Joel and Victoria Osteen, whose four English and two Spanish services in 2011 averaged more than forty-three thousand attendees per week.

The frontier is a geographical description that was especially important in the nineteenth century as more and more people moved west, claimed and cleared land, settled, and started a new life. Some were immigrants from other lands—Germany, Czechoslovakia, Mexico—but most were from other parts of the United States. The bulk of the mass migration of Europeans to the United States in the late nineteenth and early twentieth centuries never made it to Texas. Immigration from other U.S. states had a greater impact on Texas.

As economic hardships hit the farmers of mid-nineteenth-century America, especially throughout the Midwest, more and more posted a sign on their front door that simply said "G.T.T."—gone to Texas, a phenomenon so widespread that everyone knew what these three letters meant. One fascinating instance of the frontier concept at work was the "Orphan Train" movement, which brought children from New York and other Eastern cities to small towns in the Midwest and Southwest, at least four thousand of whom landed in Texas between 1854 and 1929. The westward trains brought orphans to Texas towns, "a place where children without families might find welcome homes": "The arrival of an orphan train into a small rural community often caused quite a commotion. A 1922 account of an orphan line-up in the North Texas town of Commerce noted the children attracted a crowd of 'interested spectators and others whose hearts were hungering and thirsting for the patter of children's feet in the home, or whose Samaritan spirit prompted them to noble deeds.'"[15]

The frontier refers to more than mere geography; for millions of people it has meant an attitude, an outlook on life expressing the belief that you can begin again (you can make a fresh start in life and forget the failures of the past), you can succeed through hard work (what you become depends on your own efforts), and there is opportunity to succeed when you are not limited by old barriers and traditions.

The concept of the frontier, with its emphasis on self-reliance, individualism, innovation, and experimentation, continued to draw millions to Texas even after the geographical frontier had begun to close. Today it continues as a major draw for people from other nations as well as other states, who move to Texas in search of a "new start" in life. To some proponents of the frontier concept, the old barriers that constrained them were viewed not as traditions in some settled community but, rather, the federal government. One Texas business leader in the late twentieth century saw the role of the national government as being to "deliver the mails, defend the shores, and leave me alone!"[16]

It is from this frontier concept that a belief in individual success—a faith in one's own abilities—took hold and promoted a spirit of entrepreneurship among many Texans. As one recent writer on Southern politics has noted, "The new wildcatters are entrepreneurs in the personal computer, telecommunications, and real estate business who have risk taking in their blood. They collectively echo the same values as the petroleum mavericks, but they wear suits instead of Stetsons and boots. The political culture is a product of the spirit of the oilfield, the ranch, and the Alamo."[17]

In 1962, a young salesman for IBM decided that it would be easier and more profitable to be selling computer services rather than computers to his customers. He went off and borrowed $1,000 to start his own company. He called it Electronic Data Services, and some twenty-five years later he sold it to General Motors for more than $2 billion. When he determined that the country was heading in the wrong direction, he decided to run for president and spent a considerable sum of that money on unsuccessful campaigns in 1992 and 1996. H. Ross Perot believed that he could succeed if left on his own to experiment and innovate, and so he did. Today he is one of the wealthiest men in America.[18]

Describing Texas at mid-twentieth century, the writer John Bainbridge declared it "the frontier of America—the land of the second chance, the last outpost of individuality."[19] While the neighboring state to the northeast may call itself the "Land of Opportunity," to most people in the United States and throughout the world it is Texas that is truly associated with that slogan. The frontier concept remains alive as myth and reality in the twenty-first century and still impacts not only those born in the state but also those millions who have migrated to Texas from other states and countries.

To understand Texas today it is necessary to realize the importance of the frontier. Just as many Texans still hold to values and outlooks that can be traced back to the culture of the Old South or the traditional values of Mexican culture, so too many other Texans shape their attitudes within the framework of the frontier concept and its values. These outlooks can be seen as the major sources for what Elazar labeled the traditionalistic and individualistic political cultures, the two dominant influences in Texas.

The Place

An essential element of understanding Texas is recognition of the vast space occupied by this one state. While much of Texas in the nineteenth century was the frontier, an area of wide open space and sparse settlement, even today, with more than 25 million Texans, the state still has a lot of unsettled territory. Texas is second only to Alaska in land space and second only to California in total population. Within its boundaries Texas could fit twelve of the thirteen original colonies. In fact, Brewster County alone is larger than the combined states of Connecticut, Rhode Island, and Delaware.

Traveling north to south, it is almost eight hundred miles from the tip of the Texas Panhandle to Brownsville in far South Texas. Changes in topography and climate are evident from the feedlots and grain harvests of West Texas to the citrus groves and truck farms of the lower Rio Grande Valley. It is not a rare winter weather report that shows snow in Pampa and eighty degrees with sunshine in Pharr. East to west some 770 miles stretch from Texarkana to El Paso, a distance greater than that from Boston to Washington, DC, or from New York City to Chicago. Texarkana is closer to Chicago in the cold northern Midwest than it is to El Paso, a city in the Mountain Time Zone slightly west of Denver.

Across the long expanse from Odessa west to El Paso, life can be desolate and lonely. As of the 2010 census only eighty-two people lived in

Loving County, the least populated of the state's 254 counties, and the last to be formed, in 1923.[20] Not too long ago a fire gutted what was then the only grocery store in Dell City, population 365, in nearby Hudspeth County. This tragedy forced residents to drive at least sixty miles to buy foodstuffs. As one young mother complained, "We're going to need a store, for sure, because with kids you run out of milk and bread and stuff. And ice. You can't go to El Paso for ice."[21]

The sparsely populated communities of rural Texas, many of which continue to lose population, naturally have small school districts whose pupils travel many miles each day. Those high schools with fewer than one hundred students are eligible to compete in a little-known sport: six-man football. Nearly all the six-man schools are west of Interstate Highway 35 and include some two hundred public and private institutions. The existence of the sport ensures a continuation of the "Friday Night Football" tradition in even the smaller towns that continue to dot rural Texas.[22]

Prior to the end of World War II, more than half of the population of Texas resided in rural areas. Since then, the movement to metropolitan areas has continued at an ever-increasing rate. By the time of the 2010 census, only 12.2 percent of the state's 25,145,561 residents lived in rural areas and Texas had become one of the most heavily urbanized states in the nation. Over the first decade of the twenty-first century, 79 of the state's 254 counties lost population. In 1960 only three counties had a population of fewer than 1,000 residents; by 2010 there were eight. Fourteen counties in 1960 had fewer than 2,500 residents; that number had increased to twenty-four by the 2010 census.

There is another side to the story, however. While not a high percentage of the total population, millions of Texans do live in rural communities throughout the state, especially in West Texas and the Panhandle. With a statewide total of more than 25 million residents, there are 3,060,392 people living in rural Texas. This rural population constitutes more than the total population of twenty-one other states, including Arkansas, Iowa, Nevada, New Mexico, and Utah.

Texas is obviously more than its rural areas, and in a state as vast as it is, there are many different ways of describing it geographically. In his classic work *Imperial Texas*, D. W. Meinig divided the state into nine cultural areas.[23] Most geologists follow the pattern of Elmer H. Johnson, who in his *The Natural Regions of Texas* divided the state into four regions.[24] Texas tourist officials describe the state by focusing on seven regions.[25] To simplify matters, seven general and loosely defined geographical areas will be used to describe some of the different components of the state.

East Texas is an area of small towns, large forests, and timber production, as well as some areas of substantial oil production. The region has one of the lowest per capita incomes in the state, with a sizable portion of its residents living on federal assistance of one kind or another. This area typifies the culture of the Old South more than any other part of Texas. In addition to the influence of those whose ancestors moved from other Southern states, the French Creole population of neighboring Louisiana has impacted areas in the southern part of East Texas. In the past, East Texas also had a substantial African American population, with some of its counties being over 40 percent Black. Over the past fifty years many of these individuals have moved to the major metropolitan areas, especially Dallas. Today, the population of only one East Texas county is more than 25 percent African American, while Blacks comprise 22 percent of Dallas County.[26]

The people of East Texas have generally been conservative in their social, religious, and political attitudes. At the same time, East Texas has been an area of relatively strong Populist support and even stronger Democratic Party identification. The major cities of East Texas are Texarkana, on the border of Arkansas, and the cities of Longview and Tyler. These last two cities are unlike the rest of the region in that their economy is more focused on oil and they both trended Republican in their voting behavior well before those changes took place in other parts of East Texas.

The Gulf Coast ranges from Orange and Beaumont in the northeast, close to Louisiana, over through Houston and Galveston and down to Corpus Christi in the south. The diverse areas of this region are linked by proximity to the Gulf of Mexico. The area has seen a sizable influx of newcomers from other states and counties. The 1980 movie *Urban Cowboy*, with John Travolta and Debra Winger, portrayed rural Texans moving to this area for better-paying jobs in the petrochemical industry. In the late 1970s and 1980s, Vietnamese immigrants resettled in coastal communities of this region. Many New Orleans residents fled the devastating impact of Hurricane Katrina in 2005 by relocating to the Texas Gulf Coast and then decided to remain in Texas.

According to the 2010 census, Jefferson County (Beaumont) has the highest percentage of African American residents (34%) in the state. Harris County (Houston) is majority-minority, with a population that is 41 percent Hispanic and 18 percent African American. Some smaller counties outside Houston, including Walker and Waller, have populations that are more than 20 percent Black. Suburban Fort Bend County has the highest percentage of Asian Americans, who constitute roughly 17 percent of its population.[27]

The economy of this region is based on petrochemicals, oil, insurance, shipping, and health care. It is an area of relatively strong unionization, especially in the Golden Triangle area of Beaumont, Port Arthur, and Orange. Politically, the region has been mixed; Republicans have been stronger in Houston and its suburbs, while Democrats have been more dominant in the Golden Triangle and, until recently, in Galveston and Corpus Christi.

North Texas describes an area along the Oklahoma border from Wichita Falls in the west to Sherman and Denison in the east down to the Dallas–Fort Worth (DFW) metropolitan area. Banking, finance, transportation, and commerce are the mainstays of the North Texas economy. Dallas has become the wholesale distribution center for much of the Southwest. For many retailers, going "to market" means going to the Dallas Market Center, with its showrooms of goods available from wholesalers.

The Dallas–Fort Worth metropolitan area was one of the first to experience the growth of the Republican Party in the late twentieth century, although most recently Democratic candidates have made a major comeback in Dallas County. Some cities in the region, such as Wichita Falls, Sherman, and Denison, have sizable populations of residents over sixty-five years of age, while the suburbs north of Dallas and Fort Worth have seen phenomenal growth over the last fifty years. The Dallas–Fort Worth area is home to DFW airport, the Dallas Cowboys, and the Texas Rangers; transportation and entertainment are important contributors to the economy of the region.

Although the area is predominantly Anglo, ethnic change has been occurring in both Dallas and Fort Worth, with Dallas County's population now 38 percent Hispanic and 22 percent African American, while Tarrant County comprises 27 percent Hispanic and 15 percent Black residents. Suburban Collin County is home to a sizable Asian community, which constitutes 11 percent of its population.

Central Texas is a region of great ethnic diversity. It has a substantial Mexican American population and a large number of African Americans. But it is also home to German, Czech, Swedish, Alsatian, and Polish communities, first settled in the nineteenth century. Education, tourism, government, agriculture, and high-tech industries contribute to the economy of Central Texas. One of the largest military installations in the world, Fort Hood, is located in this part of the state, as is the state capital and several major universities.

Traditionally Central Texas has been a Democratic stronghold with the exception of the Hill Country to the west, where Republicanism first became dominant after the Civil War. The major cities in this area are Austin, Round Rock, Waco, Temple, Bryan, and College Station.

Beginning in San Antonio and continuing down to the Mexican border is a region known as South Texas. The economy of this area is based on agriculture (especially citrus and truck farming), commerce and banking, international trade, and several large military installations. Of all seven regions, this area has the lowest per capita income.

While the Canadian border is far longer than the United States border with Mexico, of all fifty states, Texas has the longest border with a neighboring country. Having once been part of Mexico and sharing this continuous long border, the state of Texas has been closely related in many ways to the nation of Mexico. Much of the culture of Texas developed from the state's association with Mexico, whether in fine arts or in popular culture and folkways, an association that provides a continuing contribution to what Texas is today.

With its proximity to the border, it is not surprising that this area has the largest Mexican American population. Nearly all its counties have a Hispanic majority, with Hidalgo, Starr, Webb, Zapata, and Zavala being more than 90 percent Mexican American. Unlike other ethnic groups, which are typically separated by thousands of miles or by political barriers from their ancestral lands, those of Mexican descent are separated by little more than a day's car ride. Politically, South Texas has been a stronghold for the Democratic Party for several years and home to many "jefes," or political bosses. Although the Republican Party has made inroads in recent elections, with the exception of San Antonio and its suburbs, this area remains overwhelmingly Democratic.

Jutting out from the rest of Texas and protruding into Oklahoma and New Mexico is an area known from its shape as the Texas Panhandle. Many of the earliest settlers of this area came from the states of Kansas, Iowa, Nebraska, and the Dakotas; the region still has a strong midwestern flavor. Agriculture (especially wheat and cotton), cattle, and oil are the major contributors to the economy of the Panhandle region. Here can be found some of the largest feedlots in the nation. The population is heavily Anglo but with a sizable Mexican American contribution.

Partly due to its midwestern heritage and partly due to the influence of the oil industry, the Panhandle has traditionally been an area of relative strength for the Republican Party—one of the first areas in which it made inroads in the late twentieth century. The two major cities in this area are Amarillo and Lubbock, a city whose residents often claim is not really part of the Panhandle. Lubbock serves as a major trade center for the agricultural communities around it and is also home to Texas Tech University.

Ranging all the way from Abilene in the east out to El Paso is an area often called West Texas. This region is dependent on oil, natural gas, ranching, and farming, with the additional importance of international trade and military installations in El Paso. The area's cities include El Paso, Midland, Odessa, Abilene, and San Angelo. These last four major cities are predominantly Anglo and have been much more Republican in recent elections.

Isolated from the remainder of Texas by desert, mountains, and a different time zone, El Paso is more than 80 percent Hispanic and traditionally Democratic. The existence of "maquiladoras" located just across the border from El Paso has provided thousands of better-paying jobs for Mexican citizens and lower-cost labor for American manufacturers. Most recently, violent competition among drug cartels has led many middle-class Mexicans to flee to El Paso. At the same time, the growth of a middle class in Mexico has encouraged a sizable market for retailers in Texas cities along the border and even further north.[28]

In summarizing the various regions of Texas it is important to note that, unlike the situation in several other states, there is little sectional conflict. Texas does not divide into one major city and "upstate," or one major city and "downstate," or east versus west, or mountains versus tidelands. In fact, no single city dominates, even though both Houston and Dallas may think they dominate. There is no New Orleans, Chicago, Boston, or Little Rock in Texas. Nor is there any statewide media blanketing the entire state. Texas has twenty-seven different major media markets, more than in any other state. There is no single statewide newspaper, although the *Dallas Morning News* comes closest to being one since it circulates in a wide area of the state. Finally, while Texas can be described by the characteristics dominant in each of the seven regions, for Texans the state association and identity prevails over any loyalty to city or region. Regardless of where they are from, people tend to view themselves first and last as Texans.

The People

Although originally a Spanish and then a Mexican territory, the area that became first the Republic of Texas and then a state of the United States of America has been populated by various waves of immigration from throughout the world.[29] Clearly the most important ethnic influence on Texas today is Mexican, which itself derives from Spanish and Indian cultures. Mexican culture and values trace back to the area's time as a Spanish colony and its earliest settlers. This initial influence was added to by the various movements of people escaping from the revolution in Mexico in the early years of the twentieth century, through the more recent flow of workers seeking opportunity for employment and advancement, up to the present-day efforts of middle-class Mexicans escaping the drug violence along the American border.[30]

Whether it is Tex-Mex food, mariachis, Cinco de Mayo, or bilingual ballots on election day, the influence of Mexican culture, traditions, and values has permeated the state's culture. According to the 2010 census, 37.6 percent of the Texas population consider themselves of Hispanic origin, a percentage that has grown substantially in recent decades. While a number of Cuban Americans can be found in Texas along with small numbers from other Latin American countries, the overwhelming majority of Hispanics in Texas are Mexican Americans.[31] They constitute the leading national origin group in the state. Harris County alone is home to 1,671,540 Hispanics, followed by Bexar (1,006,958), Dallas (905,940), Hidalgo (702,206), and El Paso (658,134) Counties.[32]

In certain parts of South Texas and along the border, the Mexican American influence is dominant. Some 96 percent of Webb County, home to the city of Laredo, comprises individuals who consider themselves of Hispanic origin, with similar percentages in the rural counties of Starr, Zapata, and Zavala. Numerous towns and cities are overwhelmingly Mexican American in their population, in their culture and traditions, and in the language most often used by their residents.[33] As the number of Hispanics in the major metropolitan counties of Texas indicates, this influence is felt not only in the counties along the border but also in neighborhoods hundreds of miles from Mexico.

United by ethnicity and many other common characteristics, Mexican Americans also differ in many ways—by education and occupation, where they live, how they vote, and where they worship, as well as the extent of their assimilation into the dominant Texas and American cultures. Some have lived in the United States for generations; still others are new immigrants, whether citizens or aliens, legal or illegal.[34] Only California has more Mexican Americans than Texas. With a culture, language, and traditions that have had a great influence on what we know as Texas today, Mexican Americans are also a growing political force in

Texas. While Blacks were kept from the polling place through various means up to the abolition of the poll tax in 1966, many Mexican Americans did vote. However, in much of the state, powerful political bosses controlled their votes.[35]

Until recently, voting-age Mexican American citizens tended to participate in elections at a lower rate than either Anglos or African Americans. However, major efforts have been made to increase the number of registered voters, and both political parties have attempted to win the support of Mexican American voters. This has resulted in a number of Hispanics being appointed and elected to statewide offices, including attorney general, railroad commissioner, secretary of state, and justice on the Supreme Court of Texas. While most Hispanic legislators and local officials are Democrats, Republicans made a breakthrough in 2010 with six Mexican American state representatives sitting in the eighty-second regular legislative session and two elected to Congress.

Different names have been used—Latino, Chicano, Latin American, Spanish-origin, Spanish-surname, Hispanic—but the most accurate in many ways is Mexican American. This term describes a specific ethnic influence and people in Texas whose contributions are partly Mexican and partly American, blending both cultures together into an essential element of what we know as Texas today.

While the African American population of Texas is now approaching 3 million, it has been decreasing as a percentage of the state's total over the last several census counts. As of 2010, Blacks comprised 11.8 percent of the state's total, slightly less than in the 1990 census and below the current national total of 12.6 percent. In none of the state's 254 counties are African Americans the largest ethnic group, but in some 14 counties they constitute more than 20 percent of the total, including Jefferson County (Beaumont) at 34 percent and Dallas County at 22 percent. Historically, in the nineteenth century much of the Black population was concentrated in East Texas, but today more than half of the state's 2,979,598 African Americans live in Dallas, Tarrant, or Harris County.

Because the state seceded from the Union in 1861, President Abraham Lincoln's Emancipation Proclamation freeing Blacks from slavery did not take effect in Texas until two and one half years after it was issued, on June 19, 1865—a date now celebrated throughout the state as Juneteenth. During the decade following the end of the Civil War, most newly enfranchised Blacks supported the Republican Party, and three African Americans were elected to the Texas Senate, while several others held local offices. However, division and infighting led to the Republicans losing the governor's office in 1874, opening the way for a return of Democratic dominance that would continue for the next hundred years. Although they had won their freedom from slavery and were guaranteed the right to vote, from the end of Reconstruction forward, official and unofficial policies of segregation and discrimination limited the rights of African Americans in Texas. As one historian of the period noted, "The trends set in motion by the return of the Democrats to power could be seen by the end of the century, when of some 650,000 potential black voters only 25,000 qualified."[36]

Throughout the middle third of the twentieth century, from the beginning of the Depression to the start of the civil rights movement in the 1960s, thousands upon thousands of Blacks moved north from Texas to seek better job and educational opportunities and to escape segregation. Along with Blacks from other Southern states they settled in the cities of Chicago, Detroit, Cleveland, Philadelphia, and New York. More recently, greater local opportunities for African Americans have developed in the Texas economy, resulting in fewer young Blacks leaving the state, while others have either moved back or into the state for the first time—some seeking new jobs or being moved here by their employers. Today, Texas ranks third among the states in the total number of African American residents.

The Black population in Texas remains much more homogeneous—politically, religiously, and culturally—than other ethnic groups in the state. Being relatively unified and constituting nearly 12 percent of the total population, the Black community is an important political force in the state. Several Blacks have been elected to the Texas legislature, and three African Americans currently represent Texas congressional districts in Washington. While most Black officeholders are Democrats, the 2012 election saw three African American Republicans elected to the Texas House of Representatives. In 1990, Republican Louis Sturns became the first Black statewide official since Reconstruction when Governor William P. Clements Jr. appointed him to the Texas Court of Criminal Appeals. Since then, Republicans William Jefferson and Dale Wainwright have been elected to the Texas Supreme Court and Michael Williams to the Railroad Commission of Texas.

An even more recent influence on Texas has been made by the migration of Southeast Asians to the state. Whether Vietnamese, Thai, Cambodian, Indian, or Chinese, these people from different nations have become an important component of several communities over the last fifty years, especially in the Houston area and along the Gulf Coast. According to the 2010 census, nearly 1 million Asians make their home in Texas, comprising some 3.8 percent of the total population. More than two-thirds of Asian Americans live in Harris County and its suburbs in Fort Bend and Brazoria Counties, or in the Dallas–Fort Worth area in Dallas, Collin, Denton, or Tarrant County. With 98,762 residents, Fort Bend has the highest percentage (16.9%) of Asian Americans.

While many have moved to the United States and Texas for educational or economic reasons, still others were forced to flee their homeland. They bring a dedication to hard work, a belief in the critical importance of education, and an entrepreneurial spirit. When reviewing the names of high school valedictorians in many areas of Texas, it is common to see second-generation Asian Americans listed.

The generic term "Anglo" is used to describe a wide range of other ethnic groups residing in the state. One of the first organized migrations to the Republic of Texas began in 1838 when Friedrich Ernst transported German settlers to found Austin County. Soon thereafter other Germans settled in New Braunfels in 1845 and in Fredericksburg one year later. It was the revolutions of 1848 that brought many more Germans to Texas over the following decade. The heaviest German settlement occurred to the east and west of the cities of Austin and San Antonio, with their influence felt especially in the Hill Country area.

These German settlers differed from the other Anglos in several ways. They favored small farming and crafts. They were Lutheran or Roman Catholic in their religion. They enjoyed beer and dancing. When the 1860s arrived, they were opposed to secession and to slavery. These last positions, in particular, did not endear them to most other Texans, especially since the state joined the Confederacy.

In 1862, martial law was declared in Texas. All males aliens older than 16 were required to take an oath of allegiance to the Confederacy. Five hundred German Unionists met at Bear Creek in Gillespie County and organized three companies of militia to protect their homes and the frontier.

Fearing open insurrection, the governor sent detachments in search of the outspoken Germans. . . . The Union Loyal League, founder of the three frontier companies, disbanded but 61 men met on August 1, 1862 and headed for Mexico. In the early dawn of August 10, the poorly armed Germans were attacked by a Major Duff. Nineteen Germans were killed in the fighting; nine of the wounded were murdered. Of the others, seven more were killed trying to cross the Rio Grande. Their bodies were left where they fell for three years, until their remains could be returned to Comfort.[37]

Because of their opposition to secession and slavery, most Germans became strong supporters of the Republican Party, an allegiance that continued to differentiate them from most Anglo Texans for the next hundred years. Even today, some of the strongest support for Republican candidates can be found in the Hill Country, where the German influence remains substantial.[38]

Germans have also contributed to what is known as Texas in many other ways. Events such as the New Braunfels Wurstfest and institutions such as Scholz Garten, a gathering spot for politicians and journalists in Austin, developed out of the German culture. Communities such as Boerne, Gruene, Kerrville, and Fredericksburg still reflect the influence and impact of their earlier German settlers.[39]

Another sizable ethnic group to settle in nineteenth-century Texas consisted of immigrants from Bohemia and Moravia. While many individual Czech families came to Texas in the 1840s, the first organized group landed at Galveston in 1852. Like many of the Germans, they were refugees from the oppression that followed in the wake of the 1848 revolutions throughout much of Europe. The area of heaviest Czech settlement was in a line from Denton and Kaufman Counties to the north to Calhoun, Karnes, and Atascosa Counties in the south. Fayette, Lavaca, Austin, and Williamson Counties were the most heavily settled by these immigrants.[40]

The presence of this ethnic group is evident when one is driving along Interstate Highway 35 from Dallas to Austin. As one approaches the community of West, just north of Waco, the billboards appear beckoning drivers to "Czech Stop—Five Miles," inviting one to stay at the Czech Inn or stop at the Little Czech Bakery. Also widely seen in small Central Texas communities is the SPJST Hall, meeting place for the Slavonic Benevolent Order of the State of Texas, a Czech fraternal organization with some seventy-five thousand members throughout the state. Formed in 1897 in LaGrange, the SPJST emphasizes community service, financial services to its members, social gatherings, and the preservation of the Czech heritage and language.[41]

According to the 1990 census, Texans who listed some Czech ancestry numbered close to three hundred thousand. While the Czech communities are concentrated in some fifteen counties to the north of Austin and east of San Antonio, kolache (Czech pastry) shops can be found in most areas of the state. The Czech influence on the music of Texas is also evident, with its polkas and waltzes and accordion playing blending in to the conjunto and tejano music played by Mexican American artists across the state.[42]

Norwegian and Swedish immigrants also created settlements in the 1830s and 1840s in the Republic of Texas, continuing into the latter half of the nineteenth century. Most Norwegian settlements occurred in Bosque and Hamilton Counties, while the Swedish communities were mainly found in Travis and Williamson Counties in Central Texas. Many of the Swedish Americans in Central Texas are the descendants of about eleven thousand Swedes who migrated to the United States from the Swedish province of Smaland and settled in the Round Rock and Austin area.

Several other ethnic groups are also part of the history of Texas. Beginning in the 1850s, Polish immigrants came to the state, first settling in the village of Panna Maria, a town that even today retains its Polish influence.[43] The Polish American Foundation of Texas exists to preserve the Polish national heritage and to honor its contributions to culture and the arts. Further west of Panna Maria is the town of Castroville, where in 1844 immigrants from the province of Alsace, on the French and German border, re-created their native villages as much as local materials permitted. Today the European character of the town remains virtually intact.[44] Another ethnic influence comes from the five hundred Wendish who left an area of Germany in Saxony and Prussia to pursue freedom of religion and language in 1854 and settled in Lee County. Today the Texas Wendish Heritage Society maintains offices and a museum in Giddings, near the original settlement in Serbin. Each September an annual Wendish festival is sponsored.[45]

More recently, a sizable number of East Asians and South Asians have settled in Texas, some drawn by the high-tech industries and educational opportunities and others as refugees from Communism or other repressive regimes. Among the fifty states, Texas is second only to California in its concentration of Vietnamese, many of whom initially settled in the Gulf Coast areas around Houston but have subsequently disbursed to other Texas cities.[46]

Rather than being only an area of cowboys, Indians, Blacks, and Mexicans, Texas has been built also by the contributions of many different groups who sometimes are linked together under the general category of Anglos. All these varied ethnic influences have contributed to what is known as Texas today. In some areas the traditions of the older cultures have remained and retain their original flavor. Throughout the state in all its aspects—social, cultural, and architectural—what is known as Texas is a combination of the contributions from many different racial and ethnic traditions.

Population Distribution

Over the last fifty years Texas has undergone a tremendous expansion in population, moving from sixth to second, behind California, in overall population.[47] In 1960, the total population of Texas was 9,579,677; by the 2010 census the state's population had grown to 25,145,561, a growth rate of 162 percent over those fifty years. The most rapid growth came in the last decade (table 1.2).

It is interesting to note that most of the population growth in Texas over the past half-century came from natural growth (births minus deaths) rather than from net migration (individuals moving into the state minus those moving out). Natural growth will continue to contribute to population growth as individuals live longer and the birth rate continues to remain high. As noted in a recent study, "In 2000, Texas was second in the country (behind Utah) in state rankings for birth/fertility rates. Because birthrates change slowly over time, Texas will probably continue to see large natural increases in its population despite changes in economic conditions or immigration policies."[48]

While natural growth has been a major contributor to the state's population expansion, it has been assisted tremendously by the movement of individuals from other parts of the country as well as from outside the nation's borders. As table 1.2 indicates, migration grew from a relatively low 13.3 percent of total growth during the decade of the 1960s to its highest rate in the following ten-year period. The greatest inflow occurred in the decade of the 1970s, when 58.4 percent of the state's growth came from net migration. In the most recent period, net migration comprised 41.5 percent of the total population growth.

Net migration consists of both those who moved to Texas from other states and international migration from other countries. As economic conditions changed, so too did the pattern of migration to Texas. During the 1970s and the oil boom, tens of thousands of residents from other states moved to Texas looking for new opportunities. Likewise, in the decade of the 1990s Texas added nearly 2 million new residents from migration as individuals from other states were drawn to the strong economy or were transferred to the large number of high-tech industries, particularly

Table 1.2. Sources of Texas population growth, 1960–2010

Period	Total increase	Natural growth	Net migration
1961–1970	1,617,053	1,402,683	214,370
1971–1980	3,032,461	1,260,794	1,771,667
1981–1990	2,757,319	1,815,670	941,649
1991–2000	3,865,310	1,919,126	1,946,184
2001–2010	4,293,741	2,358,981	1,934,760
TOTAL	15,565,884	8,757,254	6,808,630
PERCENTAGE OF TOTAL		56.3%	43.7%

Source: Data from Texas State Data Center.

in the Dallas and Austin areas. Nevertheless, during the entire decade of the 1990s, some 55 percent of the net migration came from international immigration. One result of this population growth in the 1990s is that "the foreign-born population share in Texas rose significantly during the decade and in 2000 composed 14 percent of the population compared with 11 percent at the national level."[49]

The most recent decade reflects the impact of economic conditions on migration patterns. During the first five years of the decade, only some 27 percent of the total net migration came from domestic sources, with nearly three-fourths comprising those who moved from other countries. However, beginning in 2006, the pattern was reversed, with more than 60 percent of all net migration coming from other states as the Texas economy continued to provide job growth, in contrast to much of the rest of the country.[50]

In a recent issue, *Forbes* magazine attempted to predict what cities are best positioned to grow and prosper, concentrating on the fifty-two largest metropolitan areas with populations over 1 million. Among the measures employed were job growth, rates of family formation, growth in educated migration, overall population growth, and "a broad measurement of attractiveness to immigrants—as places to settle, make money, and start businesses."[51] Among the Texas metropolitan areas, Austin ranked number one, with San Antonio fourth, Houston fifth, and Dallas seventh. As writer and demographer Joel Kotkin noted, "Aided by relatively low housing prices and buoyant economies, these Lone Star cities have become major hubs for jobs and families." In concluding his study, he commented, "What is clear is that well-established patterns of job creation and vital demographics will drive future regional growth, not only

Table 1.3. African American and Hispanic population of Texas, 1960–2010

| Year | African Americans | | Hispanics | | All Texans |
	Number	Percentage of population	Number	Percentage of population	
1960	1,187,125	12.4	1,448,900	15.1	9,579,677
1970	1,399,005	12.5	1,981,861	17.7	11,196,730
1980	1,710,175	12.0	2,985,824	21.0	14,229,191
1990	2,021,632	11.9	4,339,905	25.5	16,986,510
2000	2,404,566	11.5	6,669,666	32.0	20,851,820
2010	2,979,598	11.8	9,460,921	37.6	25,145,561

in the next year, but over the coming decade. People create economies and they tend to vote with their feet when they choose to locate their families as well as their businesses."[52] If Kotkin's predictions are correct, Texas will continue to grow from both natural increase as well as net migration.

The ethnic and racial makeup of the state has changed dramatically over these last fifty years also (table 1.3). In 1960, the Texas population was 12.4 percent Black, with a total of 1,187,125 African Americans. By 2010, that number had increased to 2,979,598 but now constituted only 11.8 percent of the state, as the sizable expansion in the Black population did not keep up with the overall growth of the state. That was not the case with the Hispanic population, however, as it increased from 1,448,900 to 9,460,921 in the same period of time, going from 15.1 percent of the state population in 1960 to 37.6 percent in 2010.

In the past, Blacks were more heavily represented in East and Central Texas, while Hispanics were located mainly from San Antonio south and west along the border with Mexico, but that is no longer the situation. Today, a higher percentage of African Americans live in Dallas, while there are more Hispanics in Harris County (Houston) than in any other area of the state.

With 254 counties in the state it is impossible to analyze and understand the transitions that have occurred in Texas politics without dividing the state into more meaningful divisions. In the next chapter, Texas will be described in terms of four categories of counties, each of which contains a distinct community composition. As will be discussed later, the changes in Texas politics over the past fifty years took place in different times and in different forms in each of these four categories of counties.

CHAPTER 2

Dividing the State

Given the geographical size and population of Texas, any attempt to explain political change over the past fifty years needs to view the state in terms of manageable and meaningful categories. While others have employed sectional approaches to describing and analyzing the state's politics, the current work divides Texas into four types of communities. Texas is viewed from the perspective of the following four groupings of counties: (1) the Big 6 counties, (2) the twenty-nine counties surrounding them that are included by the U.S. census bureau as part of the Big 6 metropolitan statistical areas, (3) twenty-one other counties viewed as the focal points of metropolitan statistical areas by the census bureau, and (4) the remaining 198 mainly rural counties. These four groupings will be referred to on the following pages as Big 6, Suburban, Other Metro, and Small Town. While there are significant differences within each of these categories, they do represent useful political units for compilation, discussion, and explanation of the political changes that have occurred.

The county is used as a geographical boundary since it is both unique and permanent—unique in that there are no overlapping boundaries and permanent in that no new counties have been created since Loving in 1923. Texas cities, on the other hand, often have boundaries that can encompass more than one county and grow over time, with annexation of unincorporated areas.[1] Additionally, election data is compiled and collected at the county level, and using this unit of government facilitates comparisons over time.

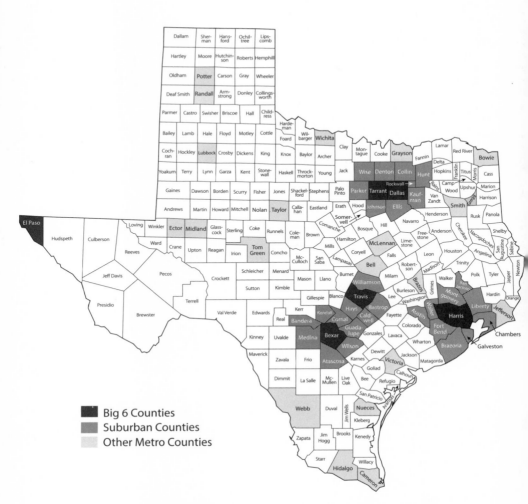

MAP 1. Map of Texas showing Big 6 counties, Suburban counties, and Other Metro counties

The Four Categories of Counties

Big 6 Counties

The Big 6 counties are the traditional major metropolitan areas of the state, ranging in size from El Paso, with a 2010 population of 800,647, to Harris (Houston), with its 4,092,459 residents. Currently they are the six most populated counties in the state, although El Paso may slide behind Collin and Hidalgo Counties if present trends continue.[2] The other four counties, with their major cities, are Bexar (San Antonio), Dallas (Dallas), Tarrant (Fort Worth and Arlington), and Travis (Austin).

Table 2.1 indicates that the six largest counties in the state nearly tripled in population during the last fifty years. Overall, the Big 6 counties grew by nearly 200 percent. Interestingly enough, Dallas County—home to Irving, Garland, Mesquite, and parts of Richardson, as well as the city of Dallas—grew at the slowest rate (149%) of the six counties, while Travis County nearly quintupled its 1960 population total.

Harris County is home to both Houston, the largest city in the state and fourth largest in the nation, with a population of 2,099,451, and Pasadena, with 149,043 residents. With more than half the county's population, Houston dominates the county. That situation is less true of Dallas and Tarrant Counties, where more than one heavily populated city can be found.

Within the boundaries of Dallas County lie the cities of Dallas and four others with populations in excess of one hundred thousand. The city of Dallas, with a population of 1,197,816, is the ninth largest city in the country, but it shares Dallas County with the cities of Garland (226,876), Irving (216,290), Grand Prairie (175,396), and Mesquite (139,824).[3] Tarrant County contains a number of communities, but its two largest cities are Fort Worth (741,206) and Arlington (365,438), which is home to the Texas Rangers ballpark and the Dallas Cowboys stadium. Bexar, Travis, and El Paso Counties, by contrast, are each dominated by one large city. Table 2.2 lists the most populous ten cities in the state.

It is among these cities in the Big 6 counties that some of the most dramatic population growth has occurred over the past fifty years. In 1960, only 186,545 individuals lived in what was the laid-back home of the state's largest university and its center of government. By 2010, the population of Austin had grown to nearly eight hundred thousand.[4] Likewise, Arlington transformed itself from a small community of less than forty-five thousand residents to the seventh largest city in the state. Simi-

Table 2.1. Big 6 counties population change, 1960–2010

County	Population 1960	2010	Percentage increase
Harris	1,243,158	4,092,459	229
Dallas	951,527	2,368,139	149
Tarrant	538,495	1,809,034	336
Bexar	687,151	1,714,773	250
Travis	212,136	1,024,266	383
El Paso	314,070	800,647	155

Table 2.2. Most populous Texas cities, 2010

State rank	City	Population	Category	National rank
1	Houston	2,099,451	Big 6	4
2	San Antonio	1,327,407	Big 6	7
3	Dallas	1,197,816	Big 6	9
4	Austin	790,390	Big 6	14
5	Fort Worth	741,206	Big 6	16
6	El Paso	649,121	Big 6	19
7	Arlington	365,438	Big 6	50
8	Corpus Christi	305,215	Other Metro	60
9	Plano	259,841	Suburban	71
10	Laredo	236,091	Other Metro	81

lar growth took place over the half-century in Garland and Irving, two cities in Dallas County.

Today, nearly 60 percent of the Big 6 counties population is either Hispanic or African American, and a similar proportion of these two groups live in the Other Metro counties. In fact, the largest percentage of Hispanics resides in the Other Metro counties, a category that includes the major population centers along the Texas border with Mexico. Anglos remain a majority of the population in the categories labeled Suburban and Small Town.[5]

Among the Big 6 counties, only Tarrant and Travis have Anglo majorities, while El Paso and Bexar are overwhelmingly Hispanic. More than half of all Hispanics in Texas live in the Big 6 counties, with Harris County alone home to more than one in six Hispanic Texans. Roughly one in five residents of both Dallas and Harris Counties is African American. Slightly less than 8 percent of both Travis and Harris Counties comprise individuals classifying themselves as other than Anglo, Black, or Hispanic. Harris, Dallas, and Bexar Counties are each approximately two-thirds majority-minority, while El Paso County is more than 80 percent Hispanic. As can be seen in table 2.3, there is a tremendous variation in the percentage of Anglos in these six counties, ranging from slightly over half of all residents in Travis and Tarrant Counties down to less than one in seven in El Paso County.

Suburban Counties

Surrounding all but El Paso is a ring of twenty-nine Suburban counties so classified because they are considered part of the metropolitan statistical areas (MSAs) of the Big 6 counties as defined by the United States Census Bureau (table 2.4). Nine counties surround Dallas and Tarrant Counties: Collin, Denton, Ellis, Hunt, Johnson, Kaufman, Parker, Rockwall, and Wise.[6] An additional nine are in the Houston MSA: Austin, Brazoria, Chambers, Fort Bend, Galveston, Liberty, Montgomery, San Jacinto, and Waller. The Suburban counties around the city of Austin are Bastrop, Caldwell, Hays, and Williamson. San Antonio's Suburban counties are Atascosa, Bandera, Comal, Guadalupe, Kendall, Medina, and Wilson.[7]

It is here in these Suburban counties that a number of rather large cities are located, with the most populous being Plano in Collin County, north of Dallas. Plano ranks seventy-first in the entire United States and is the ninth largest city in Texas. Plano is more than a suburb of Dallas as it is home to several important corporations, including the Dr Pepper-Snapple Group, J. C. Penney, Pizza Hut, and Ericsson. It has been described as one of the wealthiest cities in the United States.[8] Also among the larger cities in the Suburban category, all located in the Dallas–Fort Worth metropolitan area, are McKinney (population 131,177), Carrollton (119,097), Frisco (116,989), and Denton (113,383).

Many of the communities in these counties have experienced phenomenal growth over the last fifty years. Perhaps none is as dramatic as that experienced by Austin's northern suburb of Round Rock, located in Williamson County. Round Rock expanded from a population of 1,878

Table 2.3. Population of Big 6 counties by ethnicity or race, 2010

		Ethnicity or race[a]			
		Anglo		*Hispanic*	
County	*Total population*	*Number*	*Percentage of population*	*Number*	*Percentage of population*
Harris	4,092,459	1,349,646	33.0	1,671,540	40.8
Dallas	2,368,139	784,693	33.1	905,940	38.3
Tarrant	1,809,034	937,135	51.8	482,977	26.7
Bexar	1,714,773	519,123	30.3	1,006,958	58.7
Travis	1,024,266	517,644	50.5	342,766	33.5
El Paso	800,647	105,246	13.1	658,134	82.2

[a] "Anglo" comprises those responding as White, non-Hispanic. "Other" includes Asian, Pacific Islander, or some other race alone or two or more races, all non-Hispanic. The Other category is predominantly Asian in Texas.

in 1960 to slightly less than 100,000 in 2010 and is now home to the AAA minor league baseball team Round Rock Express, owned by Nolan Ryan.

As would be expected, the most dramatic population growth in Texas occurred in this grouping of counties, with five of them (Collin and Denton north of Dallas–Fort Worth; Montgomery and Fort Bend outside the city of Houston; and Williamson north of the city of Austin) expanding by more than tenfold over the 1960 population. Even though its population more than doubled over the half-century, Galveston County had the smallest rate of growth of all twenty-nine counties; its total of 140,364 residents in 1960 increased to 291,309 in 2010. All told, the twenty-nine counties in the Suburban category grew by 522 percent over the fifty-year period (table 2.5).

Overall, the suburbs surrounding the Big 6 counties are predominantly Anglo, but the percentage ranges from a high of 67.4 percent in the Dallas and Tarrant County suburbs to a low of 54.3 percent in the Harris County suburbs (table 2.6). The highest percentage of Hispanics live in the counties outside San Antonio, while the Houston suburbs have the greatest percentage of African Americans (13.2%) and those classifying themselves as other than Anglo, Hispanic, or African American (9.4%). Atascosa County has the highest percentage of Hispanic residents, comprising 61.9 percent of its total population, while Waller and Fort Bend Coun-

		Ethnicity or race[a]		
	Black		Other	
Number	Percentage of population		Number	Percentage of population
754,258	18.4		317,015	7.7
518,732	21.9		158,774	6.7
262,522	14.5		126,400	7.0
118,460	6.9		70,232	4.1
82,805	8.1		81,051	7.9
20,649	2.6		16,618	2.1

ties, outside Houston, both are more than 20 percent African American. While there has been significant growth in the Black population of many Suburban counties, the Other category (predominantly Asian) has surpassed Blacks as the third most populous group in several Suburban counties.

Other Metro Counties

An additional twenty-one counties represent other metropolitan statistical areas as classified by the census bureau. These Other Metro counties range in size from Victoria, with 86,793 residents, to Hidalgo, with a population of 774,769 (table 2.7). These counties have in common that they serve as trade centers for a larger area, have distinct media markets with a daily newspaper and a local television station, and in nearly all cases maintain commercial air transportation to other areas of the state.[9] These additional metropolitan counties have seen their populations more than double over the past fifty years, but their proportion of the state's total population decreased slightly during that same period.

Included in this group of counties are a number of cities that have seen substantial growth. The tenth largest city in the state is Laredo, with a population of 236,091. Located on the Mexican border in Webb

Table 2.4. Population of counties classified in Suburban category, 2010

County	Population	County	Population
Suburbs of Dallas and Tarrant Counties			
Collin	782,341	Kaufman	103,350
Denton	662,614	Parker	116,927
Ellis	149,610	Rockwall	78,337
Hunt	86,129	Wise	59,129
Johnson	150,934		
Suburbs of Harris County			
Austin	28,417	Liberty	75,643
Brazoria	313,166	Montgomery	455,746
Chambers	35,096	San Jacinto	26,384
Fort Bend	585,375	Waller	43,205
Galveston	291,309		
Suburbs of Travis County			
Bastrop	74,171	Hays	157,107
Caldwell	38,066	Williamson	422,679
Suburbs of Bexar County			
Atascosa	44,911	Kendall	33,410
Bandera	20,485	Medina	46,006
Comal	108,472	Wilson	42,918
Guadalupe	131,533		

Note: These 29 counties are included in the metropolitan statistical areas centered around Bexar, Dallas, Harris, Tarrant, and Travis Counties. Other counties are components of additional metropolitan statistical areas (categorized below as Other Metro counties) but are not included in the Suburban category for analysis here.

Table 2.5. Texas population growth by county type, 1960 and 2010

County type	1960 Population	1960 Percentage of state	2010 Population	2010 Percentage of state
Big 6 (*n* = 6)	3,946,537	41.2	11,809,318	47.0
Suburban (*n* = 29)	838,569	8.8	5,213,468	20.7
Other Metro (*n* = 21)	2,242,095	23.4	4,563,321	18.1
Small Town (*n* = 198)	2,552,476	26.6	3,559,454	14.2

Table 2.6. Suburban counties by ethnicity or race, 2010

	Anglo	Hispanic	Black	Other
	Race or ethnicity			
Surrounding Dallas and Tarrant Counties				
Population	1,475,498	362,961	160,066	190,844
Percentage of total	67.4	16.6	7.3	8.7
Surrounding Harris County				
Population	1,007,826	427,872	245,125	173,518
Percentage of total	54.3	23.1	13.2	9.4
Surrounding Travis County				
Population	420,830	195,547	37,705	37,941
Percentage of total	60.8	28.3	5.4	5.5
Surrounding Bexar County				
Population	254,684	151,190	11,610	10,251
Percentage of total	59.5	35.3	2.7	2.4

Table 2.7. Population of counties classified as Other Metro, 2010

County	Population	County	Population
Bell	310,235	Midland	136,872
Bowie	92,565	Nueces	340,223
Brazos	194,851	Potter	121,073
Cameron	406,220	Randall	120,725
Ector	137,130	Smith	209,714
Grayson	120,877	Taylor	131,506
Gregg	121,730	Tom Green	110,224
Hidalgo	774,769	Victoria	86,793
Jefferson	252,273	Webb	250,304
Lubbock	278,831	Wichita	131,500
McLennan	234,906		

County, Laredo has become an international trade center, along with its cross-border municipality, Nuevo Laredo. Also experiencing substantial growth over the last half-century are the border area cities of McAllen, in Hidalgo County, and Brownsville, in Cameron County.

With the growth of Texas Tech University, the city of Lubbock (Lubbock County), population 229,573, is now the eleventh largest in Texas. Further north, spanning Potter and Randall Counties, is the city of Amarillo, now ranking fourteenth largest among Texas cities. Not all cities in the Other Metro category grew, however. In 1960, Beaumont (Jefferson County) had a population of 119,175; its 2010 total was 118,296. Wichita Falls (Wichita County) was home to 101,724 residents in 1960, and its population in 2010 had increased to only 104,553.

A great disparity is present among the Other Metro counties scattered throughout the state. Taken together, the population of these counties grew by 104 percent. While all had more residents in 2010 than in 1960, a few had increases of less than 10 percent for the fifty-year period. The most dramatic increases in total population occurred along the Mexican border; Cameron, Hidalgo, and Webb Counties each more than doubled in residents from 1960 to 2010. The greatest increase, however, took place in Brazos County—home to Texas A&M University—whose total population skyrocketed from 44,895 to 194,851 over the fifty-year period.

Bell County, home to much of Fort Hood and located in Central Texas, tripled in population from 1960 to 2010. Randall County, in the Texas

Table 2.8. Small Town counties by population, 2010

County population size	Number of counties	County population size	Number of counties
Fewer than 1,000	8	10,000–19,999	50
1,000–2,499	16	20,000–49,999	45
2,500–9,999	62	50,000 or more	17

Panhandle, also saw its number of residents triple. Randall's growth is rather interesting in that it shares the city of Amarillo with Potter County. While Randall grew from 33,913 to 120,725 over the fifty-year period, its neighboring county saw virtually no growth (less than 5%), going from 115,580 in 1960 to 121,073 in 2010. Two other slow-growing counties were Jefferson, home to the city of Beaumont, near the Louisiana border (less than 3%), and Wichita, home to the city of Wichita Falls, on the Oklahoma border (less than 7%).

Among the twenty-one counties in the Other Metro category there are great variations in the percentage of Hispanic and African American residents. Five counties have a Hispanic majority, ranging from Webb (95.7%), Hidalgo (90.6%), and Cameron (88.1%) down to Nueces (60.6%) and Ector (52.7%) Counties. All of these counties, except Ector, are located in the Rio Grande Valley. While none of the Other Metro counties have an African American majority, Jefferson County has the highest percentage (33.5%), followed by Bowie (24.0%), Bell (20.4%), Gregg (19.8%), and Smith (17.7%). Except for Bell County in Central Texas, the other four counties are all located in East Texas.

Small Town Counties

The remaining 198 counties have been classified as Small Town counties but are home to more than 3.5 million Texans. While comprising a smaller portion of the state's population now than they did fifty years ago, the total population of these counties has nevertheless increased by more than 1 million residents since 1960. These counties range in size from the 86,771 residents of Angelina County in East Texas, where the city of Lufkin is located, down to the smallest county, Loving, in West Texas, with its 82 residents.

As table 2.8 indicates, nearly all of the counties in the Small Town category have less than fifty thousand residents and almost half are home to fewer than ten thousand. None of the 198 counties have as many residents as the smallest of the Other Metro category of counties, but a few do exceed the population of some in the Suburban counties category. The four largest counties not comprising a metropolitan statistical area or serving as a suburb for one of the Big 6 counties are Angelina (86,771), Henderson (78,532), and Orange (81,837) Counties, in East Texas, and Coryell County (75,388) in Central Texas.

While none of the counties in the first three categories lost population over the last fifty years, that is not the situation with those in the Small Town category. As a group these 198 counties grew by 39 percent, or slightly over 1 million residents, from 1960 to 2010. However, during the same period, seventy-seven counties lost population. All but ten of these are located in the western half of the state, with most in the eastern Panhandle and the plains west of a line from Wichita County in the north to Webb in the south. This loss of residents has made several counties smaller than an urban voting precinct. In 1960, fourteen counties had a population less than 2,500, with merely three counting less than 1,000 residents. Fifty years later, the number had increased to twenty-four counties with less than 2,500 people and eight with fewer than 1,000 residents.[10]

The population loss was not limited to the smallest of these counties. Thirty of the seventy-seven counties that lost population during the half-century started with over 10,000 residents in 1960. Some of the losses were dramatic. Hutchinson County, in the north central part of the Panhandle, had a population of 34,419 in 1960 and saw it decline to 22,150 in 2010. Two other Panhandle counties that had more than 30,000 residents in 1960 lost population. Hale County, home to the city of Plainview, was smaller in 2010 and Gray County, where the city of Pampa is located, lost a total of 9,000 residents over the fifty-year period.

Comparisons over Time

Population

The changing population composition of Texas is evident when one combines the number of residents living in the Big 6 counties with those residing in the twenty-nine counties around them. Together they were home to about 50 percent of the 1960 population, while by 2010 these major metropolitan areas contained more than two-thirds of the state's resi-

**Table 2.9. Percentage of total state
population by county type, 1960–2010**

County type	1960	1990	2010
Big 6	41.2	48.2	47.0
Suburban	8.8	14.1	20.7
Other Metro	23.4	19.4	18.1
Small Town	26.6	18.3	14.2

**Table 2.10. Percentage of population by county type
and ethnicity and race, 2010**

County type	Race or ethnicity			
	Anglo	Hispanic	Black	Other
Big 6	35.7	42.9	14.9	6.5
Suburban	61.2	22.0	8.8	8.0
Other Metro	40.2	48.1	8.5	3.1
Small Town	58.0	30.2	10.8	1.0

dents. The most dramatic growth has been in the counties outside the Big 6, as they more than doubled their share of the state's population. Although having grown in raw numbers the Big 6 counties now comprise a smaller percentage of the state's total than they did in 1990 (table 2.9).

Counties included in the Small Town and Other Metro categories, while growing in absolute numbers by 39 percent and 104 percent, respectively, now make up a much smaller percentage of the state's population. These changes have had an important impact on the state's politics, changes that will be discussed in future chapters. The Small Town counties have added more than 1 million residents over the fifty-year period but their percentage of the state's total has dropped dramatically.

The ethnic and racial composition of these four categories of counties provides another perspective on their differences (table 2.10). While the counties in the Suburban and Small Town categories remain heavily Anglo, Hispanics and Blacks together comprise a majority in both the

Big 6 and the Other Metro counties. In fact, it is the Other Metro counties that have nearly a majority of residents who are Hispanic, while Blacks
are most heavily represented among the Big 6 counties.

Voter Registration

The foregoing overview of the population totals, comprising individuals of all ages and of all nationalities residing in the state's 254 counties,
provides a context for looking at voter registration totals, numbers that
reflect only those who are eligible to participate in elections. Statewide,
45.3 percent of the 1990 population consisted of registered voters; this
increased to 52.8 percent of the total population in 2010. When one looks
at the number of registered voters in each group of counties, an interesting development is apparent (table 2.11). Counties in the Small Town and
Suburban groupings outperform the other two categories, with a higher
percentage of the state's total registered voters than of the population at
large. Some of the difference may be due to the higher percentage of Hispanic residents in the Big 6 (42.9%) and Other Metro (48.1%) counties,
since the population numbers reported in the decennial census count both
citizens and noncitizens.

Of the five Other Metro counties with a majority of Hispanic residents,
only Nueces County surpassed the statewide ratio of voters to total population. While all five have increased the percentage of those who are registered voters over the past twenty years, as has the entire state, the counties
of Cameron, Ector, Hidalgo, and Webb continue to lag behind overall
state performance. In Hidalgo County only 38.3 percent of all residents
were registered to vote in 2010.

Among the Big 6 counties, Travis County, with its sizable university
and state employee population, had the highest ratio of registered voters
to residents, at 53.0 percent, in 1990. This contrasted with El Paso, where
just 33.4 percent were registered to vote in that same year. Twenty years
later the ratio had increased dramatically in all Big 6 counties. By 2010
nearly six in ten Travis County residents were registered voters, but El
Paso showed the most sizable percentage increase, with 47.4 percent of
its population registered to vote.

Due to a number of discriminatory practices in place at the time, the
1960 numbers are not truly comparable. The minimum voting age at that
time in Texas was twenty-one. Individuals were required to pay a poll
tax within a four-month window ending some four months prior to the
Democratic primary and ten months before the general election. Those

**Table 2.11. Percentage of registered
voters by county type, 1960–2010**

County type	1960	1990	2010
Big 6	39.9	45.8	44.5
Suburban	9.1	14.4	21.8
Other Metro	22.1	18.9	17.3
Small Town	28.9	20.9	16.4

aged sixty and over were exempt from such payment but were required to submit a signed exemption form. Additionally, informal practices in many areas worked to discourage African Americans and some Mexican Americans from paying the poll tax and becoming eligible to vote. Nevertheless, the same relationship between overall population and eligibility to vote existed among the four categories of counties. Both the Suburban and Small Town counties had higher relative percentages of voters, while the Big 6 and Other Metro counties were slightly underrepresented among the eligible electorate.[11]

Voter Participation

It is one thing to measure the number of residents registered to vote. What is more critical, however, is the number of registered voters who actually vote on election day. To view changes in voter participation, three top-of-the-ticket contests are used; namely the race for the presidency in 1960 and the gubernatorial contests of 1990 and 2010. Two of these contests were won by a Democratic candidate and one by a Republican. The first occurred in a time of one-party (Democratic) dominance of Texas politics. The second took place during the short interim of two-party competition. The third and most recent was held when the Republican Party had become the dominant force in Texas politics. Only the last was not a close election.

When it comes to actual participation on election day, once again it is the counties in the Suburban and Small Town categories that outperformed in 2010, although admittedly the Suburban counties lagged in 1990 (table 2.12). Despite their declining share of the state's population, by participating at a higher rate the 198 Small Town counties have maintained a modicum of influence in state elections. Although they had fewer residents than the Other Metro counties in 1990, they still contributed

Table 2.12. Percentage of contribution to total state vote, by county type, 1960–2010

County type	1960	1990	2010
Big 6	40.3	45.3	44.0
Suburban	9.1	15.2	23.8
Other Metro	21.7	18.3	15.4
Small Town	28.9	21.1	16.8

a greater share of the state's total vote. With 14.2 percent of the state's population in 2010, the Small Town counties accounted for 16.4 percent of all registered voters and contributed 16.8 percent of all votes in the November election. Clearly, a higher level of civic involvement helps these areas to retain greater influence in choosing elected officials.

For the 2010 election, statewide participation overall was a low of only 37.5 percent of all registered voters. Republican governor Rick Perry carried eighteen of the twenty-one Other Metro counties in his contest against former Houston mayor Bill White. The only three counties in this group carried by White were three of the five majority-Hispanic counties, and they also had the lowest rate of participation of registered voters, with turnouts of 23.5 percent (Cameron), 24.7 percent (Hidalgo), and 27.4 percent (Webb). Overall, 18.1 percent of the state's population resides in Other Metro counties, but they contributed only 15.4 percent of the 2010 vote. While the statewide registered voter participation was much higher in 1990, the same three counties were among the lowest that year. Of the ten Other Metro counties carried by Democrat Ann Richards in her campaign against Clayton Williams, only two (Wichita and McLennan) had turnout levels above the state average, while all eleven counties with Williams majorities had above-average participation rates.

In the Suburban grouping, twenty-two of the twenty-nine counties had above-average turnout in 1990, with twenty of them doing so in 2010. By 2010 these counties had grown to be home for 20.7 percent of the state's population and had a higher percentage of registered voters, who contributed nearly one in four of all votes on election day.

Voting Behavior and Party Competition

It is clear that the distribution pattern of the state's population has changed over the past fifty years—most dramatically among those counties categorized here as Suburban or Small Town. While the suburbs have consistently grown, the relative positions of the Other Metro and Small Town counties have consistently decreased. The Big 6 counties comprise a greater portion of the state's population in 2010 than they did in 1960, but represent a smaller share than was the case in 1990.

In terms of political influence, the change has been most substantial in the Suburban category of counties. While these counties have grown from 8.8 percent of the state's population to become home to more than one of every five Texans, their residents' level of participation in general elections has made them even more influential. Likewise, the shrinking relative population position of the Small Town counties has been balanced by a higher turnout in elections.

As we have seen, the overall population totals and the population composition of these four categories and the counties identified within them—as well as their voter participation levels—have changed since 1960. Moreover, the political loyalties and voting behavior of the counties and categories have seen major transformations. As Texas moved from one-party Democratic to two-party competitive and then to modified one-party Republican, these changes occurred first in some categories and then spread to others. Most recently, another transformation of local and state political behavior appears to be taking place in some of the counties in at least one of the categories. In the following chapters, these four categories—Big 6, Suburban, Other Metro, and Small Town counties—will be used to help identify and describe the transformation that has taken place in Texas politics over the past half-century.

CHAPTER 3

A Century of One-Party Politics

From the admission of Texas as a state to the beginning of the Civil War, the Democratic Party was dominant across the state. Only during the brief period of Reconstruction after the war did anyone other than a Democrat serve as governor or hold any other statewide elective office. In fact, the Democratic candidate for president carried the state in every election save one from the time of the state's initial participation in presidential elections in 1848 up to the election of 1952. That exception occurred in 1928, when Republican candidate Herbert Hoover bested Democratic candidate Al Smith, governor of New York. Smith, the first Roman Catholic presidential nominee, was committed to ending the national prohibition on the sale of alcoholic beverages, a position unpopular with many Texans.

The Early Years of Statehood

Prior to the Civil War, the Whig Party's candidates provided minimal opposition to the Democratic Party in presidential elections, and the Whig Party was not a factor in congressional elections. Only one Whig candidate from one of the state's two districts ran in one election, in 1853, obtaining 14.9 percent of the vote. Given the Whig Party's stand on issues of great importance to the Texas electorate, this is not surprising. Nationally, the Whig Party took a clear stand in opposition to the admission of slave-owning states, including Texas, into the Union. As one historian sums up the difference and the result, "Nationally, Whigs led the opposition to Texas annexation; Democrats, increasingly the party of the South, led the fight for it."[1]

More serious competition came from the American ("Know-Nothing") Party in the elections of 1855 and 1857. In fact, American Party candidate Lemuel D. Evans was sent to Congress in 1855 from the second district with 60.2 percent of the vote, and in the first district the party's unsuccessful candidate obtained 49.9 percent of the vote. Two years later, both American Party candidates were defeated and Texas returned to its all-Democratic delegation. Through this period the state legislature remained overwhelmingly Democratic, as were all governors of the period.[2]

Reconstruction to the Twentieth Century

The national Republican Party was formed in 1854, but it was not until 1867 that the party was organized in Texas at a convention in Houston.[3] Closely associated with the Union and the abolition of slavery, its initial membership was predominantly African American. The party leadership, however, was mainly White, with a large proportion of German Americans and others who had been opposed to secession and membership in the Confederacy. As would be the case throughout its first sixty years, the new party quickly divided into two factions of more conservative supporters on one side and those allied with the Radical Republicans on the other side. While the conservatives held the regular party machinery, the Radical Republicans controlled the Union League and had the support of most Blacks.[4]

Democratic candidates for president carried the state in each of the seven elections after Texas was readmitted to the Union. But there were pockets of Republican strength during this time, when African Americans were allowed to vote and cast their ballots, predominantly for the Republican candidates. In all seven presidential elections, Republicans won the counties of Brazoria, Fort Bend, San Jacinto, Wharton, and Waller—all located just outside Harris County—as well as Kendall County.[5] Another four counties (Jackson, Marion, Robertson, and Matagorda) voted Republican in six of the seven elections, while Colorado, Grimes, Harrison, and Washington Counties supported the Republican candidate in five of the seven contests. With the exception of Kendall in the Hill Country and Harrison and Marion Counties in far northeast Texas, the nineteenth-century GOP strength in presidential contests was concentrated in the area around Harris County (table 3.1).

In the election of 1869, prior to the end of military occupation and at a time when many of those who had supported the Confederacy were

Table 3.1. Votes cast for president, by party, 1848–1896

Year	Democratic Party candidate	Votes cast	Candidates from other parties	Votes cast
1848	Cass	8,801	Taylor (Whig)	3,777
1852	Pierce	11,515	Scott (Whig)	4,185
1856	Buchanan	31,852	Fillmore (Whig)	15,130
1860	Breckinridge	47,949	Bell (Constitution Union)	15,529
1872	Greeley[a]	66,455	Grant (Republican)	47,425
			O'Conor (Bourbon Democrat)[b]	2,580
1876	Tilden	104,755	Hayes (Republican)	44,721
1880	Hancock	158,228	Garfield (Republican)	57,845
			Weaver (Greenback)	27,405
1884	Cleveland	225,883	Blaine (Republican)	92,743
1888	Cleveland	232,106	Harrison (Republican)	88,504
1892	Cleveland	244,346	Harrison (Republican)	74,572
			Weaver (Populist)	97,303
1896	Bryan	285,263	Bryan (Populist)	77,740
			McKinley (Republican)	162,766

[a] Greeley was the candidate of both the Democratic Party and the Liberal Republican Party, an entity that operated in Texas only in the 1872 election.
[b] O'Conor was the candidate of a rump body of States' Rights Democrats in the 1872 election.

not allowed to vote, Republican candidates dominated. The factional divisions within the GOP led to two candidates seeking to become governor. The candidate backed by the Radical Republicans, E. J. Davis, narrowly defeated A. J. Hamilton. Much of Davis's election could be credited to support from the newly enfranchised African American voters. As one historian reported, "In the 31 counties in which more blacks voted than whites, Davis won easily in all but three. A strong statistical correlation existed between the Davis vote and the black population."[6] The party was able to elect a majority to the Texas legislature and, in turn, the legislature selected two Republicans to represent the state in the United States Senate upon readmission to the Union in 1870.[7] In that same election of 1869, the Republicans won three of the four congressional districts, sending George Whitmore, Edward Degener, and William Clark to the U.S. House of Representatives.

The party's success was short-lived, however; the military turned over civil functions to the elected officials, Texas was readmitted to the Union, and the former supporters of the Confederacy regained the franchise. As historian Paul Casdorph concluded, "The Republicans did not threaten the Bourbon Democrats after Reconstruction because 'the party of Lincoln' had become indelibly stamped on the southern mind as pro-Negro. Indeed, for a southern white to question the supremacy of the Democratic party was tantamount to being branded as 'a renegade to race, to God, and to Southern womanhood.'"[8] This same theme was stressed by Roscoe Martin when writing in the 1930s to describe the post-Reconstruction period: "The Democratic Party was looked upon, rightly or wrongly, as the defender of all that was dearest to the hearts of Texans, and those not members of that party were regarded virtually as traitors to the State."[9]

In the election of 1871, the three Republican congressmen were defeated after serving one term, and it would be over twenty years before another Republican would be elected to Congress. In 1894, George H. Noonan served one term from a district centered around San Antonio before being defeated for re-election. Two years later, Robert B. Hawley was elected to the first of two terms representing a district that included Galveston; he did not seek a third term. In the Senate, when the terms of Republican senators Flanagan and Hamilton ended in 1875 and 1877, respectively, the party's representation in that body also ceased.[10]

In the election of 1873, with the return of former Confederates to the electorate, Governor Davis was defeated for re-election and the party's majority in the Texas House of Representatives disappeared. The party's base of voter support through most of the remainder of the nineteenth century came from African Americans. According to the party's official history, some forty-four Blacks served in the Texas legislature as Republicans during the latter part of the nineteenth century.[11] As one historian noted, "Even after the defeat of E. J. Davis and his Reconstruction government, though, Blacks continued to play a prominent part in Texas Republican politics."[12]

After leaving the governor's office, Davis remained as leader of the party until his death in 1883, when he was replaced by Norris Wright Cuney, one of the most prominent African American leaders of his time.[13] With the loss of their elected officials, the party turned more and more to an emphasis on federal patronage at a time when local postmasters and many other officials were political appointees of the national administration. The party began to play primarily national convention politics, seeking to support the proper individuals for the presidency so that state patronage would be directed to them.[14] Cuney was particularly adept at backing the presidential candidates that would ensure his control of Texas appointments when the GOP held the White House.[15]

Despite the ability of the Texas Republican leaders to control federal patronage in the state throughout most of the remainder of the nineteenth century, their ability to gain voter support and elect candidates to office was sorely lacking. From 1882 to 1900, Republicans ran candidates in slightly more than half of all congressional district elections; few of these, however, obtained more than 25 percent of the vote. Support for Republican presidential candidates during this period ranged from a low of 17.3 percent for President Harrison in 1892 to a high of 30.9 percent for President McKinley in 1900. The number of Republican state legislators declined from eight in 1881 to none at the beginning of the twentieth century. Three times during this period, the Republicans fielded no candidate for governor; never did they pose a challenge to the election of a Democrat to the state's highest office. As one Texas writer noted, in the 1890s "whole counties there were which boasted not a single white Republican."[16]

In such an environment, other challengers to the Democratic Party's dominance in Texas did come forward and attempt to elect their candidates to both the presidency and state positions. Chandler Davidson maintains that there were two periods of conflict and competition in the post–Civil War period, first with the Republicans during Reconstruction and then with the Greenback and Populist movements toward the century's end.[17] Whatever competition there was, however, was rather ineffective. The percentage of non-Democrats in the state legislature never exceeded 25 percent from 1874 forward for the next hundred-plus years. Likewise, only four non-Democrats were elected to Congress from the period after Reconstruction to the 1950s. Every governor and United States senator from 1877 to 1961 was a Democrat.

The Greenback Party arrived in Texas in 1878 and died after the 1884 election. Its candidate for governor came second in three elections, reaching a high-water mark of 40.5 percent of the vote in 1882, when there was a Greenback-Republican fusion candidate. In the three other elections the Greenback candidate for governor obtained 23.2 percent (1878), 12.8 percent (1880), and 27.1 percent (1884) of the total vote. Meanwhile, the party elected ten state representatives in 1878, but only three were re-elected in 1880 and none thereafter. Only one candidate was ever elected to Congress from Texas on the Greenback Party ticket. George W. Jones of Bastrop was elected to Congress as a Democrat in 1878 and then re-elected as a Greenback candidate in 1880. Jones ran for governor as a Greenback-Republican fusion candidate in 1882 and finally campaigned as the Republican nominee for governor in 1884.[18]

Following the demise of the Greenback effort, the People's (Populist) Party started with a number of local efforts from 1886 to 1890, when it became more formally organized and ran candidates for governor and the Texas legislature in the next five biennial elections. The party was never successful, only once besting the Republican candidate; the party's vote for governor ranged from 44.2 percent in 1896 (when no Republican ran) to 5.9 percent in its final campaign of 1900. The party sent eight members to the Texas House of Representatives after the 1892 election, increasing its delegation to twenty-two in 1894. From that point, the party went into decline, with only six legislators elected in 1896, four in 1898, and one in 1900.[19]

The Republican challenge to the Democratic Party's dominance was weak during the latter part of the nineteenth century. Beginning soon after Reconstruction and up to the 1920s, internal disputes and efforts to control the party machinery took place between the "Black and Tan" Republicans, who had the support of those Blacks remaining in the electorate, and the "Lily Whites," who attempted to win over former Confederate supporters, with little success. According to Hanes Walton the dispute did not end until 1928, when the Republican National Convention credentials committee voted to seat the "Lily White" group led by R. B. Creager. Thus, "Black and Tan Republicanism came to an end in Texas in 1928."[20]

The Democrats used their overwhelming legislative majority and control of the governor's office to impose a poll tax in 1903 and enact the Terrell Election Law in 1905, two key elements in a plan to limit the influence of those likely to support non-Democratic candidates. According to Chandler Davidson, the Terrell law "encouraged the use of the all-white primary at the county level, increased the difficulty of third party competition, and established a poll tax payment period that ended six months before the primaries and nine months before the general elections."[21] Thus, by the beginning of the twentieth century, Blacks no longer voted in any substantial numbers. According to one historian, of some 650,000 potential Black voters in Texas at the turn of the century, only 25,000 qualified under the new restrictions on the franchise.[22] Neither party appealed to the few Blacks still eligible to vote. It would not be until 1944 that the U.S. Supreme Court finally struck down the "White primary" provisions enforced by the Texas Democratic Party.[23] The combination of barriers to participation not only impacted the ability of Blacks and poor Whites to vote but also ensured virtually total Democratic dominance throughout the first sixty years of the twentieth century.[24]

1900 and Beyond

If the Democratic Party was the dominant force in the nineteenth century, it would be even more so over the first sixty years of the twentieth century. Unlike the changing nature of party opposition in the nineteenth century—from Whig to American to Republican to Greenback to Populist—only the Republicans would provide an enduring alternative to the Democratic Party in the new century, and an extremely weak alternative at that.[25]

Throughout the first fifty years of the twentieth century, Texas was clearly part of the "Solid South" save for the 1928 election, when Herbert Hoover carried the state over Al Smith. In all the other presidential elections, only once did another Republican candidate obtain as much as one-fourth of the total vote; in 1900 William McKinley received 30.9 percent of the total Texas vote. After carrying the state in 1928, President Hoover was abandoned four years later by all but 11.2 percent of the Texas electorate. This was not the lowest level of support for a Republican president seeking re-election, however. In a four-way contest in 1912, William Howard Taft's 9.4 percent of the vote barely squeezed out Teddy Roosevelt's 8.9 percent and Socialist Party candidate Eugene V. Debs's 8.3 percent of the Texas vote. The tiny Republican base was divided further with Roosevelt's campaign against a sitting Republican president and would be split again in 1920 when a "Black and Tan" faction ran its own slate of electors, polling 5.6 percent of the vote.[26] It would not be until 1952— and then only with the backing of the major Democratic elected officials in the state—that a Republican presidential candidate would duplicate Hoover's 1928 performance.

Other than in the 1928 Hoover win, the number of Texas counties carried by the Republican presidential candidate ranged from a low of three in 1912 (Kinney, Webb, and Zapata, along the Mexican border) and 1936 (Gillespie and Kendall in the Hill Country and Tyler in East Texas) to a high of twenty-six in 1920. In his classic *The Emerging Republican Majority*, Kevin Phillips claims that Republicans were beginning to make inroads in the urban areas of Texas in the 1920s, especially Dallas and Houston, only to be stopped by the Depression.[27] However, this does not

Table 3.2. Counties carried by GOP presidential candidate and percentage of statewide vote, 1900–1948

Year	Number of counties carried by GOP	Statewide percentage of vote	Year	Number of counties carried by GOP	Statewide percentage of vote
1900	19	30.9	1928	140	51.7
1904	13	22.0	1932	0	11.2
1908	11	22.4	1936	3	12.5
1912	3	9.4	1940	7	19.0
1916	9	17.4	1944	7	16.7
1920	26	23.5	1948	8	24.6
1924	14	19.8			

seem borne out by the raw data. Prior to the Hoover-Smith contest, only once did the GOP candidate carry any of the Big 6 counties, when Harding received more votes than Cox in Bexar County in 1920. In that election, Harding obtained 35.2 percent of the vote from the Big 6 counties, only slightly better than William Howard Taft's 28.7 percent of the vote in 1908. The unique factors of "Rum, Romanism, and Rebellion" in 1928 can account for Hoover carrying 140 of Texas's 254 counties, including four of the Big 6 counties.

What support there was for Republican presidential candidates in isolated areas of the state basically died out with the coming of the Depression in 1929. Even in the traditionally Republican counties of the Hill Country and South Central Texas, Franklin D. Roosevelt and New Deal politics would dominate over the next twenty-plus years. Over the thirteen presidential elections from 1900 to 1948, only three German-influenced counties supported the Republican candidate with any regularity. Gillespie and Kendall Counties provided a GOP majority in eleven of the thirteen contests while Guadalupe did so in nine. None of the three carried for Taft in 1912 or Hoover in 1932 (table 3.2).

Clearly, over this fifty-year period, setting aside 1928, Democratic presidential candidates could take it virtually for granted that they would receive the Electoral College votes from Texas. Nevertheless, Texas Democrats did play an important role in their party during this time. Congressman John Nance Garner became speaker when the party gained a majority in the U.S. House of Representatives after the 1930 election. Two years later he sought the Democratic presidential nomination, stepping aside for Franklin D. Roosevelt, who then chose Garner as his vice presidential running mate. Garner served two terms in that office and was expected to be a candidate for the presidential nomination in 1940, until Roosevelt arranged to seek a third term in office.

The situation with the Texas congressional delegation was little different. Only one Republican—Harry M. Wurzbach—won election to Congress from Texas.[28] Wurzbach represented a district centered around San Antonio and served first from 1921 to 1929. When defeated for re-election in 1928 with 49.7 percent of the vote, he challenged the outcome before the House of Representatives and one year later was seated. Wurzbach then won his last term in the 1930 elections and died in office in 1931. Wurzbach's election was warmly welcomed by most Republicans, but not by Rentfro B. Creager.[29] Wurzbach and Creager battled for control of patronage during the 1920s, including backing their own candidates for the gubernatorial nomination in the party's first primary election of 1926.[30]

Of the 470 congressional district elections from 1902 to 1950, the GOP had candidates filed in 212, or 45 percent, of all possible contests. However, only 25 of these 212 candidacies (5.3%) were able to obtain as much as 25 percent of the vote, 6 of the 25 with Harry Wurzbach as the candidate.

The elections for United States senator produced similar results. Democratic candidates won every race, and only two Republican candidates obtained over 25 percent of the vote. In 1922, George E. B. Peddy received 33.4 percent against Earle B. Mayfield, while in 1948 Jack Porter won 32.9 percent of the vote against Lyndon B. Johnson after Johnson's eighty-seven-vote primary victory over Coke Stevenson, the famous "Landslide Lyndon" election involving late-appearing returns.[31] Even with these two almost credible showings, the average Republican percentage in the ten races the party contested was 16.2 percent, slightly less than one in six votes cast.

The situation in state elections could not be described as any more encouraging. In the twenty-five biennial contests for governor, Republicans ran candidates in twenty-two elections, surpassing 25 percent of the vote only twice. The party's irrelevancy was most evident in the 1912 and 1914 elections, when its candidates received less than 8 percent of the vote each time and came in third—behind the candidate of the Socialist Party. In fact, seven of the twenty-two candidates could not reach as high as 10 percent of the vote. Only the elections involving Miriam "Ma" Ferguson in 1924 and 1932 gave Texans a reason to consider the Republican candidate. George C. Butte obtained 41.1 percent of the vote in 1924 and Orville Bullington received 38.1 percent in 1932. As would be expected, no Republican candidate was elected to any of the myriad of other state-wide offices over this period of time.

A similar situation existed with the Texas legislature. From 1900 to 1960 there were never more than three members of the Texas House and one state senator elected as a Republican.[32] The largest delegation of non-Democrats served in the 1921 regular session of the Texas legislature when four candidates elected on the American Party ticket were in the house. Only one, John H. Wessels of Fayette County, was re-elected, but as a Republican. Starting in 1930 up to 1960 no Republican served in either chamber save for Edward T. Dicker of Dallas, who was elected to one two-year term in 1950. Over the entire half-century only three others were elected to the Texas House as independents or "no party," most serving only one or two terms.

State election law required a primary to be held for any political party whose gubernatorial candidate received over one hundred thousand votes (later revised to a two-hundred-thousand minimum). Moreover, primary elections were to be conducted and funded by the party, not the state, as Texas maintained that political parties were private organizations, a key point in their defense of the Democratic Party's White primary. When University of Texas law professor George C. Butte garnered nearly three hundred thousand votes against Ma Ferguson in 1924, the Republicans were required to hold and finance the cost of a primary in 1926. Some 15,239 Texans voted in the first "statewide" Republican primary while 821,234 participated in the Democratic primary that year.[33] The party's mediocre performance in gubernatorial elections meant that only four more primaries would be held in a handful of counties until the 1960s, only one of which involved even as many voters as the 1926 primary.[34]

Democratic Party dominance of Texas politics over the first half of the twentieth century is no more apparent than in voter history in primary and general elections. It was the rare situation when more Texans voted in a general election than in the Democratic Party primary of that year. In nonpresidential years, more took part in the Democratic primary than voted in the November election each year up to 1962. Since they had to be financed and staffed by the party, Republican primaries were viewed not as a means to increase support but, rather, as a burden placed on the party. As O. Douglas Weeks noted, "The Democratic Party has always had a near-monopoly on local offices and its primaries are in fact the local elections. Hence, if Republicans cannot be induced to run for local office, there is no source of funds for holding Republican primaries even when a large vote in the previous general election of a Republican candidate for governor makes it mandatory."[35] Clearly the important choice to be made for most public offices took place in the Democratic primary, as that party's candidate was virtually guaranteed election in November. In fact, it was the rare Democratic primary in a nonpresidential year that did not attract at least twice as many voters as the November general election.[36]

Post Office Republicans

It is in such a context that a history of the early twentieth-century Republican Party is mainly a recitation of state and national convention politics. With the exception of the Wilson years, from 1913 to 1921, Republicans controlled the White House up to the election of Franklin D. Roosevelt in 1932. In Texas, federal patronage was all that kept the party alive and gave it a purpose for existence. From the 1920s to the early 1950s, Rentfro B. Creager of Brownsville was the dominant force in Texas Republican politics. Creager had been the party's candidate for governor in 1916, receiving 49,198 votes, or 13.5 percent, of the total ballots cast. But it was his support for Warren G. Harding at the 1920 Republican National Convention that initially gave him influence and power. By 1921 he was state chairman and two years later became national committeeman, holding that position until his death in 1950. After Harding's election, Creager "within two years became sole patronage referee in Texas and created a new state headquarters organization."[37]

It is important to remember that patronage was a major factor in making appointments to a number of federal positions within the states. Many party leaders became U.S. attorneys, collectors of customs, and postmasters for areas large and small. A survey in 1928, when many Texas counties did not even have a Republican county chairman, showed that thirty-six county chairmen were postmasters and another thirty-two were married to postmasters.[38] Keeping the party small and discouraging participation was one way that Creager and his allies could retain control of patronage.

When Lloyd Bentsen Sr. moved to Mission, Texas, he met with Creager and expressed a desire to become active in the party. Creager's advice was for Bentsen to join the Democratic Party, maintaining that "what's best for Texas is for every state in the union to have a two-party system and for Texas to be a one-party state. When you have a one-party state, your men stay in Congress longer and build up seniority."[39] Bentsen Sr. took his advice and his son, Lloyd Jr., was subsequently elected as a Democrat to the U.S. House and Senate before becoming the Democratic vice presidential candidate in 1988 and later secretary of the treasury under President Clinton. Meanwhile, Creager kept the Republican Party as a tight-knit group and discouraged the involvement of ambitious potential challengers to his control.[40]

Democratic Party Factionalism

With the election of FDR in 1932, the lure of patronage disappeared and the Republican Party entered into what has been called "an extended period of hibernation" that would continue into the 1950s.[41] The small band of party stalwarts occupied themselves with controlling the party machinery and the delegations to the Republican National Conventions. Texas politics shifted even more into a totally Democratic orbit. Meanwhile, the New Deal policies of the Roosevelt administration exacerbated divisions within the state Democratic Party that would have a lasting impact on subsequent partisan developments. While some in the party identified with and supported the economic and social policies associated with the New Deal, others were adamantly opposed. As Chandler Davidson notes, "In Texas, a split gradually developed along liberal-conservative lines focusing on the New Deal and early civil rights measures, especially the Supreme Court's 1944 decision declaring the Texas all-white primary unconstitutional. . . . Thus, by the mid-1940s, the broad philosophic coalitions had taken shape, developing leaders and institutions to give them cohesion."[42] With the Republican Party an empty shell devoid of the appeal of patronage and the possibility of election, it is understandable that this ideological conflict took place within the one dominant political party in the state. Throughout the 1940s, the battle was described as "the most bitter intra-Democratic fight along New Deal and anti-New Deal lines in the South."[43]

In presidential politics, this conservative opposition to the New Deal took different routes. These began as early as 1940, when there was considerable uncertainty as to whether Roosevelt would seek a precedent-breaking third term. Vice President John Nance Garner launched an effort to gain the presidential nomination, only to be stopped by FDR's announcement that he would run again. Conservative forces in control of the Texas party had pushed through the state convention a delegation pledged to Garner over a slate of FDR delegates backed by a young congressman Lyndon Johnson and the leading liberal of the day, Maury

Maverick Sr., then mayor of San Antonio.[44] Some observers viewed the 1940 Garner effort as the first clear-cut conservative-liberal conflict of the twentieth century, one that would continue for at least the next fifty years: "It was also bizarre that in one of the nation's strongest Democratic states, neither the Governor nor the Vice President of the United States, perhaps the two most powerful Texas Democrats, endorsed the Democratic President's re-election. . . . While Roosevelt won his third term, the Texas turmoil was the harbinger of the internecine warfare that plagued the state's Democratic presidential politics in future years."[45] Despite this lack of support from key state officials, Roosevelt carried Texas with ease, receiving 80.9 percent of the vote, an indication of both FDR's broad support and the weakness of the Republican label in the state.

Four years later, another battle would take place over FDR's decision to seek a fourth term. This time the strategy of the Texas Regulars was to have the Democratic State Convention nominate a slate for the Electoral College of individuals who would not vote for Roosevelt. Supported by Senator W. Lee "Pappy" O'Daniel, former governor Dan Moody, and other conservatives, the Texas Regulars won the first state convention but then lost at the second one. This led them to run their own slate of electors in the general election, but they attracted few votes and carried only one county. Nevertheless, "the precedent established by conservative Texas Democrats, unhappy with the direction of the national party and willing to abandon that party out of ideological conviction, was as significant as anything else born of the revolt."[46] An unintended consequence of the effort to deny a fourth term to FDR was that the liberal faction obtained control of the state Democratic executive committee.[47]

In 1948, conservatives were in control of the state's delegation to the Democratic National Convention, and all fifty delegate votes were cast for Senator Richard Russell of Georgia rather than President Truman. Once the national convention was over, conservative forces attempted to have the state convention name electors who would support Governor J. Strom Thurmond of South Carolina rather than Truman. Loyalist forces controlled the convention, however, and the states' rights backers walked out carrying Thurmond banners and Confederate flags. Some of those who had backed the Garner and Texas Regulars efforts against FDR as well as the Russell candidacy could be found in the Dixiecrat movement that nominated Thurmond and ran a slate of electors pledged to him. On election day, however, they could obtain only 9.3 percent of the vote as the Democratic nominee, President Truman, carried Texas handily with 65.4 percent of the vote.[48]

Although unsuccessful in opposing Roosevelt and Truman in the 1940s, conservative Democrats persisted, taking a different path in 1952: "If you can't beat them, join them." When the Democratic National Convention nominated Governor Adlai Stevenson of Illinois, he was perceived as too liberal for many Texas Democrats. Led by Governor Allan Shivers and Senator Price Daniel, many Democratic elected officials endorsed and campaigned for the Republican nominee, Dwight Eisenhower.[49] In both 1952 and 1956, Eisenhower carried the state to join Hoover as the only two Republican presidential candidates to win Texas. With the defection of the conservative Democratic officials, the liberal element in the party gained stature by their claim of being loyal Democrats.

The ideological split in the party was reflected in more than presidential politics.[50] It can be seen also in efforts by both sides to control the party machinery. As Chandler Davidson notes, this split was "at least as much a story of the battle for control of the Democratic party through the convention process as it is the much better-known account of electoral struggle between liberal and conservative candidates for public office."[51] The conservative challenge to a fourth term for Roosevelt provided sufficient ammunition for the liberal element to gain majority support on the state party executive committee. The conservative element soon regained control, but these internal party battles would continue for the next thirty years, until the liberal faction regained control in 1976.[52]

As long as conservatives remained dominant in the Democratic Party, they prevented the growth of the Republican alternative in Texas. This strategy proved unbeatable for many years and allowed the conservative Democrats to preserve their one-party domination of Texas politics.[53] According to Bartley and Graham, "The pattern in Texas illustrates the shrewd ability of conservative Democratic governors to rally to their standards in the hard-fought primaries sufficient upper-income voters to edge the liberal coalition of blacks and lower-income whites. Then in the general elections the Democratic voters remained in the fold, and the G.O.P. suffered biannual humiliation. Little wonder that the morale of both liberal Democrats and loyal Republicans remained chronically low in Texas."[54]

The liberal faction in the Democratic Party backed a number of candidates for statewide office but had little success until the late 1950s. Perhaps the first significant liberal campaign was that of Homer Rainey for governor in 1946.[55] Rainey had been removed as president of the University of Texas and used that event as a launching pad for a statewide campaign. Rainey had been labeled as "a friend of radical labor and an adherent of radical left-wing ideology" but still succeeded in reaching a runoff with Beauford Jester.[56] The more conservative candidate won the runoff, with Rainey polling some 34 percent of the vote. Nevertheless, his campaign has been described as "a harbinger of the racial-economic liberalism that was to become a fixture in Texas politics."[57]

While Rainey can be seen as the first clear-cut liberal candidate for statewide office, it is Ralph Yarborough who carried the ideological banner into a series of campaigns during the 1950s, including his victory in the 1957 special election for the U.S. Senate. Yarborough first campaigned against Governor Allan Shivers in 1952, obtaining 37 percent of the vote, a percentage slightly greater than that obtained by Rainey six years earlier. Yarborough ran again in 1954 and this time came much closer to Shivers, losing with 46.8 percent of the runoff vote. Two years later he came within 4,200 votes of gubernatorial candidate Price Daniel in their runoff. Since Daniel was a sitting United States senator from Texas, he resigned his seat to become governor, and a senate vacancy occurred. After these three unsuccessful campaigns for governor, Yarborough struck gold in the 1957 special election for the U.S. Senate. In a twenty-two-candidate race involving Republican Thad Hutcheson and conservative Democratic congressman Martin Dies, Yarborough's 38.1 percent of the vote was sufficient for victory.[58]

For the first time in a statewide race, the conservative vote had been divided between a relatively well-financed and organized Republican candidate and a traditional conservative Democratic candidate. In such a situation, the liberal faction had won due to a three-way division of the vote. Clearly, if conservatives could be encouraged to support a Republican candidate—and take part in any GOP primary—the support for a conservative Democrat would be decreased, increasing the chances for a liberal victory. Facing a conservative opponent as the incumbent in each of his next three elections, Yarborough defeated William Blakley in 1958 and Gordon McLendon in 1964 before being defeated by former congressman Lloyd Bentsen in the 1970 primary. Yarborough's situation was aided by the existence of a Republican primary in each of these elections, drawing only a handful of voters in 1958 but a sizable number in the Goldwater-Rockefeller primary of 1964. He made one last attempt to regain his seat in the United States Senate in 1972. Yarborough came in first in the regular primary but then lost an exceedingly close runoff to former U.S. attorney Barefoot Sanders.[59]

Yarborough's liberalism was of a populist nature that appealed more to rural voters than to those in the heavily urban areas. As Bartley and

Graham noted, "Yarborough ran best in the hills and piney woods of east Texas; he fared worst in the heavily Chicano machine counties of South Texas; and he lost west Texas, though usually by relatively narrow margins."[60] This alliance of support allowed him to overcome the strength of the upper-income and middle-income voters in the major urban counties, voters who had been the base of conservative support in the Democratic Party and who were to move increasingly into the Republican fold, first in general elections and eventually in Republican primaries.

Yarborough's victory gave new hope to the liberal faction in the party. As one author maintains, "The significance of the Yarborough battle for control is that it launched a grassroots effort to rid the Texas Democratic party of conservative-minded Democrats."[61] The objective was to capture the party organization when and where possible and encourage conservatives to affiliate with the Republicans by voting in their primary.[62] Such a strategy required two developments beyond the liberal Democrats' control, however—the existence of a Republican primary and a desire by the Republican leadership to seek to win major elective offices in Texas.

Mr. Republican of Mid-Century

With the coming of the New Deal and throughout the 1950s, the necessary conditions for Republican viability were seldom present. Of the twenty contests for governor and U.S. senator from 1934 to 1958, eighteen could not attract as much as one in six votes, and none received as much as one-third of the total votes cast (table 3.3). It was not until 1948 that a brief resurgence in electoral progress could be seen, coupled with a move by new leadership to actively promote candidates who could compete with the dominant party. This came with a challenge to the leadership of national committeeman R. B. Creager and his key lieutenant, state chairman Henry Zweifel, representative of the "Old Guard" forces determined to keep the party small.[63]

As in past years, the challenge centered around presidential nominating politics involving an effort by Herbert Brownell to organize support for Governor Thomas E. Dewey of New York in the late 1940s against the "post office Republicans" who supported Senator Robert Taft of Ohio. Brownell had been campaign manager for Dewey in 1944 and then served as Republican national chairman from 1944 to 1946, only to return as Dewey's campaign manager in his 1948 presidential campaign. For Texas, the results of Brownell's efforts were to create "a bloc of committed partisans with a vested interest in the GOP's future" who were interested in

Table 3.3. GOP percentage of vote for governor and U.S. senator, 1934–1954

Year	Governor	U.S. senator	Year	Governor	U.S. senator
1934	3.1	2.9	1948	14.7	32.9
1936	7.0	7.1	1950	9.8	—
1938	3.1	—	1952[a]	—	—
1940	5.3	5.7	1954	10.4	14.8
1942	3.2	4.4	1956	14.8	—
1944	9.1	—	1958	11.9	23.6
1946	8.8	11.5			

[a] In 1952, the Republican Party endorsed most statewide Democratic candidates who ran on both parties' columns. This endorsement was regarded as a "quid pro quo" for the Democratic officeholders' endorsement of Eisenhower. Democratic and Republican votes for governor and senator were counted separately and are discussed later in this chapter.

winning elections and ending the rule of the post office Republicans.[64] While Brownell succeeded in winning the nomination for Dewey once again in 1948, the outcome in Texas was less immediately apparent as Creager delivered thirty of the state's thirty-three delegates to Robert A. Taft on the convention's first ballot.[65]

Although the Dewey forces were unsuccessful in combatting Creager and Zweifel during the preface to the 1948 Republican National Convention, a more significant challenge was forthcoming. Their nemesis would be H. J. "Jack" Porter, a young businessman from Houston who was committed to growing the party and making it an electoral force in the state.[66] Still in his early forties, Jack Porter had been successful in the oil business, was a founder of the Texas Independent Producers & Royalty Owners (TIPRO) association, and dedicated to using his time and talents in civic endeavors. Wanting to become more involved in Republican politics, Porter agreed to take on the task of recruiting a Senate candidate for the 1948 elections. Porter approached former governor and U.S. senator W. Lee O'Daniel, who declined the offer. After several friends and associates encouraged him to become the candidate, Porter agreed to run. Meanwhile, the Democratic primary ended up as a contest between former governor Coke Stevenson, supported by the dominant conservative faction, and Congressman Lyndon B. Johnson, backed by the loyalist wing of the party and Speaker Sam Rayburn. After the late returns came in from South Texas, it became clear that Johnson had won the nomination by eighty-seven votes.

With only two months to election day, Porter's efforts were described as "nothing short of heroic."[67] Porter hired a professional staff, placed ads in most daily newspapers, and campaigned throughout the state, covering areas where few Republicans had ever been seen. Johnson was perceived as closely associated with Truman and the national Democratic Party, and his primary battle had been so bitter that Coke Stevenson crossed over and endorsed Porter. "Lyndon B. Johnson won the Senate seat, but Jack Porter ran well—eighty thousand votes ahead of Thomas E. Dewey. Porter carried two oil-rich cities, Tyler in East Texas and Midland in West Texas, and most of the German counties. . . . To Porter, the election returns proved that the Republican party in Texas might become effective if it had strong candidates, adequate financing, and aggressive leadership."[68] Though nowhere near victory, Porter had captured almost 350,000 votes for slightly less than one-third of the total votes cast. Two years previously the Republican Senate candidate could only attract 43,619 votes.

Jack Porter had won eleven counties, building on the traditional GOP base in the German Hill Country counties of Comal, Guadalupe, Kendall, Gillespie, Kerr, and Bandera, as well as expanding to the smaller urban centers of Midland, Gregg, and Smith Counties. In the state's three largest counties, Porter was a credible challenger, notching 48.7 percent of the vote in Harris, 48.3 percent in Dallas, and 45.0 percent in Bexar. Clearly, Porter's performance was of a different character than any of the earlier party campaigns and set a new standard, even if it was still far short of the mark.

Once the 1948 campaign was over, Porter remained committed to his belief that the Republican Party could become a competitive force in state politics. Now known to most Republicans from his statewide campaign, Porter challenged the leadership of Creager and Zweifel. As Paul Casdorph described the conflict, "It was basically a contest between the old faction of the party which sought only control of the federal patronage, and the new faction which had a real desire to build a genuine two-party system party in Texas."[69] For the next few years the old guard remained in control. When Creager died in October 1950, Zweifel had sufficient votes on the state committee to succeed him as national committeeman, and Orville Bullington, a gubernatorial candidate in 1932, became state chairman.

The year 1950 did bring two fleeting victories for the GOP, however.

After Democratic congressman Eugene Worley resigned to accept an appointment as a federal judge, eleven candidates ran in a May 1950 special election—ten Democrats and Republican Ben Guill. With some 23 percent of the vote Guill came in first and became the first Republican to serve in Congress since the death of Harry Wurzbach in 1931. Six months later, however, Guill was a former congressman, having been defeated in the November general election. Meanwhile, in that same general election Edward T. Dicker became a state representative from Dallas, the first Republican in the Texas legislature since 1930. Dicker's tenure was also short-lived as he was defeated for re-election in 1952, at which point the legislature went back to total Democratic Party control.

Porter's efforts from 1950 forward were focused on lining up support for Dwight D. Eisenhower. Porter agreed with the former general on policy matters, and he also sought to establish himself as a force in Texas politics. "Eisenhower's candidacy was exactly what Porter needed for his own purposes. With the Texas Republican organization still firmly in the hands of the pro-Taft old guard, Porter, like Creager in 1920, needed a candidate who would carry him into power. . . . Porter would have to do more than support Eisenhower; control of the delegation to the national convention was every bit as important as backing the winning candidate."[70] The conflict within the Republican Party of Texas ended up being one of the key factors in the eventual nomination of Dwight Eisenhower. In many ways it was a battle between Henry Zweifel and Jack Porter as much as it was between Eisenhower and Taft.[71]

By 1952, Dwight Eisenhower was an extremely popular leader who had served as president of Columbia University and was now supreme allied commander of the North Atlantic Treaty Organization (NATO). Activists from both major political parties attempted to recruit him, and he finally decided to become a Republican candidate for president of the United States. Building on the broad support for Eisenhower among the electorate at large, Porter and his forces convinced many who had never been involved in politics to attend the Republican precinct conventions. These "new Republicans" would then elect delegates to higher-level conventions who would be pledged to Eisenhower.[72] When the precinct conventions were held across the state in the spring of 1952, literally thousands of Eisenhower supporters swamped the longtime Republicans who were backing Taft. The result was a series of credentials challenges at the county, state, and national conventions.

Some 2,200 precinct conventions were held across the state, each electing delegates to 230 county conventions, which, in turn, elected 984 delegates to the Republican State Convention, held that year in Mineral Wells. Henry Zweifel and the Taft supporters were in control of the convention and successfully challenged the credentials of five hundred Eisenhower delegates, replacing them with Taft supporters and electing a slate of thirty-eight national convention delegates pledged to Taft. Porter and his Eisenhower backers were forced to hold a rump convention at which they selected a slate of thirty-three delegates pledged to Eisenhower and five pledged to Taft, a proportion reflecting what they believed to have been the distribution of support at the original precinct conventions. The Taft victory was short-lived, however. When the national convention convened in Chicago the delegate slate led by Porter and pledged to Eisenhower was seated in place of the rival slate backed by Zweifel and supportive of Taft.[73] Eisenhower would win the nomination and the election that November, while Zweifel's time as national committeeman and a leader in the state party would come to a close.

Jack Porter was elected to replace Zweifel as Republican national committeeman from Texas and served in that capacity for the next eight years. He devoted himself to building an effective campaign organization that served as the groundwork for future success. At the same time, some viewed Porter as autocratic, attempting to control the party organization in much the same way as Creager had from 1920 to 1950. Porter's contributions to the growth of party competition are best summed up by historian Roger Olien: "What had he accomplished? A fair answer is clearly implied by his unofficial title, 'Mr. Republican,' respectfully accorded him by Republicans and Democrats alike. More than anyone else, Jack Porter had brought the Texas GOP into competitive electoral politics."[74] It would be some time before the Republicans could become that competitive force and begin electing many of their candidates to office; the 1952 presidential campaign and its aftermath would dominate the remainder of the decade.

Shivercrats and the Co-opting of Conservatives

For all three presidential elections in the 1940s, conservative elements within the Democratic Party had opposed the national party nominee, supporting Garner in 1940, the Texas Regulars slate of electors in 1944, and the States' Rights party slate in 1948. None of these approaches had succeeded, as Roosevelt and Truman carried Texas in each election. A much different path would be taken in 1952 under the leadership of Governor Allan Shivers.

In July of 1949, Governor Beauford Jester died in office and was succeeded by Lieutenant Governor Allan Shivers. Shivers was then elected in his own right in 1950 and has been described as having "exerted as much or more influence on the earliest stages of partisan realignment and modern conservatism in Texas than anyone else."[75] That influence was not, however, to result in general partisan realignment but, rather, in the development of a breed of voters known as "presidential Republicans."[76]

As governor, Allan Shivers led the conservative forces in the Texas Democratic Party, and his allies controlled the Texas delegation to the 1952 Democratic National Convention. All fifty-six delegate votes were cast for Senator Richard Russell of Georgia, the Southern conservative candidate for president. However, Governor Adlai Stevenson of Illinois became the party's nominee. In addition to Stevenson's perceived liberalism, a major concern in Texas centered on whether the tidelands beyond the state's border in the Gulf of Mexico would be controlled by Texas or the federal government. President Truman and candidate Stevenson supported the federal position in this dispute, one that involved the potential disposition of millions in oil revenue.

Texas Democrats were so concerned about the tidelands issue that liberal activist Walter Hall commissioned a sixteen-page response, "The Truth about Tidelands," that was used to defend Truman's actions. According to the pamphlet, the issue was merely one more effort to destroy the party. "The enemies of the Democratic party in Texas, who for years have been attempting to defeat and discredit it, have thus far permitted only their side of the issue to be presented to the people of Texas." Hall realized that the issue of states' rights and state control of the offshore oil reserves could be a major weapon against Stevenson unless a response was provided.[77]

Returning from the Democratic National Convention in Chicago, Governor Shivers not only endorsed Republican candidate Eisenhower but also helped provide him with an official endorsement from the Texas Democratic Party.[78] Eisenhower had been endorsed previously by Attorney General Price Daniel, the Democratic nominee for the United States Senate, and would gain the backing of former governors Will Hobby, Dan Moody, and Coke Stevenson.[79] Just as importantly, Shivers and all but one of the statewide Democratic candidates were cross-endorsed by the Republicans and ran in the 1952 election as both Democratic and Republican nominees.[80] This bipartisanship extended to the congressional delegation, where only one of the twenty-two members of the House of Representatives was opposed by a Republican candidate.[81]

With the strong support of the Democratic governor and most other Democratic candidates, as well as the nascent Republican organization, Dwight D. Eisenhower became the second Republican presidential candidate in history to carry Texas. The Republican obtained 53.2 percent of the two-party vote statewide and carried the Big 6 counties with 58.6 percent. Eisenhower also carried the twenty-one Other Metro counties with 52.6 percent of the vote. Meanwhile, the Republican candidate nearly broke even in the twenty-nine Suburban counties around the Big 6 and in the 198 Small Town counties, losing the suburbs by 2,191 votes and the rural areas by only 14,425 votes. However, as historian Paul Casdorph noted, "It had not been a Republican victory that carried the state for Eisenhower in 1952, but a strong conservative-Democratic one."[82] This sentiment was evident in the bumper stickers displayed on pickup trucks and cars throughout the state proclaiming, "I'm a Democrat, but I Like Ike."[83]

By endorsing the Republican presidential candidate and co-opting the GOP line for most major elective offices, Shivers had ensured that conservatives would be elected to office while not allowing a competing political party to gain leverage. As T. R. Fehrenbach observed, "A majority of conservative Democrats might vote for the national Republican ticket, as they did in 1952 and 1956, but, in local control, this same majority felt the one-party system adequately served their needs. Republicans contested few local races, and won even fewer, but there was a steady, noticeable growth, fed by the unpopular policies of the nationally dominant Northern Democrats."[84] These "presidential Republicans" remained Democrats in all other elections. Historian Randolph B. Campbell notes that "Shivers and his fellow leaders continued to support the traditional one-party system and to control government at the state and local level."[85]

Thanks to Shivers's position that ideological convictions trumped partisan loyalty, Eisenhower was able to carry Texas in both of his elections, and Richard Nixon nearly won in 1960, losing by some forty-six thousand votes to a ticket featuring a Texan as the vice presidential candidate. Meanwhile, conservatives continued to dominate the Democratic primary, thereby preventing the Republicans from developing a clear-cut alternative. This strategy proved unbeatable for many years and allowed the conservative faction to remain in control of the Democratic nominations and, with them, most statewide and local offices.[86] Shivers had facilitated the growth of a new breed of Texas voters, the presidential Republicans, but, in so doing, had helped to ensure the continued conservative dominance of the Texas Democratic Party and hindered the development of a viable state Republican challenge.[87]

Eisenhower's victory had returned a Republican to the White House after a twenty-year hiatus, but there would be little to show for it among the Texas Republicans. Once ensconced in office, "Eisenhower largely ignored the state's embryonic Republican party, choosing instead to co-operate with Shivers and the conservative Democratic establishment."[88] The new administration in Washington had little interest in developing a viable Republican Party in Texas and "was not inclined to use patronage and other prerogatives in the interest of the party in Texas."[89] In fact, Eisenhower and his associates in the national party seemed to have little desire to build up the Republican presence in the South more generally, waiting until 1957 to launch Operation Dixie, an outreach program that had little success. Moreover, the only two Southerners appointed to the Eisenhower cabinet were lifelong Texas Democrats Oveta Culp Hobby as secretary of health, education, and welfare, and Robert Anderson as secretary of the treasury.[90]

The historian Roger Olien concluded, "The Eisenhower administration worked at cross-purposes with party leaders."[91] The focus of the administration's political patronage in Texas was directed from the office of Democratic governor Shivers rather than from Republican national committeeman Jack Porter, despite the fact that Porter had played a critical role in producing the Eisenhower nomination at the 1952 Republican National Convention. This decision greatly hampered the ability of the Republicans to be seen as a viable alternative force in the state. "The political consequences of the inability of Porter and the Texas Republicans to control patronage went beyond the denial of places to party faithful and the attendant failure to groom strong candidates for state and congressional offices. Equally significant was the fact that Jack Porter and other party leaders could not demonstrate to influential state conservatives that the Republican party in Texas was to be taken seriously."[92] To many of the political, civic, and business leaders of Texas, Republicans were still viewed as somewhat outside the norm.

Even into the 1950s it was deemed socially unacceptable in various parts of the state to be identified as a Republican. Writing in 1963, Clifton McCleskey could claim that "segments of the community crucial to Republican success, especially those engaged in some manner in serving the public, are often reluctant to become too closely identified with the GOP because of the fear it would lead to the erosion of their economic and even social position in the community."[93] The end result of this "social ostracism" was noted by William J. Crotty in a study of North Carolina politics. He concluded that "the minority party is in the unenviable position of molding a coalition of out group interests in accordance with classic American political practices. . . . The minority party attracts individuals less integrated into the social structure of the community and less susceptible to its mores."[94] As late as the 1960s, a study of rural Texas Democratic county chairmen found that they perceived their role as a civic duty rather than a partisan advocate for candidates, "an apolitical, nonparty, legal-duty orientation. They are neither campaign nor organization oriented, . . . confining themselves to impartially administering the election code."[95]

As the administration continued in office, its emphasis on advancing a "modern Republicanism" would only pose additional concerns for the Texas Republicans, whose ideological center was clearly further to the right. By the end of the Eisenhower administration, the Texas Republican Party was making clear its differences with the White House on policy as well as patronage matters, a conflict that resulted in some difficulties for the vice president as he attempted to win in his own right in 1960.

Despite the fact that the decision to cross-endorse so many Democratic candidates in 1952 had negated the possibility of any Eisenhower coattails, it did produce some solid evidence that there was a base of Republican voter support in the state, especially in some of its more populous counties. By running on both the Democratic and Republican tickets, Governor Shivers had provided a clear measure of partisan support, a measure that eliminated factors such as ideology and candidate personal characteristics. When a voter chose to support Democratic candidate Shivers or Republican candidate Shivers, the choice was made solely on a partisan basis. Therefore, the totals provide some interesting precursors of future voting behavior.

Statewide, both Governor Shivers and Senate candidate Price Daniel received almost exactly the same vote total on the Republican ticket (468,320 votes for Shivers and 469,594 for Daniel), constituting roughly one in four votes cast. These raw totals were more votes than any Republican candidate for any office had ever received previously in Texas. Both carried three counties as the Republican candidate—the traditional base of Gillespie and Kendall Counties, but also the second largest county in the state, Dallas. It would be this last county that would produce the first meaningful breakthrough in congressional representation since the 1920s. Republicans could take heart in the raw numbers of voters who chose their party line even if it remained only a small percentage of the total electorate and produced no officeholders.

The Eisenhower Years

Texas Republicans found themselves in a complicated situation after the 1952 elections. Their candidate was now the president of the United States and the tidelands issue had been settled in favor of Texas ownership. Republicans were also in control of both houses of Congress. They found themselves in a position of having to defend a national government sometimes advocating policies to which they, from their conservative perspective, were opposed. Moreover, at the state level they had given their party's endorsement to Governor Shivers, who remained an active leader of the opposing political party.

Since Governor Shivers had obtained more than two hundred thousand votes on the Republican line in 1952, the party was required to hold primary elections in 1954. This posed a problem for the Republican leadership due to "the desire of the organization to aid in the re-nomination of Governor Shivers in the Democratic primaries by freeing Republicans to vote in them."[96] The end result was that Republican primaries were held in 150 of the state's 254 counties but had a turnout of only 9,606 voters statewide. The party ran candidates in 12 of the 150 state house of representatives districts and for five congressional seats. In the statewide races, the GOP candidate for governor could attract only 10.4 percent of the vote, while its U.S. Senate candidate received support from 15.0 percent of the electorate. It appeared to one observer that "the Republican party, standing alone and without the benefit of cross-filing and Eisenhower, had dropped back to its normal insignificance in state politics."[97]

There was one bright spot to the election returns and it came from Dallas, one of the three counties where in the previous election Shivers and Daniel had obtained more votes as the Republican than Democratic candidate. In a contest for an open seat, Republican Bruce Alger became the lone Republican in the state's congressional delegation. Alger's success was brought about as "platoons of energetic women effectively carried out a grass-roots campaign, backed by telephone squads and canvassing teams."[98] The Alger victory was a tremendous boost for Republicans statewide, but especially in Dallas County, an area that would be a substantial base of support for the party for several years. As one GOP leader noted a few years later, "If I had to trace the one thing that got the Republicans going on a statewide level, I would say it was the election of Alger. For the first time we saw that we could elect a man to Congress from the Republican party."[99] Alger would go on to serve ten years in Congress until defeated in the Johnson landslide of 1964.

Eisenhower was re-elected in 1956, again with the support of Shivers and most conservative Democrats but without the official imprimatur of the Texas Democratic State Convention that he had obtained previously. While the president carried the state, the GOP candidate for governor, William Bryant, performed in the traditional Republican mold. In a three-way contest involving Democrat Price Daniel and W. Lee O'Daniel as a write-in candidate, Bryant could obtain only 14.8 percent of the vote. Republicans ran five candidates for Congress, but only Alger was successful, with none of the others receiving more than 35 percent of the vote. It was described at the time as "a rather poor record for a party which professed to be in the process of becoming a serious rival to the Democratic party in the politics of the state."[100]

Having been elected as governor in November 1956, Price Daniel had to resign his seat in the United States Senate, necessitating a special election in the spring of 1957. With twenty-two candidates in the race, Republicans coalesced around their one contestant, attorney Thad Hutcheson of Houston. The three main competitors turned out to be conservative Democratic congressman Martin Dies, liberal Democrat Ralph Yarborough, and Hutcheson. While Republicans were enthusiastically supporting their candidate, who campaigned actively throughout the state, Hutcheson ended up in third place with 219,591 votes, or 22.9 percent of the total. The winner was Yarborough, the first in a series of liberal Democratic victories statewide that would eventually transform the Texas Democratic Party and the framework of politics in the state.[101]

To most political observers, two messages were clear from the results of this 1957 election. Even an aggressive campaign by a highly qualified Republican in a special election ended up with less than one-fourth of all votes cast. Just as importantly, when conservative votes were divided between a Republican and a conservative Democrat there was room left for a liberal Democrat to win with a plurality. To most Republican activists, however, the glass was half full. They were more interested in creating a party organization that could compete effectively than in protecting and preserving conservative Democratic control of state government.

To these activists, the Hutcheson campaign had been one more building block in the process of establishing a statewide organization. Hutcheson was not discouraged by his loss and agreed to take up the challenge of serving as Republican state chairman, setting out to both build morale and encourage a more active party organization.[102]

Republican leaders aggressively recruited candidates and fielded a record number of twenty-nine for the Texas House of Representatives and three for the state senate in the 1958 election. In addition to Bruce Alger, two other congressional candidates sought election. Roy Whittenburg of Amarillo became the GOP candidate for the U.S. Senate against Ralph Yarborough, while Edwin S. Mayer ran against Governor Price Daniel. Since the Republican candidate for governor obtained more than two hundred thousand votes in 1956, the party was required to nominate by primary.

Turnout in the primary should have been a clue to the faithful that 1958 would not be a stellar year for the party. Republican primary voters were scarce even in areas of the state that would subsequently become party strongholds. Former first lady Barbara Bush recalled her experience in Midland: "I can still remember when George and I volunteered to work at the polls during a primary election. Exactly three people voted Republican that day. The two of us and a man who you could say was a little inebriated and wasn't sure what he was doing."[103] Only sixteen thousand votes were cast statewide in the Republican primary, and some eleven thousand of them came from Dallas County, where a liberal labor leader had challenged Bruce Alger for the congressional nomination.[104]

The results from the November election were disappointing. All the Republican legislative candidates went down to defeat, while Whittenburg obtained only 23.6 percent of the vote against Yarborough and Mayer received 11.9 percent against Governor Daniel. During this period of time ideology appeared to make little difference to Texas voters; whether one was a liberal like Yarborough or a conservative like Daniel, the important point was that they were Democrats.

By the end of the Eisenhower administration, few positive results could be shown in the development of a viable alternative to the Democratic Party. Conservative Democrats continued to dominate state politics and, by endorsing Eisenhower and encouraging the development of presidential Republicans, they had gained additional influence in the White House. Those presidential Republican voters continued to participate in the Democratic primaries, where they helped nominate conservative candidates for state and county offices who then went on to victory in the November general election, often unopposed, sometimes against weak Republican candidates. Additionally, in some areas of the state, such as Dallas, there was developing an identification of Republicans with what was viewed as right-wing extremism.[105]

The liberal faction within the Democratic Party could take satisfaction in their most significant victory in the late 1950s, with the election and re-election of Ralph Yarborough. Admittedly, their first win had occurred in a multicandidate special election where the conservative vote was split, but Yarborough had easily won renomination and re-election in 1958. For the next decade and beyond, Yarborough would be spiritual leader of the liberal forces as other candidates came forth to seek state and legislative offices.

When the decade of the 1950s ended, the Republican loyalists could point to the election of Bruce Alger as their only member of the congressional delegation, but little more. Various measures of competitiveness can be used to indicate the Republican Party's role in Texas politics. Since the state does not require a citizen to indicate party affiliation when registering to vote, one must look for alternative measures, such as self-identification and participation in a party primary election. In 1952, only 6 percent of Texas residents classified themselves as Republicans, while 66 percent said they were Democrats. Ten years later the Belden Poll found the Republican ranks to have increased to 9 percent and the Democratic self-identifiers to be at 59 percent.[106] After eight years of a Republican presidency, less than 10 percent of Texans identified with that party.

A second, even more dramatic, indicator of the weakness of the Republican Party is voter participation in primaries. In 1958, some 1.3 million Texans chose to vote in the Democratic primary, while only sixteen thousand took part in the Republican primary. Democratic dominance is reflected also in the fact that only 790,000 Texans cast votes in the November general election, more than 500,000 fewer than had voted in the Democratic primary that year. Clearly, the important choices had been made among the Democratic candidates rather than between the candidates of the two parties. Republicans had succeeded in electing one of the twenty-two congressmen from Texas but had nary a member of the Texas legislature or any statewide elective officials. The number of county officeholders who were Republican was less than 1 percent of the state's total.

As another presidential election approached, conservative Democrats were in control of the Democratic Party of Texas; their main challenge came not from the Republican Party but from liberal Democrats. Democratic dominance nonetheless seemed secure. Their senior senator was a candidate for the party's presidential nomination, and a Texan was proudly serving as speaker of the U.S. House of Representatives. However, the transformation of Texas politics would soon be under way.

CHAPTER 4

Stirrings and Small Cracks

On January 20, 1961, as a new president was inaugurated, Texas Democrats could be proud of the fact that they had carried the state for John F. Kennedy in a very close election. After defecting Democrats, led by their own governor, had delivered the state twice to Dwight D. Eisenhower, they had returned it to the Democratic column. For the first time, both major party candidates had been born in the twentieth century. For only the second time, a major-party candidate was Roman Catholic. Unlike the situation some thirty-two years earlier, religion did not keep Texas from its traditional loyalty to the Democratic Party. Undoubtedly, Kennedy had been aided by the presence of a Texan on the ticket, as Lyndon Johnson became the second vice president of the United States from the Lone Star State, following in the footsteps of John Nance Garner, who had served in the first two terms of Franklin D. Roosevelt.

Below the presidential race was a sea of Democratic elected officials. Every statewide elected official as well as every member of the Texas legislature was a Democrat. Only one of the state's congressional delegation was a Republican. County government was, with rare exceptions, totally controlled by the Democratic Party. To employ an apt description, Democratic activists and supporters were in "high cotton" after the 1960 election. The widespread support for the party and its candidates, especially those seeking county and state offices, would continue for some time. As political observers noted about the situation, "There were thousands of Texans alive in the 1960s who had never met an actual Republican (or at least one out of the closet). Loyalty to the Democratic Party was so deeply embedded in Texas' political culture that a great many partisans were aptly described as 'yellow-dog Democrats,' voters who would rather vote for a yellow dog than any Republican."[1] Another writer claimed that the Republican Party wasn't a shambles, "because it really didn't have enough individual pieces to constitute a shambles. It was the irrelevant, all-but-silent opposition. Throwing their votes away was an intramural sport for Republicans."[2] Texas was clearly Democratic country as a new Democratic president and Democratic-controlled Congress took office in Washington to complement Democratic control back home.

Over the next two decades, only minor changes were to appear in the partisan composition of Texas elected officials. But there would be some significant Republican breakthroughs in the one-party dominance of Texas politics, coupled with some close losses as well as many hopes deferred. Until the election of 1978, the period after 1960 can be seen as a series of lost opportunities in the effort to introduce two-party competition, if not two-party government, at all levels of Texas government. What did develop, however, was top-of-the-ticket competition that can be described as a "two-tiered system." While the two parties vigorously contested statewide federal offices (president and United States senator), little real competition took place for all other elected positions, and the Texas electorate, in general, remained as committed to the Democratic Party as it had been since the state's admission to the Union in 1845.

The Two-Tiered System of Competition

For Texas Democrats, the high of January 20 would be followed by the shock of May 27, 1961. The first successful challenge to Democratic hegemony in the twentieth century came about because of the actions of Lyndon Baines Johnson. Leading up to the 1960 election, Johnson was majority leader of the United States Senate and wanted to become president. However, his Senate seat was up for election in 1960. As a firm believer in the golden rule ("he who has the gold, makes the rules"), Johnson convinced the Texas legislature to change the state's election law so that a candidate could run for two offices at the same time. This meant that Johnson could seek the Democratic presidential nomination while still running for re-election to the Senate. His presidential campaign was unsuccessful, but John F. Kennedy then picked him to be his vice presidential running mate. This is how it came to be that Johnson appeared twice on Texas ballots in 1960, as vice presidential candidate and also as candidate for re-election to the Senate.

Since Johnson won both contests and could not serve in both offices at the same time, he had to decline either the office of vice president or his position in the Senate. This created a vacancy in the Senate that was to be filled by a special election in 1961. The contest produced seventy-one candidates, only one of whom was a Republican. That Republican, John G. Tower, had been the party nominee against Johnson in the 1960 general election, polling a respectable 41 percent of the vote. While far short of victory, his performance surprised most Texas observers. Speaking of the political environment in 1960, Tower claimed that "we were dismissed as naïve visionaries and worse. The idea that the entrenched Texas Democratic party would ever be forced to share political power was considered by the experts about as foolish as 'a dog walking on his hind legs.'"[3] In the 1961 special election, Tower came in first but far short of a majority, thus requiring a runoff between the top two candidates, Tower and William Blakley, a conservative Democrat who had been appointed to serve until the election by Governor Price Daniel.

Tower, a little-known thirty-five-year-old college professor from an obscure university in a small city near the Oklahoma border, produced a major upset in Texas politics by polling 448,217 votes in the runoff to Blakley's 437,874. In so doing he became the first Republican ever elected to the U.S. Senate from Texas. Tower's runoff victory came about due to his performance in the Big 6 counties, where he carried all but Travis and built up an unsurpassable lead over Blakley of 61,121 votes. Blakley carried the Suburban and Small Town groupings of counties, while the two candidates basically split the Other Metro counties.[4]

An important element of support for Tower in 1961 came from liberal Democrats who were unwilling to vote for a conservative such as Blakley and saw a Tower victory as a step toward cleansing the Democratic Party of conservatives by encouraging the development of a two-party system. Like many other observers, they expected Tower to be defeated for re-election five years later in a contest where the Democratic candidate would be more representative of their ideological position. As David Richards, an active leader in the liberal Democratic Rebuilding Committee of the time, noted: "The Rebuilding Committee urged liberals to support Tower in both of his early races as the least offensive alternative and as a way of fostering the emergence of a real Republican Party."[5]

Moreover, it was felt that Ralph Yarborough, the sitting liberal Democratic senator from Texas, would control patronage from the Kennedy administration more easily with the Republican Tower as his colleague, while having a conservative Democratic colleague would present serious problems. The state's leading liberal publication, the *Texas Observer*, formally endorsed Tower in an editorial maintaining that the state needed a two-party system.[6] Still others, such as liberal leader Frankie Randolph of Houston, urged those who could not vote for Tower to "go fishing" on runoff election day.[7] As John Knaggs, long a key advisor to Tower, summarized the situation in the 1961 runoff, "How many liberals voted for Tower will never be known, nor will it be known how many 'went fishing.' But in reviewing Tower's razor thin 10,343-vote margin out of 886,091 cast, it must be concluded that the liberal element was pivotal in electing the first Republican United States Senator to represent Texas during the twentieth century."[8] With the support of some liberals and the abstention of others, Texas had elected its first Republican senator since Reconstruction and the only Republican senator from the eleven former states of the Confederacy.

Most political observers regarded the Tower victory as a fluke and predicted that he would serve only one term in office. However, Tower went on to win re-election in 1966, 1972, and 1978, serving nearly twenty-four years in the United States Senate. The support of many liberal Democrats was critical to Tower, not only in his initial election but also in his first re-election campaign against Attorney General Waggoner Carr, a leading conservative Democratic officeholder. Distaste for Carr and a desire to drive conservatives out of the Democratic Party led David Richards to do the unthinkable in 1966: "We'd rather go down in flames than be trapped supporting reactionary Democratic candidates. Thus it was that I cast my one and only vote for a Republican candidate for public office. I am sure that many Texas liberals joined me, and Tower won re-election handily."[9] Six years later Tower was opposed by a more moderate Democrat and, with George McGovern at the top of the Democratic ticket, Texas liberals were inclined to vote for their party's candidate. In the Nixon landslide of that year Tower easily won re-election to a third term. Tower won one more critical re-election and until 1978, he was the sole Republican to win statewide office in Texas.

The Tower election produced a wave of enthusiasm among the hard core of Texas Republican supporters as well as among many new, younger voters. John Knaggs, an active participant in the politics of the time, credited much of this new support to the appeal of Barry Goldwater and William F. Buckley Jr: "Goldwater conservatism, keyed by rugged individualism, was taking hold in early 1961. Young conservative Texans, eager to learn, related to the novels of Ayn Rand, particularly *The Fountainhead*, and the *National Review* magazine whose editor, William F. Buckley Jr., had gathered a stable of strong conservative writers to complement his incisive writing. Politically, they related to Goldwater and, in turn, to Tower."[10] Still others thought the Tower victory proved that the Republican Party "was not simply a protest party or a safety valve for the raging Democratic civil war, but a power that the state must recognize."[11] While that optimism would produce a series of competitive, but unsuccessful, top-of-the ticket contests for Republican candidates over the next two decades, the Democratic Party would for the time being remain firmly in control of the state's political arena. Not able to take electoral success for granted, Democratic candidates put forth the effort needed to ensure eventual victory in nearly every contest.

The First Tier of Federal Elections

Although Tower was the only successful Republican senatorial candidate, his 1961 election was one of six two-party competitive contests in the 1960s and 1970s. During this period each party won three senatorial elections, with the Democratic candidates receiving slightly more than half of all votes cast (51.8%). A similar situation existed for the five presidential elections from 1960 to 1976. While Democratic presidential candidates carried the state in four of the five elections, they actually received less than half of all votes cast for the two major parties.

The geographical pattern in presidential elections throughout the two decades was similar to that which had existed in the Eisenhower victories of the 1950s. In 1960, Nixon carried the Big 6 counties by a margin of 72,986 votes but lost the other three categories of counties to end up 46,233 votes short of Kennedy. Eight years later he once again built a lead of 51,955 votes over Humphrey in the Big 6 counties only to lose in the Suburban, Other Metro, and Small Town counties, thereby losing the state by 38,960 votes.[12] The same pattern held true in 1976, with Ford building a sizable lead out of the Big 6 counties but losing in the other three categories. Only the Johnson landslide of 1964 and the Nixon re-election landslide of 1972 broke with the pattern, as the winning candidates carried all four categories of counties in each election (table 4.1).

In John Tower's four successful campaigns, he was able to build a substantial lead over his Democratic opponent each time in the Big 6 counties, ranging from lows of 61,121 in 1961 and 56,186 in 1978 to more impressive leads of 140,265 in 1966 and 148,625 in 1972. In his two closest contests it was the lead he produced in the Big 6 counties that provided victory. Those same counties were a base of support in the losing GOP Senate campaigns also, although only in 1970 did George H. W. Bush

Table 4.1. Number and percentage of votes cast for president and U.S. senator, by party, 1960–1976

Year	Democratic candidate	Votes cast	Democratic percentage	Republican candidate	Votes cast
			Presidential election		
1960	Kennedy	1,167,932	51.0	Nixon	1,121,699
1964	Johnson	1,663,185	63.4	Goldwater	958,566
1968	Humphrey	1,266,804	50.8	Nixon	1,227,844
1972	McGovern	1,154,289	33.4	Nixon	2,298,896
1976	Carter	2,082,319	51.6	Ford	1,953,300
TOTAL		7,334,529	49.2		7,560,305
			Senatorial election		
1961	Blakley	437,874	49.4	Tower	448,217
1964	Yarborough	1,463,958	56.3	Bush	1,134,337
1966	Carr	643,855	43.3	Tower	842,501
1970	Bentsen	1,226,568	53.4	Bush	1,071,234
1972	Sanders	1,511,985	45.3	Tower	1,822,877
1976	Bentsen	2,199,956	57.3	Steelman	1,636,370
TOTAL		7,484,196	51.8		6,955,536

carry them, with 53.5 percent of the vote. Bush had lost the Big 6 by 51,103 votes in his first campaign in 1964, while Alan Steelman garnered 49.3 percent of the vote to lose the Big 6 counties by 23,267 in his 1976 campaign against Lloyd Bentsen. Clearly the highest level of votes for top-tier Republican candidates in the 1960s and 1970s was centered on the Big 6 counties, which had experienced an influx of new residents from other states, a major source of Republican support at the time.

At the level or tier of statewide federal elections, neither party could take Texas for granted throughout these two decades. Three times the Democratic presidential candidate carried the state by close margins while three senatorial candidates won with less than 55 percent of the vote. Reflecting this new party competition at the top of the ticket, from 1960 forward more Texans voted in the November general election than took part in the Democratic primary, the place where nearly all election contests had been settled in the past.[13]

The Second Tier of State Politics

While Republican candidates were occasionally having a measure of success and even providing a serious challenge to the Democrats for the offices of president and United States senator, it would not be until 1978 when the party would finally be able to win a statewide state elective position. Although making some progress during the period for state legislative, congressional, and county offices, the party seldom even contested half of the positions up for election.

Statewide State Elective Offices

Texas has an abundance of statewide elective offices. Not only do voters select two United States senators and governor, but they also choose who will fill eight other executive positions as well as nine members of the Texas Supreme Court and nine justices of the court of criminal appeals. During the time period being reviewed here, all thirty positions were filled in partisan elections.[14] With the exception of John Tower, each of these offices was held by a Democrat until 1979, when a Republican took office as governor.

The most visible, although arguably not the most powerful, position in Texas state government is the office of governor. Only Democrats had held this office since the term of E. J. Davis ended in controversy in 1874. During the 1960s and 1970s, Republicans sporadically provided competition for this office. If one uses the commonly accepted measure of competitiveness (within a range of 55 to 45 percent of the vote), then four of the nine elections in these two decades could be described as such. At the same time, another four of these contests saw the Republican candidate receive less than one-third of the total vote. Only in the ninth and final contest of the period was the party able to produce the first Republican gubernatorial victory in more than one hundred years.

Former Democratic state representative and candidate for governor in 1960 Jack Cox switched parties one year later and obtained the Republican nomination in 1962. Cox came close to defeating John Connally after Connally defeated Governor Price Daniel and attorney Don Yarborough in the Democratic primary. Eight years later, Paul Eggers came close in a rematch with Governor Preston Smith. Eggers had lost his first race against Smith in 1968 when he received 43.0 percent of the total. In terms of raw votes, Senator Hank Grover came closest to victory of all the Re-

Table 4.2. Number and percentage votes cast for governor, by party, 1960–1978

Year	Democratic candidate	Republican candidate	Republican percentage[a]
1960	1,625,699	610,295	27.3
1962	846,586	714,025	45.8
1964	1,878,793	661,560	26.0
1966	1,037,416	368,025	26.2
1968	1,662,019	1,254,333	43.0
1970	1,232,506	1,073,831	46.6
1972	1,631,246	1,534,486	48.5
1974[b]	1,016,806	514,268	33.6
1978	1,166,919	1,183,828	50.4

[a] Percentages shown are of the two-party vote totals for governor.
[b] Beginning with the 1974 election, the term of office for Texas governor was extended to four years.

publican candidates to that time, losing to banker and rancher Dolph Briscoe in 1972, a year in which a majority of Texans gave their support to President Nixon and Senator Tower (table 4.2).

In the three losing contests where the Republican candidate reached a level of competitiveness, it was the Big 6 counties that provided the greatest support. Jack Cox, Paul Eggers, Hank Grover, and Bill Clements all carried this group of counties, although by varying amounts. While the three unsuccessful candidates lost each of the other categories of counties, Clements was able to become governor by barely winning the Suburban and Other Metro groupings of counties while substantially reducing his net loss in the Small Town counties.

As in the contests at the first tier, for president and United States Senate, Republican inroads were most evident in the Big 6 counties. As the suburbs of these counties expanded, they became a source for a larger percentage of the candidate's vote (from 7.8% of Cox's total vote in 1962 to 11.3% for Clements in 1978) as well as becoming a net plus in terms of overall votes (table 4.3).

While the party periodically nominated candidates for various other positions, few Republican candidates for any of the myriad of other statewide elective offices received as much as 45 percent of the vote in any

Table 4.3. Republican vote for governor by county category

GOP margin and percentage of vote	Jack Cox (1962)	Paul Eggers (1970)	Hank Grover (1972)	Bill Clements (1978)
	Big 6 counties			
Margin versus Democrat	+1,916	+74,905	+128,602	+50,523
Percentage of vote in category	50.1	53.7	54.2	52.4
Percentage of total vote	45.3	52.4	53.6	47.2
	Suburban counties			
Margin versus Democrat	−26,053	−27,956	−23,780	+4,511
Percentage of vote in category	40.5	43.5	46.2	50.9
Percentage of total vote	7.8	8.9	9.4	11.3
	Other Metro counties			
Margin versus Democrat	−27,276	−49,999	−31,946	+10,622
Percentage of vote in category	46.0	44.4	47.5	51.2
Percentage of total vote	21.7	19.2	19.4	20.0
	Small Town counties			
Margin versus Democrat	−81,148	−157,316	−169,636	−48,777
Percentage of vote in category	40.8	36.0	38.1	45.6
Percentage of total vote	25.2	19.5	17.6	21.6

election during these two decades.[15] Clearly, up to the historic election of 1978 the Republican Party occasionally provided a serious challenge to continued Democratic control of the Governor's Mansion, but just as frequently those candidates were more nuisance than competitor.[16]

State Legislative Elections

Only twice in the 1960s did Republicans constitute as much as 5 percent of the Texas legislature. During the 1970s, the party's adherents held approximately 10 percent of the house and senate seats. Only once, in 1962, did the Republicans compete for more than half of the house districts and not until 1974 did they begin competing for at least half of the state senate seats up for election.[17]

It would not be until 1966 when a Republican candidate would win election to the Texas Senate, a body that had been totally Democratic since Julius Real of Kerrville completed his last term of office in 1929.[18] Hank Grover of Houston was soon joined by O. H. "Ike" Harris, the winner of a special election in 1967. By 1972, Grover was a candidate for governor and his seat was taken by another Republican, Walter Mengden, and the party's membership was increased by one with the election of Betty Andujar of Fort Worth. Former congressman Bob Price won a special election from Senate District 31 in 1977 but was subsequently defeated in the November 1980 general election. With the switch in party affiliation of Senator Bill Braecklein of Dallas in 1979, by the end of the two decades Republicans temporarily held five of the thirty-one state senate districts.[19]

Republican success in elections for the Texas House was not much greater. Total Democratic control was broken when two special elections in 1961 brought Republicans Kenneth Kohler of Amarillo and George Korkmas of Texas City to the state capitol. Both were then defeated in the 1962 general election. During the two decades Republican candidates won eleven special elections for the Texas House and two for the Texas Senate. Unfortunately for the party, it was difficult to consolidate these wins, as only four of the house members were re-elected and only one senate candidate served a second term. Most had been won with small turnouts in traditionally Democratic districts, and the brief period of incumbency was insufficient to ensure re-election at the next general election. One contemporary study of state campaigns found that "legislative elections remain very much matters of mobilizing partisan electorates. Transmission of partisan cues, together with aggressive campaigning for office, clearly perform central roles in the popular choice of legislators."[20]

During this period of weak party competition, mobilizing partisans appears to have been especially critical in special elections for Texas state legislative districts.

The earliest development of Republican competitiveness beyond the traditional bases in the Hill Country and the Panhandle took place in the most urbanized parts of the state, the same areas that had first displayed support for Republican presidential, senatorial, and gubernatorial candidates. Until the latter part of the 1970s, Republican representation was concentrated in the upper- and middle-income areas of the state's largest cities, along with two of the Other Metro category of counties in West Texas. Thus, after the 1978 elections, eighteen of the twenty-four Republican state representatives came from Dallas, Tarrant, and Harris Counties. The GOP held senate seats in the same three counties where their representatives were concentrated (Dallas, Tarrant, and Harris) and briefly added a fourth seat from the Panhandle in the 1977 special election (table 4.4).

By the end of the 1970s, Republican representation in the Texas legislature had gone from nonexistent to slightly more than 10 percent of both the state senate and house. The party was fielding candidates in approximately half of the senate contests and in slightly more than a third of the house districts. Despite the small number of Republicans, given the prevalent nonpartisan nature of the two bodies, some GOP members had already been appointed committee chairmen and were exerting influence over potential legislation beyond their party's numbers. Nevertheless, the Democratic Party's control of the Texas legislature would continue for many more years.

Statewide Competitiveness

Various comprehensive methods of determining party competition at the state level have been employed. Austin Ranney developed an early measure that is based on the proportion of success a party obtains (calculated on the percentage vote won for statewide offices and percentage of seats in the legislature), the duration of success (amount of time each party controlled statewide offices and the legislature), and the frequency of divided control (the percentage of time the governor and legislature were controlled by different parties). Using a scale from 0.0000 (all GOP) to 1.000 (all Democratic), Ranney measured the average percentage of the popular vote for the Democratic candidate for governor, the average percentage of seats held by Democrats in the state legislature, and the percentage of all terms for governor and legislature where the Democrats controlled. Based solely on state offices, he found Texas to be the fifth-most one-party Democratic state in the period from 1946 to 1963, ranking behind only South Carolina, Georgia, Louisiana, and Mississippi. By the next period measured, Texas had become slightly more competitive, but it still ranked fifth-most Democratic. In the last time frame shown, Texas had begun to move in a clearly more competitive direction (table 4.5).[21]

A similar measurement differentiates between party control and party competition, providing a measure that ranges from 0.000 to 1.000 for the extent of Democratic Party control and from 1.000 to 0.500 for competition, with the lower score being the least competitive between the two parties. With this measure, Jewell and Morehouse found Texas to be the sixth-most Democratic state and also the sixth-least competitive state during most of the 1960s and 1970s.[22] Clearly, both of these compara-

Table 4.4. Republican members of the Texas House of Representatives, by county type, 1961–1979

Year	Big 6	Sub- urban	Other Metro	Small Town	Total
1961	0	1	1	0	2
1963	8	0	2	0	10
1965	0	0	1	0	1
1967	4	0	2	1	7
1969	5	0	1	3[a]	9[a]
1971	8	0	1	1	10
1973	16	0	1	0	17
1975	15	0	1	1	17
1977	16	0	2	1	19
1979	19[b]	1	2	2	24[b]

[a] Includes John Poerner, who was elected as a Republican in a 1969 special election. According to his Legislative Reference Library profile, "Republican John Poerner changed party to Independent after the election . . . Party listed as Independent on member card; original listing as Republican marked through." For the party's reaction, see Knaggs, *Two-Party Texas*, 142.
[b] Includes Representative Anita Hill of Garland, who switched parties and became a Republican in 1979.

**Table 4.5. Interparty competitiveness scores,
1946–1978**

Period	Score	National ranking
		Ranney measure
1946–1963	0.9590	Fifth-most Democratic
1962–1973	0.8780	Fifth-most Democratic
1974–1980	0.7993	Eleventh-most Democratic
		Jewell and Morehouse control measure
1964–1978	0.848	Sixth-most Democratic
		Jewell and Morehouse competition measure
1964–1978	0.652	Sixth-least competitive

Source: Data for 1946–1963 are from Jacob and Vines, *Politics in the American States*, 1st ed., 63–65; data for 1962–1973 are from Jacob and Vines, *Politics in the American States*, 3rd. ed., 59–61; data for 1974–1980 are from Gray, Jacob, and Vines, *Politics in the American States*, 4th. ed., 65–67; data for 1964–1978 are from Jewell and Morehouse, *Political Parties and Elections in American States*, 28–32.

tive measures support the assertion that at least up until the election of 1980, Texas remained overwhelmingly Democratic in state elections, yet saw small spurts of competitiveness from a weak but growing Republican Party.

Congressional Elections

As the decade of the 1960s began, Republicans held one congressional seat from Texas, that of Bruce Alger from Dallas. After a slow process of expansion, set back by the Johnson landslide of 1964, the party's representation had grown to four members by the end of the 1970s. Over the two decades Republicans had, at one time or another, elected candidates from six of the state's congressional districts. Although congressional dis-

Table 4.6. GOP performance in Texas congressional districts, 1960–1978

Year	Number of districts	Number of GOP candidates	Number of GOP victories	Individual elected
1960	22	5	1	Bruce Alger (Dallas)
1962	23	18	2	Alger; Ed Foreman (El Paso)
1964	23	23	0	
1966	23	6	2	George H. W. Bush (Houston); Bob Price (Amarillo)
1968	23	12	3	Bush; Price; James Collins[a] (Dallas)
1970	23	11	3	Price; Collins; Bill Archer (Houston)
1972	24	13	4	Price; Collins; Archer; Alan Steelman (Dallas)
1974	24	16	4	Collins; Archer; Steelman; Ron Paul[b] (Houston)
1976	24	19	2	Collins; Archer
1978	24	21	4	Collins; Archer; Paul; Tom Loeffler (San Antonio)

[a] Collins won a special election in 1968.
[b] Paul won a special election in 1976 but was defeated in the 1976 general election by 236 votes, only to win back his seat in the 1978 general election.

trict lines extend into different kinds of counties, it is safe to say that all but one of these districts comprised mainly, or extended into, the Big 6 counties (table 4.6).

In the 1976 and 1978 elections, seven Republican congressional candidates lost competitive races, but they did garner more than 45 percent of the vote. Among those competitive losers was future president George W. Bush, who lost to Kent Hance in a district running from Lubbock to Midland and Odessa. Hance was one of two Democrats first elected to Congress that year who would subsequently change parties and be elected to statewide office as a Republican. The other congressional winner, who would change parties five years later, was Phil Gramm.

County Competition

With 254 counties, Texas has literally thousands of elected county officials, not counting the various judges and district attorneys whose electoral districts comprise more than one county. At the heart of county
government is the commissioners court, presided over by a county judge
(the county executive), who is elected countywide, and four county commissioners, who are elected from districts, plus a number of other elected
officials such as sheriff, tax assessor-collector, clerk, and a varying number
of constables and justices of the peace. For more than a hundred years it
was the county courthouse that served as the center of Democratic Party
control of Texas politics.

It was at the county level, especially in the state's 198 Small Town
counties, where the personal nature of politics was most evident, with
voters knowing most of the candidates for county office, seeing them at
church, school, or community functions, and being aware of their family
roots. Loyalty to the Democratic Party resulted not only from such relationships with individual candidates but also from the lack of any Republican competition. In such an environment, "social attitudes, cultural
patterns and decades old alliances [are] not easily replaced, much less completely destroyed."[23]

A critical element in Democratic domination of county politics in
much of the state was that often voters simply had no other choice. Any
contest for public office took place in the Democratic primary or not at
all. Throughout the 1960s and 1970s, roughly 20 percent of the state's
counties, almost all in the Small Town category, were without anyone
willing to serve as a Republican county chairman. The absence of a willing
volunteer chairman meant that no primary election could be conducted.
No primary meant that no Republican candidates for county office could
be nominated. Even where individuals could be convinced to hold forth
the Republican banner, they were frequently perceived as alien interlop-
ers. In fact, a study of county chairmen in the 1960s found that almost half
of all Republican chairmen had lived in the state less than twenty years.
For Democrats, 97 percent had been Texas residents for at least twenty
years, with most of them native Texans.[24]

At the beginning of the 1960s, the Republican Party could claim only
3 among the state's 254 county judges and an additional 8 of the state's
1,016 county commissioners.[25] After the 1962 elections, the number of
county officials had increased to 28, including the election of the state's
only woman county judge, Barbara Culver of Midland. Symptomatic of

the times and the regard in which Republicans were held was Culver's response when asked whether she faced a political problem with voters accepting the idea of a woman being county judge: "The beautiful thing was that being a Republican was so much worse. They got off of being a female pretty quickly."[26] Culver would go on to serve several terms as county judge and later briefly on the Texas Supreme Court by appointment.

The 1964 Johnson landslide delayed any further growth of the party at the local level. Writing in 1965, Kenneth Thompson, at the time editorial editor of the *Dallas Morning News*, observed that "except for a few mayors, city councilmen, local judges and other minor officials, the Republican Party of Texas has no representation in government offices and little to build upon."[27] Prior to the 1966 elections, the Republican Party held the office of county judge in only Midland, Kerr, and Harrison Counties, with an additional twenty-five other county officials throughout the state, including county commissioners, constables, and justices of the peace.

Statewide, the Republican Party focused most of its effort in 1966 on re-electing Senator Tower, at the time the only party member holding an office above its single state representative, Frank Cahoon of Midland. For the amount of effort extended, however, Republicans did not do too poorly in contests for county judge. In the 254 counties, the GOP fielded eleven candidates and four were successful as Gray County joined Midland, Kerr, and Harrison with Republican county judges. Having run county commissioner candidates in twenty-eight counties, ten Republicans from nine counties won. Nevertheless, as John Knaggs noted, after the 1966 elections the Democratic Party controlled all 254 county courthouses and the GOP only held a total of thirty-six public offices (table 4.7).[28]

During the 1970s, the Republican Party made small but significant gains in its representation in county government. After the 1972 election the party held fifty county offices, including five county judges and seventeen county commissioners. Following the disastrous Watergate election of 1974, the party's total stood at fifty-three county offices, but this included nineteen county commissioners and eight county judges. Most significantly, Republicans picked up the key offices of county judge in the state's two largest counties as Jon Lindsay began a twenty-year tenure in Harris County and John Whittington won in Dallas County. The suburban growth of the party was led by new county judges Nathan White in Collin County and Arthur Evans in Kendall County.

Over the next two election cycles, Republicans continued to expand their small base of county officials, increasing to sixty-seven after the

Table 4.7. Number of Republicans on county commissioners' courts, by county type, 1967–1975

| Year | County type | | | | Total |
	Big 6 (n = 6)	Suburban (n = 29)	Other Metro (n = 21)	Small Town (n = 198)	
1967	2	0	4	8	14
1973	3	3	6	10	22
1975	5	7	5	10	27

1976 election and eighty-seven by the end of the decade. It would not be until the 1980s and 1990s when any significant growth would occur, first appearing in the Big 6 and Suburban groupings of counties along with selected counties in the other two categories.[29] Despite its emergence as a presence and a competitor, many political observers still agreed with commentator Paul Burka, who maintained that "except in wealthy Southwest Houston and North Dallas, [the Republican Party] is still regarded largely as an organization for people of principle rather than ambition. That is fine for churches, but not so good for political parties."[30]

Party Identification and Affiliation

Self-identification as to partisan loyalties provides an additional measure of the level of party competition during the 1960s and 1970s. So too does the choice of whether to vote in a party primary election and the party in which a voter participates. Both of these measures point to the continued dominance of the Democratic Party in Texas until the beginning of the 1980s.

Party Identification

Unlike the majority of American states, Texas does not include party affiliation as an element of voter registration. Absent party registration, one must look to self-identification provided in response to public opinion surveys. While more contemporary surveys have shown a sizable increase in the percentage of voters who decline to express a partisan attachment, this was less the case in the 1960s and 1970s. The authors of the classic study of political behavior at mid-twentieth century, *The American Voter*, maintained that "few factors are of greater importance for our national elections than the lasting attachment of tens of millions of Americans to one of the parties."[31] They found that two-thirds of all voters still identified with the party for whose presidential candidate they cast their first vote. In analyzing one Texas gubernatorial election, Richard Murray found that party identification was the strongest predictor of vote choice.[32]

In 1966, the John F. Kraft Company was retained by the John Tower campaign to conduct public opinion surveys. When Texas registered voters were asked whether the support of a political party would influence them to vote for a candidate, the results were illuminating of the attitude at the time. Eleven percent said the support of the Republican Party would favorably dispose them to a candidate, while 25 percent said it would not. Conversely, 32 percent had a favorable reaction to Democratic Party support for a candidate and only 8 percent would be negatively impacted. The report concluded, "The Democratic Party support helps define the character of the State, and in this sense: to a Texan the Democratic Party is something which is locked into tradition. It hasn't really much to do with whether one is a moderate or a conservative or a liberal. By the same token, the fact that the Republican Party produces an over-all negative reaction is little more than confirmation of the same point, or the same analysis."[33] To a broad swath of the state's citizens in the 1960s, being a Texan and being a Democrat were almost one and the same. Clearly, some of them could depart from the faith for one candidate in one election, but many such defectors still considered themselves adherents of the Democratic Party.

Party identification has also been seen as a prime mover of other political attitudes in that it can provide a cue to the citizen on a range of issues where the party takes a distinct stand.[34] For most Texans of the time, the Democratic Party was seen as reflective of their prevailing views, attitudes, and interests. Sean Cunningham called this outlook "populist cowboy conservatism": "The Democratic Party dominated Texas politics until the 1960s and 1970s in large part because it was seen as the party of populist cowboy conservatism. . . . This perception fomented loyalty and loyalty evolved into tradition; Texans trusted the Democratic Party. . . . the vast majority of white Texans supported the Democratic Party simply because they believed the Democratic Party supported them."[35] In many ways, party identification may be viewed as a lagging indicator in that voting behavior often changes first. Thus, individuals may break from party

Table 4.8. Percentage Texas voters' party
identifications, 1952–1978

Year	Republican	Democrat	Independent
1952	6	66	28
1962	9	59	27
1964	8	65	27
1966	22	68	10
1972	19	52	28
1974	16	59	25
1978	14	48	37

voting before modifying their party identification. While at the first tier of presidential and senatorial elections Republicans were clearly competitive over the twenty-year period, party identification remained overwhelmingly Democratic. Although the percentages vacillated over time and with different polling methodologies, in every survey except one, from the 1950s to 1980, Democratic identifiers maintained a three-to-one margin over Republican identifiers.

In 1952, while Texas voters were supporting the Republican candidate for president, only 6 percent identified with the Republican Party. By 1978, the level of Republican support had increased to only 14 percent. Clearly, during the 1960s and 1970s few Texans thought of themselves as Republicans. What had happened, however, is that fewer and fewer were calling themselves Democrats, with that identification decreasing from roughly two-thirds of all voters to around only 50 percent of the electorate.

By the mid-1970s, especially with the nomination of George McGovern, "the brand name loyalty that had kept many conservative Democrats loyal to the party almost all of their lives no longer had as much appeal. The national party had changed direction over the years, leaving many conservatives unsure of where they now fit."[36] No longer comfortable in the Democratic Party, many Texans were nevertheless not comfortable with the Republican Party. Thus, by the end of the 1970s less than two-thirds of all registered voters proclaimed any identification with either of the two major parties (table 4.8).[37]

By the time of the 1978 election, self-described independents had become a formidable component of the electorate, and the Democratic Party could no longer rely on the loyalty of a majority of Texas voters. Such a situation, with more voters in a fluid state, left an opening for a Republican Party that still obtained the support of fewer than one in five Texas voters. Nevertheless, until the 1978 election and the final breakthrough by a Republican gubernatorial candidate, the Democratic Party clearly remained the dominant element among the Texas electorate.

Primary Participation

In Texas a registered voter officially becomes a party member by choosing to participate in its nominating process, whether convention or primary election. Thus one measure of change in party competition consists of primary voter turnout by party. Changes in primary participation and party affiliation, however, are likely to occur more slowly than changes in general election behavior. This phenomenon was noted by Malcolm Jewell and David Olson in a work on state politics published in 1978: "If we are interested in finding trends in party competition, we should recognize that voters are often slow to change their registration from one party to another, and similarly slow to shift from voting in one primary to the other. Therefore, partisan trends are likely to appear first in general elections, and later in primaries and registration."[38] Texas voting behavior substantiates this conclusion as more and more Texans chose the Republican candidate in top-tier federal contests while remaining attached to the Democratic Party and supportive of its candidates in other races. This competition at the top tier contributed to the shift in voter participation as more Texans began to vote in the November general election than in the Democratic primary, a move that occurred when it became the arena of final choice.

As has been discussed previously, there developed throughout Texas an accepted tradition of "Democrats for . . ." committees supporting various Republican candidates, with Allan Shivers being the most prominent Democrat to lend his name and support to several such efforts. Although most apparent in the Eisenhower elections of 1952 and 1956 and the Nixon contest of 1960, the phenomenon of the "presidential Republican" was observed even earlier by V. O. Key in his classic work of 1948: "Indigenous to the South is a strange political schizophrenic, the Presidential Republican. He votes in Democratic primaries to have a voice in state and local matters, but when the presidential election rolls around, he casts a ballot for the Republican presidential nominee. Locally he is a Democrat; nationally, a Republican."[39] While speaking of the South in general, Key's point is especially applicable to Texas in the 1960s and 1970s and is clearly descriptive of the two-tiered system of party competition. Even though the Democratic candidate was able to carry Texas in four of the five elections from 1960 to 1976, the presence of thousands of presidential Republicans produced close contests in 1960, 1968, and 1976 as well as the landslide victory of 1972.

A second factor affecting primary turnout is that until very recently the primary election was administered by the political party rather than the state or county government. A minority party's first task in such a situation is the recruitment of sufficient personnel to simply conduct an election. This is a more considerable task than it may at first appear. While all of the state's 254 counties held a Democratic primary during the 1960s and 1970s, fewer than 200 provided an opportunity to vote in a Republican primary in most years. Thus, in several counties it was literally impossible for a registered voter to participate in a Republican primary. Even when a primary is held in a county, in its initial years the minority party is likely to have fewer and less convenient polling places. During the 1960s and 1970s, a voter was required to make a conscious, public act of going into a Republican polling place, often only one location in a county that might be several miles from the general election precinct polling place.

During most of the twentieth century the cost of conducting the primary was borne by the political party, mainly through funds obtained from candidate filing fees. Thus, the fewer the candidates for public office, the less money is available to the party to pay for the primary election. According to one observer, the end result was that "the law severely handicaps the growth of the Republican party by placing impossible financial hurdles in its way."[40] Short of volunteers to conduct an election, short of sufficient polling places to make voting accessible, and short of candidates for local office to provide funding, the Republican alternative was frequently not available to much of the electorate.

For more than one hundred years, virtually all elective offices in Texas were filled by voters in the Democratic primary, a tradition that continued throughout most of the two decades from 1960 to 1980. As has been discussed previously, there were few years up to 1960 when the Republican Party even conducted a primary election. Participation in the Democratic primary was perceived by most Texans as the means by which public officials were selected rather than as a partisan commitment or as a more general desire to be involved in the nominating process. The critical importance of the Democratic primary can be seen not only in the number of

Democrats holding public office but also in the attitude and outlook of those assuming the responsibility of conducting the primary. In a study of rural Texas Democratic county chairmen in the 1960s, David M. Olson found that they perceived their role as performing a civic duty rather than carrying out a partisan function: "They have an apolitical, nonparty, legal-duty orientation. They are neither campaign nor organization oriented. They have no concept of party as organization . . . [they] endeavor to remain acceptable to all candidates in the Democratic primary by confining themselves to impartially administering the election code."[41] With the primary funded by candidate filing fees and administered by the party's county chairman, and with the results determining who would hold public office, it is little wonder that these Democratic county chairmen would regard their responsibility as community service.

Beginning in 1962 and on to the present, Republicans have held a primary election every two years. Only in 1976, with its seriously contested presidential nominating campaign, did this primary entice the participation of more than 160,000 Texas voters, while the Democratic primary was drawing as many as 2 million participants.

Building on the success of Ralph Yarborough, the liberal faction in the Democratic Party put forth a number of strong, albeit unsuccessful, candidates for governor. Attorney Don Yarborough (no relation to the senator) carried the liberal banner three times, falling to John Connally by less than twenty-seven thousand votes in a 1962 runoff and finishing first in 1968, only to lose to Preston Smith in a runoff. Conservative Dolph Briscoe was able to hold off Frances "Sissy" Farenthold in both 1972 and 1974, but then lost renomination to Attorney General John Hill in 1978. Conservative victories in the Democratic primary, coupled with the party's almost total domination of local races, proved to be a major handicap to Republican growth. "The Republicans, when nominations stayed in the conservative Democratic faction, had little room to maneuver for the general election and could not put together a majority. This strategy proved unbeatable for many years and allowed the conservative Democrats to remain in power."[42] Indeed, it was only when the liberal faction succeeded in nominating their candidate in 1978 that the Republicans were able to elect their first governor in more than one hundred years.

During the two decades of the 1960s and 1970s there was virtually no growth in the Republican primary, and the variance in Democratic participation related more to levels of nonvoting than to any shift from one party to another on primary day. Writing in 1980, Malcolm Jewell noted this lack of growth and the small percentage of the party's general election voters who took part in the Republican primary.

> The Republican primary vote generally has been 5 to 8 percent of the total primary vote, less than 2 percent of the voting age population, and 8 to 13 percent of the general election vote. . . . There is no sign that in any of these elections the Republican primary turnout made a dent in the Democratic primary vote. There certainly is no reason to believe that in any year the Republican primary in Texas has drawn enough voters out of the Democratic primary to affect the outcome of the latter.[43]

From 1960 until 1980 the levels of participation in the Democratic primary varied from a low of 1,255,397 to a high of 2,192,903. Nevertheless, Democratic voters constituted at least 90 percent of the entire primary electorate in each year except 1976. Other than the Ford-Reagan primary contest, Republican totals peaked at 142,918 in 1964, when the party conducted a nonbinding presidential primary involving Barry Goldwater. Participation twice fell considerably below one hundred thousand during this two-decade period. As Jewell noted, there was no significant and lasting movement of Texas voters from the Democratic to the Republican primary.

Although Republican candidates became more competitive during the 1970s and eventually won election in 1978, the percentage of both the primary electorate and the party's general election vote remained small. With the exception of the two presidential primary years of 1964 and 1976, those who were affiliated with the Republican Party by voting in its primary remained a small proportion of the electorate. With most county and state offices held by Democrats, voting in that party's primary remained the only means of choosing local officials: "The strength of the Democrats on the local level resulted in many Republicans voting in the local Democratic Primary elections in order to have a voice in the local races often uncontested by the party. The 'Presidential Republicans' thus maintained at least a passing loyalty to the Democrats, frustrating Republican attempts to build a sustainable voting base."[44] The decision of these conservative Democrats and presidential Republicans to continue voting in the Democratic primary also served as a barrier to the growth of the liberal faction's influence in the party. As Monroe Lee Billington wrote in 1975, "As long as conservative Democrats are firmly in the Texas saddle, the Republican party has little chance for additional significant growth."[45]

Table 4.9. Number and percentage of GOP primary and general
election votes, 1960–1978

Year [a]	Number of GOP primary votes	GOP as percentage of total primary votes	Number of GOP general election votes	Primary as percentage of GOP general vote
1960	—	—	610,295	—
1962	115,330	7.4	714,025	16.2
1964	142,918	8.1	661,560	21.6
1966	49,568	3.8	368,025	13.5
1968	104,765	5.6	1,254,333	8.4
1970	110,465	6.7	1,037,577	10.6
1972	114,007	4.9	1,534,486	7.4
1974[a]	69,101	4.3	514,268	13.4
1976	456,822	23.0	1,636,370[b]	27.9
1978	158,403	8.0	1,183,828	13.4

[a] Beginning in 1974 Texas governors were elected to a four-year term of office.
[b] Totals for 1976 are for Republican candidate for United States senator. All other years reflect votes for Republican candidate for governor.

However, by the end of the two decades, a liberal-moderate coalition had gained control of the Democratic Party machinery and had finally nominated their candidate for governor. It was then that the first substantial Republican breakthrough in Texas politics would occur (table 4.9).[46]

Those who chose to affiliate with the Republican Party by voting in its primary were predominantly urban residents. More specifically, the GOP primary base resided in Dallas and Harris Counties, with these two counties alone producing anywhere from 36.9 percent of the total primary vote in 1962 to as high a proportion as 55.9 percent in 1972. As late as 1978 nearly half of all Republican primary votes came from Dallas or Harris County. Overall, Republican primary voters were concentrated in the Big 6 counties, which comprise the major metropolitan centers of the state. It was in these counties that Texas first experienced a substantial influx of new residents from other states. The number of Texans born outside the South went from 9 percent in 1950 to 20 percent in 1980.[47]

As historian Roger Olien noted, "Economic growth in the major cities brought new industries and with them members of the technical and professional middle class, at least good prospective Republicans in Texas and often self-identified conservatives before their arrival" (table 4.10).[48]

Throughout the two decades reviewed, the Republican primary electorate became even more concentrated in the Big 6 counties, with the party having little success in attracting primary votes from residents of the Small Town counties. As discussed earlier, it is in these Big 6 counties where the party first began to make significant inroads into county government by the middle to late 1970s. Conversely, Small Town county government remained, with few exceptions, in the control of Democratic officeholders, and in several of these counties no one could be located to administer a Republican primary. From 1966 to 1980 more than fifty counties each year failed to hold a Republican primary, nearly all of these being among the Small Town group of counties. As Olien noted in his 1982 history of the Texas Republican Party, "A great many of those who have remained loyal to the Democratic party have done so out of inertia. Tradition has been Democratic, and small town voters take longer to break with tradition. One reason for this is no doubt personal contact and friendship between the voters and the Democratic candidates."[49] The greater percentage over time of primary voters from Suburban counties is reflective as much of the growth of population in these counties as it is

Table 4.10. Percentage of Republican primary voters by county category, 1962–1978

		County category		
Year	Big 6	Sub- urban	Other Metro	Small Town
1962	59.6	4.5	23.6	12.3
1964	59.7	4.9	22.9	12.5
1966	65.8	4.6	19.0	10.6
1968	66.6	4.5	20.7	8.2
1970	70.3	5.5	16.1	8.1
1972	74.5	5.2	13.8	6.5
1974	67.7	7.4	17.3	7.6
1976	62.8	8.2	20.7	8.2
1978	66.8	7.5	17.7	8.0

in the building of a viable party organization. In 1960, the twenty-nine Suburban counties had a population of 838,569, comprising 8.8 percent of the state's total. Twenty years later they had nearly doubled, to a total population of 1,664,511, with 11.7 percent of the state's total population.

As the decades of the 1960s and 1970s came to an end, the Republican Party had begun to build a base of support in the state's major urban counties but still remained a small minority of the electorate. Few voters self-identified themselves as Republicans, and still fewer chose to vote in Republican primaries. Partly cause and partly effect, these two facts contributed to the lack of Republican candidates and officeholders.

CHAPTER 5

Toward a Two-Party Texas

Political trends and developments do not always occur in neat chrono-
logical order or in predetermined time frames. That is certainly true of the
various factors that contributed to the movement toward two-party competition in Texas politics, a movement whose success became apparent
in the decade of the 1980s but had its origins in events that occurred one
or even two decades before. This chapter focuses on four factors that impacted how Texas moved from an environment in which only one political
party represented the broad range of beliefs and interests of nearly all who
participated in the state's elections to an era when the two national political parties competed for control on a more equitable basis.

One cannot overlook the significance of the 1961 special election of
John Tower to the development of two-party competition, an event that
had an impact lasting even beyond the twenty-three years during which
he represented Texas in the United States Senate. A second development
that is equally important as a precursor to this era of competition is the
dedication of a band of liberal Democrats who correctly determined that
their ideological positions could best be furthered by encouraging conservatives to leave their traditional party home and, in so doing, help to
create two-party politics. Third, much of the acceptance of the Republican Party as a viable alternative force in state politics would not have come
about without the election and performance of Bill Clements as the state's
governor over two nonconsecutive terms of office. There is no question,
however, that the most lasting influence on the growth of the party was
the appeal, both personally and politically, of Ronald Reagan both before
and after he became the fortieth president of the United States.

At the beginning of the 1980s, each of these four factors was in place
to help usher in a new era of politics in Texas, a period in which the state

moved significantly toward a two-party system. Each factor deserves more attention and discussion.

Cadres to the Right: The Tower Legacy

Party competition in a state develops not only with temporal victory on election day but, even more importantly, from the efforts of literally thousands of individuals whose names are seldom cited in the history of the times. This is true of those dedicated efforts on the right by individuals who worked to promote the Republican Party as a viable alternative to the prevailing establishment. It is equally true of those on the left committed to reforming the Texas Democratic Party into an electoral force dedicated to advancing liberal ideas and interests consistent with the direction of the national party. To understand the transformation of Texas politics over the past half-century it is important to view the contributions of certain key individuals who served as mentors and leaders but also to discuss the efforts of the various organizations and entities that motivated and organized the grass roots of volunteers who helped to bring about change.

The effort to nominate and elect Dwight Eisenhower in 1952 brought an influx of new activists into the Texas Republican Party, a movement that also resulted in the election of Bruce Alger of Dallas to Congress two years later. To a large degree these efforts, while led by political professionals, relied on the contributions of a large number of political neophytes. In his classic work on the development of club politics within the Democratic Party in New York, Chicago, and Los Angeles during the middle of the twentieth century, James Q. Wilson provides a useful definition of this relatively new element then appearing in both political parties.

> An amateur is one who finds politics intrinsically interesting because it expresses a conception of the public interest. The amateur politician sees the political world more in terms of ideas and principles than in terms of persons. . . . The amateur takes the outcome of politics—the determination of policies and the choice of officials—seriously, in the sense that he feels a direct concern for what he thinks are the ends these policies serve and the qualities these officials possess.[1]

While the initial Eisenhower contest and the Alger campaign started the involvement of more and more ideologically motivated "amateurs" in Texas Republican politics, it would require the breakthrough of a Republican victory in 1961 to see this movement grow to a continuing force in the party. Of particular importance, as had been stressed by Wilson in his study of urban Democratic politics, was the development of political clubs, often officially outside the formal party structure but essential in recruiting, training, and motivating new workers for the party.

There are several elements that helped to develop cadres of volunteers and campaign workers on the right. Without question, the Tower victory of 1961 brought about a surge of new support for the Republican Party, including the organized and coordinated defection from the Democratic Party of many voters at "resignation rallies" held throughout the state.[2] The presidential candidacy of Barry Goldwater brought more activists into the party, many of whom would remain and assume leadership positions over the next few decades. Perhaps even more significant, however, was the senator's re-election in 1966, coming just two years after Goldwater's demoralizing landslide loss. While Tower's initial victory showed that a Republican could be elected statewide in the unique environment of a special election, his winning a second term by a decisive margin meant that there would be a Republican in high office for another six years. Tower epitomized the Texas Republican Party of the 1960s and 1970s, serving as the symbol of the party and a mentor to many younger Texans whose involvement in politics started with the senator.[3]

Tower as Mentor

The twenty-three-year tenure of John Tower in the United States Senate provided an essential training ground for the development of a core of campaign and policy professionals who would play important roles in the development of a viable political force in Texas. It was on the senator's staff in Washington and at his various district offices that many of those who assumed important roles in the development of the Republican Party received their political experience. Among this cadre were two future members of Congress: Tom Loeffler, chief counsel in the early 1970s, and Larry Combest, legislative assistant from 1971 to 1978. Both Loeffler, who served in Congress from 1979 to 1987, and Combest, a congressman from 1985 to 2003, won seats that had previously been held by Democrats and were replaced by other Republicans when they retired from Congress. Another Tower staffer from the mid-1970s was Cyndi Taylor Krier, who subsequently served eight years in the Texas Senate and another eight years, from 1993 to 2001, as Bexar county judge, the first Republican in history to hold that office.

Still other former Tower staffers held important positions in government and civic affairs. Will Ball, former chief of staff for Senator Tower,
served on the White House staff and as secretary of the navy during
the Reagan administration. Longtime chief aide to the senator Carolyn
Bacon was until recently executive director of the O'Donnell Foundation,
founded by Edith and Peter O'Donnell of Dallas. Fred McClure was legislative director for Senator Tower before assuming White House legislative affairs positions for both Presidents Reagan and George H. W. Bush.
McClure became executive director of the George H. W. Bush Presidential Library Foundation in 2012.

Bob Estrada served John Tower as his state director for several years before forming the investment banking firm of Estrada Hinojosa and Company. He served on the board of the Federal Reserve Bank of Dallas and
the board of regents for the University of Texas system. Tom Kowalski
was a senior staff member for Senator Tower as well as for Governor Bill
Clements and Congressman Jim Collins. A former regent of the Texas
State University system, he is president and CEO of the Texas Healthcare
and Bioscience Institute in Austin. Dan Branch served on the senator's
staff near the end of his twenty-three-year career and since 2003 has represented a Dallas County district in the Texas House of Representatives
as well as being secretary of the board of trustees for the Fund for American Studies. While it is impossible to cite all who gained political experience with Tower and went on to serve the party and the state in various
capacities, the names of Ken Towery, John Knaggs, Dottie de la Garza,
Jose Martinez, and Molly Pryor, who later became Harris county clerk,
deserve mention.[4] The list of former Tower staffers and volunteer workers
who helped to build a viable alternative political force in Texas goes on
and on.

Youth and the Republican Rise

Tower's contribution as a mentor did not reside solely with those serving
on his Senate staff or those who worked as volunteers in his campaign organization. Only thirty-five years old when first elected, he was a source of
pride and encouragement for many other young Texans. As one of those
younger Republicans put it, "This younger element of conservatives had
broken with their parents' conservative Democrat politics. They believed
a clean break was needed with a strong Republican Party controlled, beyond a shadow of a doubt, by conservatives. To them, it was a cause."[5]
Their interest in changing the political climate would lead many of them

to become active in one or more of the young conservative organizations active on campuses and in communities around the state.

For most of his time in the United States Senate, Tower was a member of the national advisory board of the Young Americans for Freedom (YAF), an organization formed in 1960 and dedicated to making the Republican Party more consistently conservative. YAF was committed to nominating Senator Barry Goldwater for president, an objective YAF shared in common with Senator Tower and the leadership of the Texas Republican Party. Tower was a featured speaker at the 1962 YAF rally, held in Madison Square Garden, New York City. As one attendee noted in a letter to her parents, "The speakers were excellent. My favorite was Senator Tower—what a little fireball he is."[6] Tower would speak at numerous YAF conferences and other gatherings over the next twenty years, noting that "YAF has provided the muscle that is vitally needed in political organizations for sound, conservative politics."[7]

Among those who earned their spurs through involvement in Young Americans for Freedom were two future Members of Congress, Jack Fields and Tom DeLay. Fields was active in YAF while a student at Baylor, while DeLay was a YAF member in Houston. Elected to Congress at the age of twenty-eight, Fields served from 1981 to 1997. DeLay won election to the Texas House in 1978 and to Congress in 1984, rising to the position of majority leader before his resignation in 2006. An active leader in YAF while an undergraduate at Yale and then a student at Yale Law School, Jerry W. Smith was appointed to the Fifth Circuit Court of Appeals by President Reagan in 1988. Previously he was Harris County GOP chairman and a member of the state Republican executive committee.

Several other YAF members were integrally involved in the Reagan presidential efforts of 1968, 1976, and 1980. After being active in the 1968 effort to corral delegates for Reagan, Ron Dear worked as a national YAF staffer, as legislative assistant to Congressman Bill Archer, and as executive director of the American Conservative Union before returning to help coordinate the 1976 Reagan operation in Texas. He was aided in the latter campaign by James Meadows, Coby Pieper, Gary Hoitsma, and Terry Quist. Two years later, YAF alumni Pieper, Hoitsma, and James Foster were serving on the staff of the Republican Party of Texas.

Perhaps the most prominent Texas YAF alumnus, however, is Steve Munisteri, who became Republican state chairman in 2010. Munisteri was also the founder of the Young Conservatives of Texas (YCT), which broke away from the national YAF organization to start a state-specific group. Among the former YCT members currently in prominent positions are

Congressmen Jeb Hensarling and Steve Stockman. For more than thirty years the YCT has been an active presence on many Texas college campuses and is well known for its biennial ratings of Texas state legislators on a number of issues prioritized from a conservative perspective.

Even more important, perhaps, as a training ground for future leaders is the Young Republicans (YR) and its now-distinct subset, the College Republicans. First organized in Texas in 1930 by Carlos Watson and Thomas E. Ball, the organization soon faded into inactivity, only to be reorganized by Jack Porter after his 1948 senatorial campaign. The Young Republicans served as a base of support in the early battles against R. B. Creager and Henry Zweifel for control of the Texas party.[8] With the Eisenhower nomination and election, the Young Republicans became even more active as an organizing base for new cadres. Sylvia Nugent, active in the Dallas County Young Adult Republicans during the 1950s and 1960s, has said, "[We] were 22 to 40 years old basically. It was designed in such a way to attract young people. There was a big social component, with a happy-hour type meeting every month, ski trips, and that sort of thing. Then we did a lot of things to help 'down ballot' candidates. It was a very grassroots kind of an operation."[9] By the 1960s, the excitement surrounding a possible Goldwater candidacy was enhanced by the 1961 victory of John Tower. Arriving as a keynote speaker at the national Young Republicans convention in Minneapolis one month after his election, Tower was received as the conquering hero, the man who had demonstrated that a conservative Republican could win in the South.[10]

Both in communities and on campuses throughout Texas, more and more young people were becoming politically involved at a time when the minimum voting age was still twenty-one. In the period before the assassination of John Kennedy and his replacement by Lyndon Johnson, thousands of young Texans looked to the 1964 presidential election as a clear-cut philosophical battle between left and right: "Flamboyant, enthusiastic and youthful conservatism characterizes Texas Republican supporters. By 1963, the largest and most active political organization on Austin's University of Texas was the Young Republicans club; a miniature of the statewide picture, the campus was no longer an exclusively Democratic preserve."[11] Tower's ability to win election and his mentorship while in office provided encouragement to young Republicans, while Goldwater appealed to them as a dedicated conservative candidate for the presidency.

Ernest Angelo Jr., who would later serve several terms as mayor of Midland and twenty years as Republican national committeeman, decided to help form a Young Republicans club in 1961; the following year the club helped to elect Bill Davis to the Texas House, the first Republican from what would become a GOP stronghold: "We started a Young Republicans club and had a mimeograph machine in one of the guys' garages. We put out a monthly with reproduced articles from different sources and mailed them to about three or four hundred people who were not in the Young Republicans. Then we started trying to find people to run for office."[12] Angelo emphasizes the important role that the Young Republicans played in building a state party in the 1960s. The organization attracted "a number of young people who didn't know it could not be done."[13]

One individual who was attracted to political activity by Goldwater was Tom Pauken, later to serve as chairman of the Republican Party of Texas. As he explained, "Goldwater's message appealed to young people like me. He spoke up for the individual in a society increasingly dominated by large, impersonal institutions. He stirred the idealistic instincts of young people who sensed that America somehow was coming unraveled." Pauken joined the College Republicans while an undergraduate at Georgetown University: "I became a foot soldier in a small but steadily growing conservative army which was winning converts among college students and young people across the country."[14] He would go on to be elected College Republicans national chairman in 1965.

By the mid-1960s, Young Republicans politics had become a focal point for many up-and-coming political leaders engaged in battles between the "white hats" and the "black hats," two political factions in the organization divided more by personal appeals and personality than by philosophy. In 1968, Steve Bartlett, who would later serve in Congress and as mayor of Dallas, became YR state chairman, and James Oberwetter, a future ambassador to Saudi Arabia, was YR national committeeman.[15] Other active leaders in the organization were Neil Calnan, Tom Quirk, Gary Bruner, Linda Underwood, and Anne Quirk Erben. As Erben noted about the various Young Republicans conventions she attended, "The Young Republicans were always very competitive, with lots of money spent on these conventions. I put Watts lines in our house in order to make phone calls in the state for free. It was a really sophisticated and wonderful training ground for convention politics."[16] Angelo maintained that in the early 1960s, it was not uncommon for the YR state conventions to be better attended than the state party gatherings.[17]

Linda Underwood worked for national committeeman Albert Fay and on the staff of Youth for Nixon in the 1968 campaign. To her, the most significant contribution of the Young Republicans was registering young people and other Republicans. "That was where we felt we could do the most. We went to shopping centers and grocery stores."[18] As Erben noted, during the 1960s and 1970s it was difficult for the minority party to obtain workers to do the grunt work of politics: "The pool of people to move into campaign volunteer activity or to work on campaigns was quite a bit smaller. The impact of a bus of Teenage and College Republicans on a special election in the Valley or in Dallas for a weekend of block walking was a real shot in the arm to a candidate, particularly in a special election."[19] It was the College Republicans that served as the entry point for one of the leading Republican strategists of the twenty-first century, Karl Rove. As he notes in his memoirs,

> Being a College Republican gave me and other political junkies a sense of efficacy. We could do this. We learned the power of mastering new technologies to communicate our message. We saw that politics was not about power or status, but about ideas and ideals. CRs connected me with the GOP's leadership, helped me realize I was good at this stuff, could do it as well as others much older than me, and gave me a sense that I could contribute.[20]

As the College Republican national chairman in the mid-1970s, Rove developed a relationship with the Republican national chairman at the time, George H. W. Bush, and first met his eldest son, George W. Bush. Twenty years later Rove would be "the architect" of George W. Bush's two gubernatorial and two presidential victories.

Perhaps one of the most influential groups of younger Republicans in the late 1970s and throughout the 1980s was not a formal organization at all but rather Camp Wannameetagop, the brainchild of Doug Harlan and Cyndi Taylor Krier, who, along with Andrew Sansom, Kay Bailey Hutchison, and Chase Untermeyer, dedicated themselves to building a cadre of campaign activists. From 1979 to 1991, this informal networking group met for a weekend each year at Camp Allen, near Brenham. Camp Wannameetagop is best described as a gathering of Republican activists of a certain generation, since nearly all had been born in the 1940s or early 1950s. As Untermeyer, later a state representative, director of presidential personnel, and ambassador to Qatar, explained, "The idea of the camp was to bring together younger Republicans from around Texas for endless political talk and grudge matches of volleyball."[21]

Clearly the sparkplug for the camp was Harlan, who kept it alive and active throughout its thirteen years. As he said in the initial letter of invitation, which was sent to Republican contacts throughout the state, "We're billing this as the 1st Annual Camp Wannameetagop gathering at Camp Allen. If all goes as planned our 3rd annual meeting may be held at Camp David!"[22] That initial gathering included a number of future officehold-ers, including the county judges of Bexar (Cyndi Taylor Krier), Dallas (Lee Jackson), and Harris (Ed Emmett) Counties, Congressmen Tom DeLay and Lamar Smith, federal district judge Ricardo Hinojosa, Ambas-sador Chase Untermeyer, and Texas House speaker Joe Strauss III. Later annual gatherings included future state treasurer and United States sena-tor Kay Bailey Hutchison, Congressmen Steve Bartlett and Mac Sweeney, and a number of state legislators, including state senators Jeff Wentworth and Buster Brown, and representatives Frank Hartung, Alan Schoolcraft, Bill Hammond, Ashley Smith, Chip Staniswalis, and Terral Smith.

Referring to the progress this group had made in a short period of time and noting the presence of "two nursing babies" and "two pregnant women" at the 1982 gathering, Harlan posed the question: "Who knows where those kids might wind up? Two Wannameetagop alums are now in the West Wing of the White House. Three hold key positions in the Justice Department. Some are bound for the U.S. Congress. Many serve, have served, or will serve in the state legislature. Still others hold city and county offices. Those are examples the kids can follow."[23] Camp Wanna-meetagop has been described as "a small group that brought together Re-publican politicians from across the state to strategize about transform-ing themselves into a governing majority" at a time when "it seemed like an impossible dream."[24] As time went on, these participants assumed more important roles in the state and nation, leading Harlan to admit in a 1985 column, "We used to call it a retreat for 'young' Republicans, but enough years have passed that we now have to say 'youngish.' And that may stretch it a bit."[25]

When Harlan passed away in 2008, *Texas Monthly* columnist Paul Burka, who had been a Rice University classmate, commented that "Doug was a staunch Republican in the days when the GOP was strug-gling to establish itself as a force in this state."[26] Twice a candidate for Congress in the difficult days of the mid-1970s, Harlan contributed much to the party's long-term growth and success, including his efforts to cre-ate a cadre of "youngish" Republicans who would assume leadership posi-tions in the party and the government. Jim Moseley, a justice on the Texas Court of Appeals and a frequent attendee, summed it up upon hearing of Harlan's death: "He was the kind of guy with whom you loved to talk politics even if you didn't agree on every detail. [T]he camps had a lot to do with fomenting the future leadership of the Republican Party of Texas.

The state of Texas and political discourse are poorer for his passing."[27] Harlan paved the way with his campaigns for Congress from a district that two years later would elect a Republican and that has remained in GOP hands ever since. More than this, however, Harlan remained an active writer and participant, helping to mold and encourage a cadre of committed partisans who would transform Texas politics.

Republican Women

As the Republican Party began to expand its base of support with the Eisenhower campaign of 1952, one essential source of volunteers was women, many of whom were organized into Republican women's clubs in the major metropolitan areas of the state. Mid-century America was a time when few women worked, especially married women, and housewives had the flexibility to devote time to civic and political endeavors. Most of the organized women's clubs met during the middle of the day, a schedule that necessarily appealed more to those not employed. The efforts of women volunteers were key to the victories of Dwight Eisenhower in Texas and to the election of Bruce Alger to a Dallas congressional seat in 1954. One historian summarized their contribution by noting that "women volunteers, organized into twenty-eight clubs— fourteen of them in Dallas County—had demonstrated through the 1952 and 1954 campaigns that they were the organizational sinews of the Republican party."[28] Through volunteering, telephoning, and canvassing, these women were essential to the successful grassroots campaign for Alger, a key breakthrough election in developing party competition in Dallas County.

With the development of clubs in three-fourths of the state's congressional districts, an organizational convention was held in October 1955 with the aim of creating the Texas Federation of Republican Women (TFRW). Convening the meeting was Beryl Milburn of Austin, an up-and-coming leader who would later become president of the TFRW, vice chairman of the state party, and chairman of the Ford campaign in the 1976 Texas primary.[29] Milburn later concluded, "I really think that the Republican Women's Clubs were the real levers that got people going because the women were freer economically to join and be Republicans than their husbands were. They were very devoted and dedicated. Republicans were ideologically committed."[30] This point was echoed by Louise Nixon, a pioneer in the development of the Republican Party in Fredericksburg, deep in the heart of the German Hill Country: "Men were not speaking up about Republicans. There was pressure on businessmen to be non-committal. We took a stand for Republicanism. We wanted a voice in our town. Gillespie County was Republican, but no one would speak up."[31]

By the 1960s, a growing force of Republican women was available to help bring about the election and re-election of John Tower. As Virginia Eggers, wife of a future gubernatorial candidate, recalled, "When John Tower ran in the special election, we had what we called the Tower Belles. . . . I am sure to them it was rather odd to see all of these young girls all dressed up coming to their town." According to Jane Anne Stinnett, a longtime party worker in Lubbock, "Women did the legwork, put rallies together, did the conventions, built precinct organizations, and did the phoning. They did everything." Tower was aware and appreciative of these efforts. Cyndi Taylor Krier, onetime Tower staffer, reported that "I heard him say a hundred times he was elected because of Republican women in tennis shoes who told their neighbors, held teas, walked with him and for him, and then voted."[32]

From an initial twelve clubs in July of 1952, the Republican women's clubs expanded to roughly 100 by 1963; to 130 in 1978, with six thousand members; and on to its current roster of 164 local clubs with slightly more than ten thousand members. New clubs were formed and new members recruited, and the cadre of campaign volunteers expanded.[33] As Mary Teeple, an active leader in the party during the 1980s and 1990s, concluded, "Women are good at enlisting people and convincing others that causes are important. They make it a lot of fun to work. Women have no fear of going to their peers or even people that are outstanding in the community and asking."[34] It has been estimated that in the critical break-through election of 1978, volunteers associated with the TFRW provided more than thirty-eight thousand hours of candidate support, many working in call centers and campaign headquarters around the state.[35]

While Republican women provided the volunteers needed for many campaigns in the 1950s and beyond, it was not long before some of their number would take the next step and become candidates themselves. In 1962, Barbara Culver of Midland broke through the glass ceiling to become the only Republican county judge and, just as pioneering, the only woman county judge in the 254 counties of Texas. Ten years later, Betty Andujar of Fort Worth would win election as the only woman in the Texas Senate and the only Republican state legislator from Tarrant County. Andujar served ten years in the senate and, from 1976 to 1980, also served as Republican national committeewoman from Texas. Kay Bailey Hutchison was a state legislator from Harris County in the 1970s and later was elected as state treasurer and United States senator. She concluded, "If you are going to talk about building the party in Texas, you have got to talk about the Republican Women's Clubs."[36] In addition to Senator Hutchison, who retired from Congress in 2013, the Texas congressional delegation includes Congresswoman Kay Granger of Fort Worth. In Austin, as of 2013, there are three Republican women in the Texas Senate, with fourteen female GOP members in the Texas House of Representatives.

Associated Republicans of Texas

If the Republican Party was to provide a viable alternative to the Democratic establishment, more than grassroots enthusiasm and commitment of youth and women would be needed. Without attractive and competent candidates, the party could not provide a real choice to the Texas electorate. Without adequate funding and campaign management, even attractive candidates were not likely to win. It was in such an environment that a new political organization dedicated to electing Republican candidates came into being.

After the 1974 elections, Republicans were left with only 20 of the 181 Texas state legislative seats and nineteen of the more than one thousand county commissioners in the state. Committed to building the party from the grassroots up, some one hundred Republicans met in Irving to create the Associated Republicans of Texas (ART). Serving as the initial chairman was Julian Zimmerman, a former federal housing administrator who was then president of Lumberman's Investment Corporation, with Norman Newton Jr., a past Texas GOP executive director, as the organization's director. Although not designed exclusively as such, the new group's board of directors basically consisted of men who had gained prominence and success in business or community service.[37]

Although some in the official party organization viewed the new group as a competitor for contributions and influence, ART's status was secured when Senator Tower formally endorsed it in the spring of 1975.[38] Soon thereafter, Ambassador John Hurd accepted the position as chairman of the ART Finance Committee, and the organization recruited several business and political leaders, including recent gubernatorial candidate Paul Eggers, to serve as directors. Relations with the official party were smoothed over with ART's pledge to stay out of contested primaries and limit its involvement to assisting Republican nominees for legislative and local offices.

In the nearly forty years since its founding, ART has played a critical role in assisting the Republican Party grow from little more than 10 percent of the Texas legislature to its 2012 high point of two-thirds (121 of 181) of all members. The approach taken by ART has focused on targeting winnable districts, recruiting qualified candidates, assisting with survey research and campaign management, and providing direct financial assistance. An essential strength of the organization since its founding has been its liaison with key members of the Texas lobby community, building a relationship over time that would result in political action committee contributions to targeted ART candidates. Frequently, ART would introduce new candidates to lobby representatives through informal meetings and receptions held at downtown Austin clubs, providing a "getting-to-know-you" opportunity for candidates from around the state.[39]

Currently the co-chairmen of ART are businessman George Seay of Dallas and attorney Hector De Leon of Austin. The ART board of directors includes business leaders such as Lowry Mays, Red McCombs, Tom Hicks, and Harlan Crow, as well as such familiar political figures as George P. Bush, Henry Bonilla, Cyndi Taylor Krier, Harriet Miers, and Ed Emmett. Seay, the grandson of former governor Bill Clements, recently explained his group's approach to the election of state legislators and county officials: "ART's mission hinged on recruiting and vetting of principled conservative candidates of integrity, training of those candidates in public policy and being media savvy, providing accountability and oversight to insure campaigns were run effectively, and funding the right candidates adequately."[40] With its recent legislative success, the organization is committed to building a strong "farm team" of new candidates at the local level. One specific project that ART has undertaken is called the Hispanic Voter Network, the goal of which is to "build a statewide network of pro-business, pro-family minded conservatives who are passionate about the role that Hispanics must play in the future of the Republican Party."[41]

If there was one single individual linking the various youth groups and the Republican women's clubs as well as the creation of an independent candidate-support organization, that person was John Tower. From his time as a thirty-five-year-old pioneer Southern Republican in the United States Senate to his tenure as a senior member of that body, John Tower served as a mentor and model for those committed to building a viable Republican Party in Texas. During his twenty-three years in the U.S. Senate, Tower witnessed the GOP begin its gradual growth in the state, including the election of a Republican governor, and saw his seat remain in the party's hands with the election of Phil Gramm in 1984. When fellow Texan George H. W. Bush became president, he nominated Tower to become secretary of defense, but his nomination was rejected by the Senate in a contentious and close vote.[42] Tower and one of his three daughters, Marian, were killed along with twenty-one other passengers in the crash of ASA Flight 2311 at Brunswick, Georgia, in April 1991.

With a range of assets and abilities from youth and women combined with the technical and financial resources provided to state and local candidates from a dedicated campaign support group, these cadres of volunteers helped to change the political environment in Texas. Nevertheless, they could not have succeeded in these efforts without the active involvement and dedication of some highly unlikely allies.

Forces to the Left: The Two-Party Democrats

An old saying declares that "the enemy of my enemy is my friend." This perspective was to take hold among some players in the Texas political arena in the 1960s, leading to some interesting alliances on election day. In their effort to make the Texas Democratic Party more consistently liberal and more closely in tune with the policies and philosophy of the national party, one element of Texas liberals realized that their goals could be achieved only by driving conservatives out of the party, and especially its primary elections.

As discussed previously, ideological divisions began to appear clearly within the Democratic Party in the 1940s.[43] While some of the more conservative elements in the party opposed a third term for President Roosevelt, others rallied behind FDR in the 1940 election. Four years later the party was split between the "Texas Regulars" and the supporters of the New Deal. This split at the level of presidential politics was to continue in 1948 within the party and from 1952 through 1960, when several Democratic leaders endorsed the Republican presidential candidate.

According to Chandler Davidson, the first serious liberal-conservative contest for statewide office took place in 1946 when Homer Rainey lost to Beauford Jester in the gubernatorial runoff primary. Rainey had been president of the University of Texas at Austin but had been fired by the board of regents and then launched his campaign for governor. Clearly from that time forward Austin, home to UT and state government, has been the center of liberal activity in Texas.[44] Six years later Ralph Yarborough challenged Governor Allan Shivers, and from then on "there was a liberal-conservative contest for major statewide office almost every two years for the next twenty-two years." No single individual personifies the liberal effort to dominate the Texas party better than Ralph Yarborough, who, for more than twenty years, was that faction's candidate in a statewide race; his career was topped by his thirteen years' service in the United States Senate.[45]

While Ralph Yarborough, along with the unrelated Don Yarborough and Frances "Sissy" Farenthold, were the dominant liberal statewide candidates from the early 1950s to the late 1970s, many others played essential roles in the development and expansion of liberal influences in the Texas Democratic Party. Among the individuals associated with these efforts were Creekmore Fath of Austin, Margaret B. Carter of Fort Worth, Maury Maverick Jr. of San Antonio, Walter Hall of Dickinson, Billie Carr of Houston, and David and Ann Richards, first of Dallas and later Austin.[46]

Beginning in the late 1940s, the liberal faction emphasized the importance of securing control of the party machinery. After briefly gaining control of the state Democratic executive committee, they lost out when Alan Shivers assumed the governor's office in 1949. With conservatives back in control of the state party, liberals continued to concentrate their efforts on turning out supporters at the precinct caucuses held on primary night, where delegates were elected to the county and eventually state conventions. This approach was viewed as a way to recruit new activists for the cause as well as to regain control of the state party. To keep these activists involved in a network of like-minded liberals, various extra-party organizations were formed with names such as the Democratic Organizing Committee, Democrats of Texas, and the Democratic Rebuilding Committee.[47] As they gained more influence within the party, these liberals "hoped that eventually their conservative opponents would move to the Republican Party. This, some theorized, would give the state a two-party system similar to that in many other parts of the nation."[48]

One of the most important liberal leaders during the 1950s and 1960s was R. D. "Frankie" Randolph of Houston. The wife of a prominent banker, Frankie Randolph was one of the founders of the Houston Junior League. She became a strong supporter of FDR and the New Deal and a financial contributor to Adlai Stevenson in his 1952 presidential campaign. As one of her allies later described her, "Taking into account controversiality as well as importance, Frankie Randolph was to Texas what Eleanor Roosevelt was to the United States. . . . Her wealth gave her an easy familiarity with men of power, but she cared about working people, the union movement, racial equality, social justice, and peace. . . . Earthy, blunt, and honest, she had more independent political power than any woman in Texas history."[49] Randolph later helped form the Democrats of Texas and was elected Democratic national committeewoman in 1956 over the opposition of conservative Democrats and Lyndon Johnson.[50]

Perhaps the most lasting contribution of Frankie Randolph, however, was her involvement as one of the founders of the liberal periodical the *Texas Observer*. Edited at various times by Ronnie Dugger and Willie Morris, this small-circulation magazine became a vehicle for developing liberal writers, many of whom would later spend their careers at Texas daily newspapers, as well as providing a flow of information and opinion to liberal allies throughout the state. One of its best-known writers and onetime co-editor was Molly Ivins. In an obituary on Ivins's death in 2007, Katharine Q. Seelye noted, "Rarely has a reporter so embodied the ethos of her publication. On the paper's 50th anniversary in 2004, she wrote: 'This is where you can tell the truth without the bark on it, laugh at anyone who is ridiculous, and go after the bad guys with all the energy you have.'"[51] As the conservative author John Knaggs described it, the *Texas Observer* was "considered to be the most influential liberal journal in Texas."[52] One of the magazine's readers commented on its value when he wrote in 1976, "You can't imagine how good it is to be reassured by you that we aren't the only ones with 'strange notions.' Without the *Observer*, we might become paranoid."[53]

Ronnie Dugger served as the founding editor of the *Texas Observer* and in that role played a critical part in advancing liberal influence in the Democratic Party, especially from the 1950s to the 1980s. By the 1960s, Dugger was one of a small group of key liberal activists who took what was perceived as a radical step: endorsing selected Republican candidates as a means of defeating conservative Democratic candidates, an approach that had limited success. As the author Sean Cunningham notes, "Liberals like Ronnie Dugger undermined the established Democratic power from within while, at the same time, enhancing the Republican image and even supporting Republican candidates as a form of protest."[54]

The 1961 Tower-Blakley runoff election was the first occasion when liberal Democrats encouraged their supporters to either vote for the Republican Tower or "go fishing" on election day. The *Texas Observer*, then edited by Dugger, openly endorsed Tower as preferable to the conservative Democrat Blakley. Not all liberals supported the idea of backing a Republican when faced with a conservative Democratic candidate. Most of organized labor and some leaders of ethnic and racial minority organizations rejected this view.[55] But for those who pushed for a two-party system, composed of a clearly liberal Democratic Party and a conservative Republican Party, their enemy was "any candidate for public office who was connected with the ruling conservative clique headed by Lyndon Johnson, later joined by John Connally."[56] By the late 1950s, Johnson had replaced Shivers as the dominant force in the state party, and Connally was viewed as his lieutenant.

In the 1962 Democratic primary, Price Daniel was seeking a fourth two-year term as governor. Liberal senator Ralph Yarborough was alarmed that then vice president Johnson was recruiting John Connally to run for governor. At that time Connally was serving as secretary of the navy in the Kennedy administration. Senator Yarborough let it be known that he would also return from Washington and run for governor to stop Connally unless an acceptable liberal candidate could be found. When labor leaders made evident their desire to keep Ralph Yarborough in the United States Senate, Don Yarborough, who had sought the lieutenant governor nomination in 1960, became the liberal candidate in a multicandidate primary for governor.[57]

When the votes were counted in the 1962 primary, Governor Price Daniel had been squeezed out and the top two candidates for a runoff were John Connally and Don Yarborough. The final totals in the runoff showed Connally with 565,174 votes and Yarborough with 538,924—a margin of slightly more than 26,000 votes. With such a close loss and enmity toward Connally running high, one of Don Yarborough's campaign aides formed "Texans for a Two-Party Texas" and, for the second time, began the process of rallying liberal support for a statewide conservative Republican candidate. That person was Jack Cox, a former Democratic state representative and candidate against Governor Daniel in the 1960 Democratic primary. As one participant in the effort explained, "The issues were clear to all parties involved. The two-party leaders knew that liberal and conservative protest votes for Cox might bring about his election paving the way for the two-party system. The conservatives knew this also and worked to keep it from happening."[58] Cox garnered more than 700,000 votes, but he nevertheless lost by some 130,000 votes to Connally. Apart from presidential candidates, this was the greatest number of votes that any Republican candidate had received in Texas, though still short of victory.

By late 1963, with Connally in the Governor's Mansion, Johnson was concerned that Don Yarborough would run again, defeat Connally in the primary, and drive conservative Democrats into supporting a Republican candidate in 1964, thereby threatening Kennedy's chances of carrying Texas again. Johnson convinced Kennedy that a presidential visit would help unite the party.[59] After Kennedy was assassinated, Johnson persuaded conservatives not to oppose Senator Ralph Yarborough's renomination, and Connally, having survived being shot in Dallas, defeated Don Yarborough easily in their rematch. Since the liberal hero Ralph Yarborough was a candidate in 1964, nearly all liberals supported him, and there was no "two-party Texas" effort behind the Republican senatorial nominee, George H. W. Bush.[60]

Two years later John Tower was a candidate for re-election. When less than fifty thousand voted in the GOP primary, conservatives were able to nominate Attorney General Waggoner Carr as the Democratic U.S. Senate candidate. Once again, a segment of liberal Democrats, organized as the Democratic Rebuilding Committee, refused to back Carr and rallied behind Tower.[61] According to the rebuilding committee, "Sometimes party loyalty asks too much."[62] Tower also received endorsements from the Committee for a Two-Party Texas, comprised mainly of Mexican American Democrats. At St. Mary's University in San Antonio, Tower was introduced by the chairman of the Political Science Department, an academic advisor to Bexar County liberal Democratic groups.[63] Meanwhile the leader of the group Amigocrats for Tower, M. P. Maldonado, maintained that if former governor Shivers was allowed to lead Democrats for Eisenhower in 1952, Mexican Americans need not apologize for leading Democrats for Tower.[64] Tower was able to win re-election easily with substantial liberal support.

In 1968, the Democratic Rebuilding Committee was reformulated after the liberal candidate Don Yarborough lost the primary to Preston Smith, a West Texas conservative who had been lieutenant governor but was not identified as the Johnson or Connally candidate. This time these liberal Democrats backed the GOP's Paul Eggers, and he was endorsed by the *Texas Observer*.[65] As the Democratic Rebuilding Committee stated in a flyer, "The election of a Republican Governor in 1968 will attract hundreds of thousands of conservatives into the 1970 Republican primary, taking them out of our primary. Otherwise, Texans will be faced with two years of Preston Smith and lobby dictated rule. Real Democrats will never have a strong voice in their own party until a two-party Texas is a working reality."[66] This time the effort was much more difficult, since a presidential election would result in a higher voter turnout with more straight-ticket voting. The focus of the media would be on presidential politics and national issues such as Vietnam, the assassinations of Martin

Luther King Jr. and Robert F. Kennedy, and the riots confronting many of the nation's cities.

As John Knaggs, then a Republican Party strategist, noted in his book *Two-Party Texas*, "Cross pressures were soon evident among liberal-labor ranks in which pro-Eggers sentiment was growing, but anti-Nixon sentiment was strong. Thus the ticket-splitting had to be promoted and that was not easy for so many leaders who had so often preached straight Democratic voting in presidential years."[67] This problem was apparent in a note from Dave Shapiro of the Democratic Rebuilding Committee to some GOP political strategists: "We have more leadership-types solidly on this program than ever before . . . our problems are of an entirely different kind than in '66 and in '62. This time we've got to really take the message to the grass roots, re-write the message into a ticket-splitting proposition instead of a 'go-fishin' deal."[68] The Texas electorate's Democratic Party allegiance proved sufficient, however, as Hubert Humphrey overcame both Richard Nixon and George Wallace to ensure a third straight Democratic presidential victory in Texas, while Preston Smith was elected governor. Narrow as the two victories were, they nevertheless indicated the resilience of Democratic loyalties in Texas.[69]

Throughout the 1960s, the two-party liberal Democrats had succeeded only in electing and re-electing John Tower. Their long-term goal was not to elect conservative Republicans but to move conservatives out of the Democratic primary. The year 1970 would indicate the failure of that policy over the short term. While 1,540,763 Texans chose to vote in the Democratic primary that year, only 110,465 participated in the Republican primary.[70] Clearly, most Texas conservatives were still taking part in the Democratic nominating process. When the more conservative Lloyd Bentsen defeated liberal hero Ralph Yarborough in the 1970 primary, the Democratic Rebuilding Committee was activated once again. In a mailing to Democratic voters it proclaimed, "The one-party system is the ideal atmosphere for Shivers-Connally-*Dallas News* candidates to clobber good Democrats like Senator Yarborough and that one-party system must be replaced by a competitive two-party system."[71] Nevertheless, it was even more difficult to rally support for the Republican Senate candidate, George H. W. Bush, and Bentsen won election rather easily, while Preston Smith was re-elected governor, once again defeating Paul Eggers.

By 1972, liberal Democrats nationwide had succeeded in nominating their candidate, George McGovern, for president. The McGovern campaign involved a number of younger activists, including three who would play important roles in Texas and national politics: Garry Mauro, Bill

Clinton, and Hillary Rodham. Despite their best efforts, President Nixon carried Texas and forty-eight other states in his landslide re-election. While a majority of Texans had supported GOP candidate Eisenhower in 1952 and 1956, each time it was in agreement with the endorsement of their own Democratic governor. The year 1972 was different, as Texas voters "overwhelmingly rejected the party to which most had been at least nominally loyal since birth."[72]

In 1973, the leading nemesis of the liberal faction announced that he was officially changing parties. When John Connally switched, the Democratic Rebuilding Committee said "good riddance" and expressed the "hope that the tens of thousands of other Republicans who have voted in our Democratic primary elections and dominated the government and politics of Texas while flying the flag of the Democratic Party, will follow."[73] In many ways, this was also the final gasp of the two-party Democrats. McGovern's nomination and the departure of Connally gave new hope to liberals in the Texas party. As Karl Rove has commented, "The liberals who had been an embattled minority within the Democratic Party in the 1950s and 1960s were becoming an emboldened majority that didn't think twice about driving their opponents out of the party. Most conservative Democrats parked themselves on Independent Street. Some drove on over to Republican Boulevard."[74] When Connally, a recognized leader of the conservative element within the party, abandoned the Democrats, other conservatives were motivated to follow him and added respectability to the Texas Republican cause.[75] As one writer described his actions, "The John Connally switch is significant in that it was the first attempt by an extremely successful Democrat to denounce the Democratic party completely and seek a new home in the opposition party."[76] Perhaps it was, after all, possible for one to be a loyal Texan and a Republican at the same time.

Throughout the 1960s and early 1970s, the Republican Party began holding primaries, but they attracted less than 9 percent of all primary voters and a minuscule portion of the entire electorate. This would not be the case, however, in 1976 as the GOP held its first binding presidential primary, which became a donnybrook between Gerald Ford and Ronald Reagan.[77] Nearly a half-million voters ignored the Democratic primary and chose to vote with the Republicans. This defection of many conservatives resulted in greater liberal influence within the caucus and convention process, where party leadership is selected. After the 1976 state conventions, "something important had happened. It began to look as though the liberals had taken de facto control of the party for the first time since 1948."[78] "This change in the SDEC's membership drew a new breed of party activist into party leadership, members who had cut their political teeth in the raucous days of the 1960s on college campuses and in the fields with migrant farm workers. This new group of party leaders effectively controlled the party machinery to stymie the conservative wing of the party."[79] More than half of the members of the new state Democratic executive committee were self-described liberals or moderates.

In effect, the "two-party Democrat" cause was no longer a relevant strategy. There was no need to support a Republican when the liberals now felt that they could control the Democratic Party machinery and its nominating process. The year 1976 became, in many ways, a watershed in the development of a liberal Democratic Party in Texas. Even though Jimmy Carter carried Texas and the nation and Lloyd Bentsen was re-elected to the Senate, 1976 also produced the germinating seeds of a growing Republican force in Texas politics.

The 1978 Democratic primary and conventions reinforced the liberal movement within the party. Roughly two-thirds of the state Democratic executive committee were now liberals or moderates, and their candidate, Attorney General John Hill, defeated the incumbent conservative governor Dolph Briscoe for the party's gubernatorial nomination, while moderate congressman Bob Krueger gained the senatorial bid. As one writer noted, however, "The liberal Democratic faction was successful in achieving its goal of party control, but the result was stereotyping the Texas Democratic party as solely a liberal party."[80]

Although Hill became the Democratic candidate, he never reached the office of governor. Republican Bill Clements broke the glass ceiling of state offices, appealing to conservatives regardless of party. From the primary to the November election, the Democrats lost 610,939 votes, more than one-third of their primary electorate. While some did not vote in the general election, the vast majority switched to the conservative Republican candidate.[81]

Four years later liberals consolidated their control of the party. A cadre of younger liberal candidates, comprising Ann Richards, Jim Mattox, Jim Hightower, and Garry Mauro, were elected to statewide offices and would continue to play important roles in state politics throughout the 1980s and into the 1990s. The significance of the 1982 victories was noted at the time in an article by Bo Byers, veteran political writer for the *Houston Chronicle*.

The ratio on May 1 was almost an exact 60:40 in favor of liberal candidates against conservative candidates when you total the votes for all conservatives and all liberals in the races for governor, attorney general, treasurer, land commissioner and agriculture commissioner. On the basis of that analysis, I wrote that the shift from conservative toward liberal in the Democratic Party indicated "perhaps the most profound shift in political sentiment in the Texas Democratic rank and file in the 20th century."[82]

What could be viewed as the last crucial liberal-conservative battle in the Democratic primary was the 1984 senatorial runoff between liberal Lloyd Doggett and conservative Kent Hance. Hance's defeat and subsequent party switch removed one of the last viable statewide conservative candidates in the Texas Democratic Party. As Chandler Davidson observed, "It was clear by the 1980s that candidates for the Democrats' nomination for important statewide offices could seldom succeed unless they were moderates or liberals."[83]

Doggett lost the race for the United States Senate in the 1984 Reagan landslide. His opponent was Phil Gramm, an individual who epitomized the changes that had been occurring in Texas partisan politics. Initially running in the 1976 Democratic primary as a conservative challenger to Senator Lloyd Bentsen, Gramm was elected to Congress two years later and subsequently re-elected twice as a Democrat. One of the leaders of the "Boll Weevil" faction of conservatives in the Democratic congressional delegation, Gramm had frequently supported the economic policies of President Reagan while serving on the budget committee. When the national Democratic leadership threatened to remove him from that committee in 1983, Gramm announced that he was resigning his seat and then filed for the special election to fill his vacancy as a Republican. Easily returned by his constituents, he then sought the Republican senatorial nomination in 1984, defeating Congressman Ron Paul and businessman Rob Mosbacher. As one writer noted,

> Phil Gramm's switch to the Republican party had a mammoth impact on Texas partisan politics. Gramm was the first Texas politician to define the Republican party as the sole "conservative" party in Texas. He made the "liberal" label the identifying and predominant philosophy of the Democratic party. . . . The genius of Gramm's maneuver is that it isolated the conservative Democratic faction in Texas. He redefined the term conser-

vative and placed it solidly and only in the Republican party. Conservative Democrats were left without a political home.[84]

Phil Gramm won the Senate seat vacated by John Tower, held it for eighteen years, and turned it over to the current incumbent Republican, John Cornyn, in 2002. Since the 1961 special election, the Republican Party has held this seat continuously.

With the liberal element in control of the party, it is no surprise that the 1990 gubernatorial contest in the Democratic primary was between Ann Richards and Jim Mattox—two of the younger liberals first elected to statewide office in 1982. Richards prevailed and went on to defeat Clayton Williams. She would be the last Democratic governor until at least 2015. That same 1990 election also produced two Republican victories for lower-level statewide offices featuring individuals who would continue to play important roles in Texas politics for many years—Kay Bailey Hutchison and Rick Perry.

The two-party Democrats correctly perceived that liberals could gain control of the Texas party only when conservatives were motivated to leave the Democratic primary. Throughout the 1960s and early 1970s, the two-party Democrats backed Republican candidates against conservative Democratic nominees in an effort to drive more conservatives out of the party. With the exception of helping elect and re-elect John Tower, this approach did not prove successful. By the late 1970s liberals were able to gain control of the party machinery and the gubernatorial nomination. Yet their success came more from the appeal of Ronald Reagan in attracting conservatives to the GOP primary in 1976 and the election of Bill Clements as governor in 1978 against a moderate to liberal Democratic nominee.

The unintended consequence of the liberal control of the Texas Democratic Party has been the growth and success of the Republican Party. What the liberals failed to consider is that as they gained control of the machinery and nominating process, the party label was becoming less of a draw to the electorate. In effect, the days of the "yellow dog" Democrat majority had passed. "The Texas Democratic liberal faction thought that the Texas electorate could be manipulated by Democratic party loyalty and the power of the 'Democrat' label. This perception was wrong and it eventually led to ostracizing certain conservative supporters in the Democratic party. The liberal faction did not take into account that political party labels never meant much to the Texas electorate."[85] As the Democratic Party became more closely associated with a liberal philosophy, the Texas electorate remained predominantly conservative. Over time this resulted in what the two-party Democrats desired, namely the movement of conservatives out of the Democratic Party and its primaries and conventions. Combined with the passing of the Depression generation and the influx of new residents from other states, this shifting of partisan loyalties has contributed to Republican success. The end result as of the early twenty-first century is not a two-party Texas but, rather, a partisan shift of conservative politics to the Republican side.

Bill Clements: Breaking the Glass Ceiling

For more than one hundred years Texas Republicans had succeeded in electing only one individual to statewide office. That person, John Tower, would be up for re-election in 1978. Nevertheless, unless and until the GOP could break through and win other statewide offices, and especially the most visible position of governor, there would not be two-party politics in Texas. It would take a wealthy businessman from Dallas to produce that initial victory as governor, coming 104 years after the last Republican left office in ignominy.

William Perry Clements Jr. was the successful candidate and his victory would have lasting significance for the party and the state. Clements was viewed by his campaign and much of the media as a businessman and not a politician who would appeal to what he called the "Texas ticket-splitters." The reality was more complicated. As early as 1964 Clements had been approached by GOP state chairman Peter O'Donnell Jr. to run for the United States Senate, an offer he quickly declined while agreeing to serve as finance chairman for the party's eventual candidate, George H. W. Bush. Four years later O'Donnell came calling again, asking Clements to consider a race for governor, which he again refused.[86] In 1971 he was chairman of a fund-raising dinner for John Tower, an event described at the time as the most successful GOP dinner ever. In 1972, he was co-chairman of the state's campaign to re-elect President Nixon. That same year he was nominated to be deputy secretary of defense, a position he held under both Nixon and Ford.[87]

Just as significant was the political background of his wife. Rita Crocker started her political involvement as a college student during the Eisenhower campaign, married Richard D. Bass, and became involved in a number of GOP campaigns, rising to the office of Republican national committeewoman from Texas in 1973. Shortly thereafter she divorced Bass and in 1975 married Clements.[88]

Perhaps no two people were more important in Clements's decision to seek office than his wife and Peter O'Donnell Jr., former GOP state chairman and national committeeman. As John Knaggs reported, "The former Deputy Secretary of Defense had considered such a race in 1968, when Paul Eggers became the nominee. Then and for the 1978 race, the ubiquitous O'Donnell wanted Clements. O'Donnell was prominent in this campaign from the inception with superb talent that could get things moving rapidly, not the least of whom was Clements' wife, Rita, who knew politics from the precinct level upward."[89] Throughout his three campaigns for governor, Rita Clements would be the most important political advisor to her husband and an effective surrogate throughout the state.

Clements had to maintain a balance between the traditional Republican base and the newer element that had rallied around Ronald Reagan in his overwhelming primary win of 1976. As one who had served in the Nixon and Ford administrations and whose key political advisors were former state party leaders Peter O'Donnell and Rita Clements, he was clearly a traditional Texas Republican. Yet, given the influx of so many new voters into the 1976 primary who might well vote in the GOP primary again in 1978, Clements had to reach out to the Reagan forces who had dominated the last primary. After much cajoling he convinced George W. Strake, a wealthy businessman from Houston who had been part of the Reagan delegation to the national convention in 1976, to serve as his campaign chairman. Clements was aided also in this outreach to the Reagan backers by the fact that his primary opponent, Ray Hutchison, had defeated Reagan co-chairman Ray Barnhart to become GOP state chairman.

Clements was also a contrast in terms of his personal style and background. On the one hand he was a very successful businessman with a wealth estimated at $30 million in 1978, who lived in toney Highland Park and had a ranch in Forney and a summer home in Taos, whose personal friends and associates were the business barons of Dallas. On the other hand, he was a self-made entrepreneur who could never be mistaken for a country-club Republican. Strake accurately described Clements as "a roughneck who lives in a big house."[90] Instead of the finely tailored Saville Row suits favored by John Tower, Bill Clements preferred loud plaid sport coats and open collars in the heat of summer.

When Clements announced his candidacy on November 16, 1977, he was met by initial skepticism from much of the media and party activists. Most expected the party's candidate to be Ray Hutchison, a well-regarded former state representative and party chairman who had made moves to run in 1974 before backing away. In what had been traditionally a small universe of primary voters, Hutchison was personally known to most of the party leadership across the state. For those who knew Clements personally, there were questions as to whether he had the personality to be a candidate for public office. As George H. W. Bush said, "When I first heard he was going to run, I was not sure he would adjust to it. Here was a guy making million-dollar decisions all the time, dealing in a tough environment in the offshore drilling business. It's extraordinarily tough. Difficult risk taking. Ups and downs. Victories and defeats. Calm weather and tropical storms. But he went after it with a vengeance and worked like the dickens."[91] It was clear, however, that Clements would bring to the campaign one essential ingredient that had been missing too often in past Republican campaigns. Clements had wealth and was willing to spend it to be elected. As he stated about previous GOP gubernatorial candidates, "Every one of them ran out of gas in the fourth quarter. . . . I'm not going to fold."[92]

Clements's first challenge was to become known among the party activists across the state and show them that he could bring about a Republican victory in November. As Ann Quirk Erben, who served in the Clements primary organization, noted, "Clements spent a lot of money to get people to come to events. It was difficult to recruit volunteers because the activists were supporting Ray. We had to spend money, so people would at least think Clements was credible."[93] His campaign organization attracted a number of younger Republican activists. Jim Francis, the executive director of the Dallas County party, signed on as campaign manager, along with George Bayoud, Allen Clark, Scott Bennett, and Dary Stone. Bill Elliott became Clements's Dallas County chairman, and the team began lining up other county chairmen. The local party activists were assisted by a number of campaign professionals from around the country.

While Bill Clements concentrated on the handful of counties where the majority of GOP primary votes would be cast, Rita visited many of the smaller counties, where her involvement in party affairs meant that she had already established personal relationships. As she recalled the campaign, "It was very helpful to have the political experience I had. A lot of the people in the Republican Party—the workers, the Republican club members—said, 'Who is Bill Clements?' They really didn't know. A lot of them knew me better than they knew him. . . . I enjoyed campaigning with Bill, and I enjoyed campaigning on my own."[94] Clements spent some $2 million acquiring name recognition and building support. When the results came in from the May primary, he had trounced his opponent. In a traditionally low turnout primary, Clements received 115,345 votes to Hutchison's 38,268.[95] Meanwhile, on the Democratic side, Attorney General John Hill defeated incumbent governor Dolph Briscoe. The race was on between the conservative underdog and the presumed winner, liberal Democrat Hill.

With the primary successfully concluded, the Clements campaign determined that if they were to win in November they would need to solidify their support in the major urban counties, ensure unified Republican support, and limit their losses in the state's more rural counties. While previous candidates had done well in the state's six largest counties and had kept as much as 90 percent of the small Republican base, it was the nearly two hundred less populated counties that stymied any GOP victory. Ray Hutchison quickly endorsed Clements and the party activists came on board with little reluctance. The largest urban counties would have the campaign's attention over the fall months and organization efforts were already under way. The rural and less populated counties were what needed immediate attention, however.

The campaign determined that Clements needed to introduce himself and line up local support in the state's 230 smallest counties. Over the summer months, when few were focused on politics, the Clements campaign toured the rural counties in a mobile home, meeting with local officials at the county courthouse, visiting the radio station and weekly newspaper, and holding an event to attract rural conservative voters.[96] As Clements's pollster Lance Tarrance noted, "Bill did something no other Republican had the discipline or the patience to do—to go into the rural counties. It was a brilliant move, to do it in the summer, when the Democratic guard was down and people weren't watching."[97]

Project 230 became the name given to this targeted approach to campaigning over the early months of the campaign. It was a viable approach given the defeat of a conservative Democratic incumbent whose best showing had been these very same smaller counties. Soon after the primary Clements recruited David Dean, who had been Briscoe's general counsel, to become deputy campaign manager, and placed trusted aide Omar Harvey in charge of Project 230. By the end of summer they were successful in getting conservative Democrats to head up the Clements campaign operations in 130 of these smaller counties, filling in with traditional local Republicans in the remaining areas.[98]

There is no question but that the defeat of an incumbent conservative governor combined with the campaign's emphasis on making a presence in the rural counties paid off for Clements. Of those who voted for Briscoe in the primary, 47 percent voted for Clements in the November election.[99] Traditionally, Democratic candidates had been strongest in the rural areas of the state, but the lasting impact of Project 230 was that by his third campaign (1986), Clements was running strongest in these same rural areas.[100] In the immediate 1978 campaign he was able to improve substantially over previous Republican gubernatorial candidates in the Small Town category while building his majority in the other three groupings of counties (see table 4.3).

From Labor Day forward the Clements campaign focused on the six major urban areas, their suburbs, and the other smaller urban areas around the state. These areas became the focus of both paid and earned media as well as a massive coordinated telephone bank program using volunteers to identify and then turn out supporters. Traditionally the Big 6 counties provided the best showing for GOP candidates, while the remaining urban counties were a mixed bag, including some strongly Republican areas as well as traditionally Democratic counties. The campaign also placed major emphasis on attracting the votes of those who had moved into Texas since 1970, roughly 20 percent of the electorate. It was to the growing suburbs that many of these new residents had moved, carrying with them no lasting attachment to a Texas Democratic Party.

The strategy paid off as Clements squeaked out the closest Texas gubernatorial victory in the twentieth century. Clements held on to a majority of the votes from the Big 6 counties, carried the Suburban group of counties and the Other Metro counties for the first time, and improved dramatically in the 198 Small Town counties of the state. Texas politics would never be the same, especially as the rural and suburban base of the Democratic Party began to crumble.

Some have said that the Clements victory overcame the personalism that had dominated the Republican Party and proved the importance of professional organization for campaigns and the party. With his victory, Republicans were able to build a broader base of donors and voters.[101] Still others have said that the Clements victory helped to heal some of the Ford-Reagan divisions from the 1976 primary.[102] George Strake felt that "Bill Clements was a party builder just by winning and being there. He proved people were not going to break out in a terminal rash if they voted Republican, and the more you win, the more people want to be with you."[103]

At the time of his inaugural, one reporter put the partisan challenge confronting Clements in perspective: "He knows the Republican party's fate may very well be resting upon his shoulders. It's taken more than 100 years for a Republican to win the governorship in Texas, and if Clements bungles the job, it might be another hundred years before they get another shot at it."[104] As the new term began with a Republican in the governor's office, even his harshest critics had to conclude that "Clements proved that Republicans would not do anything horrible the instant they got control of state government."[105] According to Karl Rove, who served briefly as deputy chief of staff to Clements, the new governor made it respectable to be a Republican in Texas and through his appointments and policies increased the party's support in rural counties and small cities beyond the major metropolitan areas.[106]

When he passed away in 2011, biographer Carolyn Barta reflected back on what Clements had achieved in his three campaigns and two terms as governor of Texas.

> He proved . . . that not only could a Republican be elected governor but he could function in the traditionally Democratic environment that was state government. With his appointment power, Clements brought a generation of young Republican activists to the Capitol. He made it respectable to be a Republican at a time when the GOP primary only drew about 150,000 people. His ability to deal successfully with conservative Democrats created the environment that made conservatives comfortable in switching parties. As a result, he hastened the emergence of Republicans down to the courthouse level.[107]

The Clements campaign in 1978 proved to be essential to one other Texas Republican; John Tower barely won re-election to his fourth term, by slightly more than twelve thousand votes, a margin even closer than that of Clements. Without the strong gubernatorial campaign of Clements and its extensive "get-out-the-vote" efforts it is possible, if not likely, that Tower would not have been re-elected.

Although Clements lost his re-election battle in 1982, he came back and reclaimed the governor's office in 1986, becoming only the second individual to win nonconsecutive terms as chief executive in Texas. Clearly, in terms of partisan transformation, Clements had broken through the glass ceiling, showing that the party could come back from defeat and win again. In this regard he paved the way for the next two Republican governors, who between them have governed continuously since 1995. More than this, however, is Clements's contribution in attracting many more activists to the Republican cause and greatly expanding the base of support for the developing party. Without the victory of Bill Clements in 1978, the future success of the Republican Party in Texas over the next thirty-plus years would have been much less likely.

The Reagan Revolution

If anything positive can be said to have come out of the Goldwater disaster of 1964, it is a single event, a moving thirty-minute speech by a Hollywood actor and television series host. Titled "A Time for Choosing," this one speech, shown on national television prior to the election, would propel Ronald Reagan into a new career as candidate, officeholder, and recognized advocate for conservatism. In his autobiography Reagan credits it with changing his life: "Of course, I didn't know it then, but that speech was one of the most important milestones in my life—another one of those unexpected turns in the road that led me onto a path I never expected to take."[108]

After some recruitment and convincing, Reagan would go on to be elected governor of California in 1966 and then be the featured speaker at a number of Republican fund-raising dinners and campaign rallies around the country in 1967 and 1968.[109] During this time Reagan appeared at numerous such events in Texas and developed a loyal following of supporters who saw in him the makings of a presidential candidate. Reagan's approach was one that was inclusive, regardless of party, and designed to make conservative Democrats feel comfortable with a Republican's message. Inevitably he would mention that he had been a Democrat up until 1962 but that from his perspective the Democratic Party had left him.[110]

In Texas, it was a difficult time for a Republican speaker with Texan Lyndon Johnson in the White House and most conservatives backing his policies in Vietnam. Regardless of the opposition that was developing in certain circles of other states, Johnson remained popular in his home state. To criticize Johnson took a skill that Reagan was effective in administering. "LBJ-bashing in Texas was a fine art and one that could succeed only by prioritizing Johnson's liberalism while calling upon LBJ to do more, not less, to win the war in Vietnam. In 1967 and 1968, nobody was better at this balancing act than Reagan."[111]

By the end of 1967 it was evident to many in the party that Reagan was stirring the troops and a movement was developing that wished to see him become a candidate for president in 1968. A division was developing between those who shied away from another clear-cut ideological battle for the presidency, seeking someone who was perceived as more winnable, and those who wanted a candidate to carry on the conservative crusade begun by Goldwater. To some extent, this division reflected differences between the existing party leadership in Dallas and those active in party politics in Houston. Much of the state party's leadership was lining up behind Richard Nixon as the most winnable candidate.

Peter O'Donnell Jr., GOP state chairman, who had been chair of the national Draft Goldwater Committee, was already part of the Nixon campaign's inner circle.[112] O'Donnell determined that if a movement for Reagan could not be stopped, then it should be controlled. He called a meeting with a number of prominent party people in Houston on December 18, 1967. According to one report at the time, "O'Donnell laid it on the line: there was a grass-roots Reagan movement starting in east Texas, fueled by people who might politely be called hotheads—Birchers, et al. O'Donnell felt that if there was to be any kind of Reagan activity in the state, it ought to be steered away from extremes and, most important, be under their control. By the end of the Houston Club session one of those present, J. R. (Butch) Butler, had been drafted."[113] Butler, an independent oilman from Houston, was designated chairman of "Texans for Reagan," and his effort attracted support from a small number of party leaders, including the powerful and effective Harris County GOP chairman, Nancy Palm.[114]

Among the general electorate, many Texans viewed Reagan much differently than they had perceived Goldwater four years earlier. According to one author, "Nearly 50 percent of Texans had found Goldwater too 'radical' to risk a vote on in 1964, but only 10 percent of Texans felt the same way about Reagan in 1968."[115] Throughout most of 1968 up to the Republican National Convention in Miami Beach, Reagan continued as a noncandidate, allowing his name to remain on the ballot, however, in those states where removing it would require a Sherman-like statement. His strategists' hope was that he would acquire increasingly strong showings in these states that would provide momentum for a possible declaration of candidacy. In the many states where delegates were selected at conventions, the appeal was for party leaders to remain uncommitted. To avoid another divisive primary in California, Reagan would serve as the state's favorite son, thus keeping Nixon, New York governor Nelson Rockefeller, and any other potential candidates from seeking delegates in his state.[116]

The Texans for Reagan effort picked up steam throughout the spring of 1968, including support from former national committeeman Jack

Porter, state senator Hank Grover, and financier Jimmy Lyon, all of the Houston area; West Texans Jim Campbell of Pampa and J. Evetts Haley of Lubbock; and East Texans Richard Harvey of Tyler, Bruce Eberle of Port Arthur, and Chick Dollinger of Beaumont.[117] Reagan's failure to attract substantial votes in the various primaries where his name was on the ballot did not discourage his supporters in Texas. When Reagan received only 23 percent of the vote in Oregon, Butch Butler "reckoned Reagan had done as well as he could considering the nature of the Oregon political terrain which, from his vantage point, looked like a 'socialist state . . . where they spend Federal money like it was going out of style.'"[118]

The Republican Party of Texas chose not to hold a presidential primary in 1968, thus allowing its fifty-six delegates to the national convention to be chosen in the much smaller venue of the state convention. On the night before that convention was to convene in Corpus Christi, the Reagan forces sponsored an all-night "Reagan Movie Marathon" to attract support from the delegates. When the gathering convened the next day, over three hundred Reagan supporters marched through the convention waving placards backing him for president. O'Donnell was concerned that the Texans for Reagan he had helped create was now out of control. "In the end, so as not to reveal how badly his delegation was split, Tower opted for, and got, the role of favorite son candidate. This suited the Reagan people, as it denied votes to Nixon; at Miami Beach, however, Nixon needed first-ballot votes too badly to allow Tower this face-saver and forced him to release his divided delegation."[119] By the end of the state convention the names of the actual delegates were known, but the battle for their votes continued.

During the weeks after the state convention and before the national convention, the Reagan forces attempted to win away the Tower "favorite son" delegates. Operating out of a small office in Houston, volunteers led by Nancy Palm, Iris Manes, and Marguerite and Warren Binkley began an effort to sway the delegates. They engaged the efforts of Ron Dear, then a law student who was active in both the Young Republicans and the Young Americans for Freedom. Dear was designated to travel to East and South Texas, meet with the elected delegates to the national convention, and leave with them material on Reagan, including a recording of his 1964 "A Time for Choosing" speech. Dear also organized a group of YAF and YR members to go by bus to Miami Beach and rally support for Reagan. When the presidential roll-call was taken, the Texas delegation cast forty-one votes for Richard Nixon and fifteen votes for Ronald Reagan.[120] While Nixon was able to win nomination on the first ballot by a margin of twenty-five votes, the abortive Reagan effort was the beginning of an insurgent drive that would remake the party in the 1970s and 1980s.

In many respects the 1968 Reagan effort in Texas constituted an inside-the-party dispute involving insurgents against the establishment, much like the efforts of Jack Porter and his associates in 1952. It focused on convention politics and a small group of decision makers within the party structure. The next Reagan-focused challenge, in 1976, would be quite different, reaching out to the general Texas electorate and involving thousands of individuals who had never previously been involved in Republican politics. To this extent, its significance was greater and its effects more lasting.

As early as the 1974 Republican state convention it was evident that a sizable number of Texas Republicans were unhappy with the new Ford administration and especially Ford's selection of New York governor Nelson Rockefeller to be his vice president. State Representative Ray Barnhart of Pasadena sponsored a resolution expressing concern over the direction of the administration that passed in a close vote and was seen as a challenge to the party leadership.[121] By 1975, Senator Tower and most state party officials were firmly behind the pending candidacy of President Ford. When Mayor Ernest Angelo of Midland informed Tower that he would be supporting Reagan, he was told that it would be "the dumbest thing he would ever do politically."[122]

It was the ambitions of a Texas Democrat, however, that would put in motion the process by which a Reagan candidacy could take hold in the state. Senator Lloyd Bentsen decided that he would seek the presidency in 1976. To assist him in this effort his allies in the Texas legislature enacted what became known as the "Bentsen Primary" law, establishing for both political parties a presidential primary. While the Democrats opted for a nonbinding "beauty contest," for the first time Republicans would have a binding presidential primary. This meant the contest would be taken to the voters rather than being limited to the smaller number of party activists attending the precinct caucus and conventions. The existence of a binding primary was critical for the Reagan backers, who might well be outnumbered by party regulars at conventions, as they had been in 1968.[123]

As it turned out, the Bentsen candidacy never obtained traction and he withdrew from the race shortly after the filing deadline. With Bentsen out, the Democratic primary lost much of its appeal and more voters became attracted to the heated contest between Ford and Reagan.[124] Kent Hance, then a Democratic state senator, saw the irony in the situation of unintended consequences. "The funny thing about it: the whole thing was to help Bentsen, and it didn't help him a lick, it helped Reagan."[125]

After Reagan announced his candidacy, a campaign team was put in place led by three co-chairs: Mayor Angelo of Midland, Barbara Staff of Dallas (at the time president of the Council of Republican Women's Clubs of Dallas County), and former state representative Ray Barnhart (then the Harris County GOP chairman).[126] Nearly all the prominent names in the party were signed up as Ford delegates since voters would be casting ballots for delegate names rather than the presidential candidates. Most prominent among the Reagan delegates were two state senators, Betty Andujar of Fort Worth and Walter Mengden of Houston. Lined up against them was the long-standing leadership of the state party, led by Senator Tower, National Committeeman Fred Agnich, and former state chairman Peter O'Donnell, while state party vice chairman Beryl Milburn headed up the Ford primary campaign. Among those on the Ford delegate slate were former statewide candidates Paul Eggers, Byron Fullerton, and Zack Fisher, county judges John Whittington of Dallas and Julius Neunhoffer of Kerrville, State Representative James Nowlin, and business leaders Trammel Crow and Robert Mosbacher.

To some degree the 1976 primary was a reflection of long-standing divisions in the party between the two major population centers of Houston and Dallas. As one writer noted, "Dallas aspired to sophistication and gentility, while Houston had a new-money earthiness. . . . Dallas had dominated the Republican Party for years, and its country-club, don't-make-waves aesthetic was emblematic of the party's pallid history of failure."[127] Paul Burka, the longtime political editor of *Texas Monthly*, believes that this primary campaign was a seminal moment in redirecting the Republican Party of Texas. "Until Ronald Reagan came along in 1976 to challenge President Gerald Ford, the GOP in Texas had typically been run by rich folks from Dallas and Houston. The struggle between the GOP establishment and the more conservative populists has been a major theme of Republican politics ever since."[128]

Ford's primary campaign was a centralized effort with direction coming from state GOP leaders that was enhanced by the prestige of the presidency. His camp established phone banks in the top twenty-six counties, where it was expected that up to 90 percent of the vote would be cast. Neither candidate was able to recruit a person to hold a primary election in 44 of the state's 254 counties, which prevented voters from participating in the Republican primary in those areas.[129]

Reagan could not match Ford in money or endorsements but had the enthusiasm of the grassroots troops.[130] As author Craig Shirley summarized the situation across the nation in his detailed study of the 1976 primary campaign, "In primary after primary, it was the same story. A small group of dedicated conservatives were backing Reagan while the state GOP and local party apparatchiks were supporting Ford. These grassroots conservatives did not know that 'it could not be done,' so they simply did it."[131] Since there was no party registration in Texas, any and all voters could participate in the Republican primary. The difficult task, however, was to convince those with a lifetime of voting in the Democratic primary that it was acceptable to vote with the small band of Republicans on primary day. The Reagan campaign distributed a flyer assuring Democrats that this was both legal and appropriate. In the month before the primary the Reagan campaign released a list of ten prominent Democratic supporters, most eminent among them W. St. John Garwood, former associate justice of the Texas Supreme Court, and legendary wildcatter Michel Halbouty.[132] Just as the Goldwater campaign had done twelve years earlier, the Reagan effort provided an infusion of new supporters into the party.

When the votes were counted, over 450,000 Texans had cast ballots in the GOP primary and the Reagan slate of delegates had won in all twenty-four congressional districts, producing ninety-six convention delegates for Reagan and none for Ford. Reagan lost only 3 of the 210 counties, by margins of 192 to 123 (Webb County), 24 to 2 (Jim Hogg), and 7 to 5 (Kenedy).[133] His win in Texas not only kept his campaign against Ford alive but also set in motion a process that moved the party from control by a small body of predominantly country-club Republicans to a more widely dispersed and populist movement.

In many ways the 1976 primary had a lasting significance well beyond internal party politics. It may be viewed as a turning point for partisan allegiances among Texas voters, as the Democratic Party became more clearly liberal and in line with its national party priorities while the Republican Party was viewed as a viable ideological and political alternative. From that point forward it was the Republican Party in Texas that was perceived as the vehicle for conservative politics, just as it was viewed in the nation at large.[134] In his important work analyzing the significance of the 1976 primary, Gilbert Garcia maintained that "with one dramatic presidential campaign Reagan lured tens of thousands of Texas Democrats and political fence-sitters into the GOP fold for a single day, and before long many of them began to identify themselves as Republicans."[135]

Although Reagan lost the nomination in 1976, his showing and his personal appeal put him in the position as front-runner for the 1980 campaign. After a number of other candidates tested the waters and dropped out, the contest would end up being between Reagan and Texas's own George H. W. Bush. Tom Pauken, later a GOP state chairman, noted that now "everybody calls himself or herself a Reagan Republican. But in those days it was a very divided situation within the Republican party. The lines were clearly drawn. It was . . . Reagan against Ford, and then Reagan against Bush."[136]

The 1980 primary would be much closer in Texas, attracting slightly over one-half million voters to the Republican side. Overconfidence and poor budgeting led the Reagan campaign to devote few dollars to the Texas effort, while the Bush team put on a major drive to maximize support in his home state. Many in the state knew Bush from his time as Harris County GOP chairman and two terms in Congress as well as his two statewide campaigns for the United States Senate. As Craig Shirley noted in his classic work on the 1980 campaign, "Reagan had a following in Texas but Bush had one as well. The national Reagan office failed to appreciate the severe split in the Texas GOP between the Reagan folks and the Bush brigades. The divide was exacerbated when Reagan had campaigned against young George W. Bush in his 1978 congressional primary."[137]

When the votes were tallied, Reagan had won the popular vote but only by a margin of less than twenty thousand votes: 268,798 (51.0%) to 249,819 (47.4%). Unfortunately for Bush, his support was concentrated in a few counties and this meant a majority in only six of the state's twenty-four congressional districts, the unit from which the vast majority of delegates were apportioned. Overall Bush carried only 18 counties to Reagan's 213, with most of his support centered around Houston and Austin as well as one congressional district in Dallas. Of the Big 6 counties, Bush carried his home area of Harris County and Travis County, plus six suburban counties in these two areas. Brazos County, home to Texas A&M University, was the only one of the twenty-one Other Metro counties to provide a majority for Bush. His remaining nine areas were Small Town counties, some carried by minuscule margins, such as Kenedy (5 to 4), Trinity (23 to 22), Rains (18 to 15), and San Saba (28 to 20). The end result was that in terms of the all-important delegates to the national convention Bush was apportioned nineteen delegates to Reagan's sixty-one.[138]

Reagan would go on to win the nomination and the election in 1980 as well as a landslide re-election in 1984. After eight years in the White House, Reagan was able to see his vice president follow in his footsteps as

George H. W. Bush carried the state and the nation in 1988. From 1980 forward, Republican candidates have not only carried the state in each presidential election but also received a higher percentage of the overall vote in Texas than in the nation. Prior to Reagan's election, only Nixon's re-election campaign in 1972 produced a higher percentage in Texas than nationally.[139]

Reagan deserves much of the credit for moving conservatives out of the Democratic Party and eventually into the Republican Party. By 1984, he had broken the Democratic hold on Texas and by 1988 more than 1 million Texans were voting in the Republican primary.[140] But it was more than voters who would change loyalties. It is claimed that during Reagan's term of office, more than fifty-eight Democratic officeholders in Texas switched parties.[141] As one reporter summed up Reagan's influence on Texas politics: "He recruited a new generation of young conservative activists ('the Reaganauts'), inspired social conservatives ('the Religious Right'), taught two generations of conservative Democrats ('the Reagan Democrats') that the world would not end if they voted Republican, and brought high-profile Texas Democrats into the GOP fold, including Reps. Phil Gramm of College Station and Kent Hance of Lubbock."[142] While some have argued that there was no mass conversion of officeholders in Reagan's time, it can nonetheless be concluded that he "left a powerful legacy that involved a longer-term, less tangible component. By the start of the twenty-first century, the party contained many politicians and activists who considered Ronald Reagan as their political inspiration. In time, the Reagan effect was therefore more significant as a force for mobilization rather than for conversion."[143]

Ronald Reagan had made it more than acceptable to be a Republican; for Texas conservatives, he had made it expected. In so doing, he had broken away one of the critical bases of the Texas Democratic Party—its "yellow dog" conservatives, whose loyalty to the party had been built on tradition and conformity. For the next two decades, this base would continue to turn out for local Democratic candidates in much of rural Texas, but the base was eroding away as the twenty-first century began. Indeed, it had already faded in most of the state's suburbs and many of the middle-sized counties of the state.

By the 1980s, Texas had clearly become a two-party state. While many individual campaign workers, donors, and candidates contributed to this development, the dramatic change from a century-long history of Democratic Party dominance came about primarily due to the contributions of John Tower, Bill Clements, and Ronald Reagan, as well as those within the Democratic Party dedicated to moving their party in a liberal direction. These four factors set the stage for a period in which the two political parties were nearly evenly matched in competition for statewide and congressional races, with the GOP gradually making inroads into state legislative and county politics.

CHAPTER 6

The Two-Party Interlude

Between 1978, when Republicans won their first race for governor, and 1996, when the GOP won all statewide contests, Texas experienced a time of two-party competition that gradually moved the state from predominantly Democratic to Republican dominant. As early as 1989, the director of the Texas Poll concluded that "clearly, Texas has become a two-party state. . . . It is simply a fact that nearly balanced two-party competition has arrived in Texas politics."[1] It was a time when neither party could take for granted the success of its candidates for top-of-the-ticket contests, and in many areas of the state that competition had reached down to the level of county and district offices.

While the Democratic Party won most lower-ballot positions during this period, winning is only one measure of two-party competition. Many political scientists and campaign professionals regard an office as competitive when a candidate wins with less than 55 percent of the vote. Since the competitiveness of a contest involves more than simply winning or losing, it is important to consider the extent of such contests and any changes in their frequency and composition from 1978 to 1996. However, measures of party competition can go beyond election day. Although Texas does not have voter registration by party, individuals can affiliate with a party by voting in its primary. Moreover, the results of public opinion surveys measure individual self-designation of party identification. Party support can also be evaluated in terms of the number of straight-ticket votes cast in a general election.[2] This chapter considers each of these measures of two-party competition and, where possible and appropriate, views the level of competition for each of the four categories of counties.

Competitive Elections

Statewide Competition

Beginning with the election of 1980 the Republican presidential candidate has carried Texas in all nine contests. While this record is impressive in terms of party strength, it should be noted that in six of the seven races from 1980 to 2004 a Texan named Bush was on the ballot. Moreover, the margin of victory declined substantially from the 1980s to the 1990s, as did the overall election fate of the candidates. Breaking down the presidential elections by type of county shows significant changes from the previous period of 1960 to 1976. In each period five presidential elections took place. Democratic candidates carried the state in four of the five contests from 1960 forward, the lone exception being the Nixon landslide of 1972. In each of these successful Democratic campaigns the GOP candidate did best in the Big 6 counties while losing the other three categories. Clearly, during the earlier period presidential Republicans were more concentrated in the state's largest counties, the area that had also been the base of Eisenhower support in the 1950s (table 6.1).

Not only was the Republican support greatest in the Big 6 counties, but the margin by which the GOP candidate carried this category was sufficient to overcome the Democratic advantage in the Suburban and Other Metro counties—but not the Democratic lead coming out of the Small Town category of counties. Without the Democratic lead in the Small Town counties, Richard Nixon would have carried the state in both 1960 and 1968, and Gerald Ford would have been successful in 1976. Only in the 1972 landslide was this pattern reversed, as these more rural counties' opposition to the McGovern candidacy caused them to produce the highest percentage of the vote for Nixon.

From 1980 to 1996, a number of changes in the distribution of Republican presidential support can be seen. Previously the base of GOP support, the Big 6 counties witnessed a declining margin for Republican presidential candidates, turning an earlier lead of more than three hundred thousand votes to a deficit in 1996. While the Big 6 counties continued to grow in absolute numbers, the suburbs surrounding them were increasing in numbers even more rapidly. Many of these new suburban residents were transplants from the Republican-leaning precincts of the Big 6. Nevertheless, three of these counties—Harris, Dallas, and Tarrant—were carried by the Republican candidate in all five elections, just as they had been GOP strongholds in all but the 1964 election during the previous period.

Table 6.1. GOP margin and percentage of vote in presidential elections, by county category, 1960–1976

| | County category | | | | | | | |
| | Big 6 | | Suburban | | Other Metro | | Small Town | |
Year	GOP margin vs. Democrats	GOP vote as percentage of total	GOP margin vs. Democrats	GOP vote as percentage of total	GOP margin vs. Democrats	GOP vote as percentage of total	GOP margin vs. Democrats	GOP vote as percentage of total
1960	+72,986	54.0	-19,571	45.3	-26,914	47.3	-72,734	44.5
1964	-237,096	39.4	-89,573	31.0	-131,951	38.0	-245,979	32.8
1968[a]	+51,955	52.2	-22,050	45.1	-8,040	49.2	-60,825	44.9
1972	+487,475	64.6	+224,829	67.4	+253,868	68.3	+286,943	69.0
1976	+68,824	51.8	-26,368	47.0	-13,557	49.1	-157,918	41.3

[a]For 1968, percentage shown reflects only a two-party vote. With the votes for George Wallace added, Republican support is Big 6, 44.5%; Suburban, 35.2%; Other Metro, 39.6%; and Small Town counties, 33.9%.

It is among the expanding population of the Suburban counties that the GOP made its most substantial growth in presidential support. A majority of these twenty-nine counties voted Republican during the earlier period only in the 1972 Nixon landslide, with Kendall County the only one to go with the Republican candidate in all five elections. From 1980 to 1996, however, twenty of the twenty-nine counties were carried by the GOP presidential candidate in all five contests. The Suburban category became the most Republican in terms of percentage of votes cast, producing roughly six in ten votes and sizable overall majorities for the GOP candidates. In terms of raw votes, this category of counties not only vastly expanded its electorate through population growth but also became, by the 1990s, the major contributor to the Republican presidential candidate vote advantage (table 6.2).

As with the Suburban counties, the Other Metro grouping of counties had provided small margins for the Democratic presidential candidates in all but the 1964 campaign. Only a subset of five oil-related counties (Ector, Midland, Randall, Smith, and Gregg) produced Republican majorities in all five elections during this earlier period. In the later period, fourteen of the twenty-one counties were carried by the GOP presidential candidate in all five elections, with a countervailing subset of three counties (Hidalgo, Webb, and Jefferson) remaining consistently Democratic. During the 1980s, the Other Metro counties shifted from support for the Democratic candidate to providing a sizable margin for the Republican candidate, a margin that dropped off in the 1990s when the party had less successful campaigns.

The more rural areas of the state consistently had been strongholds of the Democratic Party, but this bulwark of support was overcome in the Nixon landslide of 1972 and then began to slip slightly in the Clements election of 1978. Beginning with the 1980 election, the group of 198 counties in the Small Town category started producing Republican pluralities, albeit at percentages in the low fifties.

Growing Republican support in the Suburban and Small Town categories can also be seen in the gubernatorial elections during this period. These contests from 1978 to 1994 were all very competitive, with the winning percentage ranging from 50.4 percent to 53.8 percent of the two-party vote. In fact, the three Clements campaigns of 1978 and the 1980s and the two Richards election efforts of the 1990s were roller-coasters. Clements's initial victory was secured by acquiring pluralities in the Big 6, Suburban, and Other Metro categories to overcome a 48,777 shortfall in the Small Town grouping of counties. Four years later he lost his re-

Table 6.2. GOP presidential margin and percentage of total vote, by county category, 1980–1996

	County category							
	Big 6		Suburban		Other Metro		Small Town	
Year	GOP margin vs. Democrats	GOP vote as percentage of total	GOP margin vs. Democrats	GOP vote as percentage of total	GOP margin vs. Democrats	GOP vote as percentage of total	GOP margin vs. Democrats	GOP vote as percentage of total
1980	+344,381	58.5	+99,143	59.4	+137,060	58.0	+48,974	52.5
1984	+643,038	62.7	+268,594	68.9	+298,617	64.3	+273,903	62.4
1988	+306,783	56.1	+176,581	61.3	+136,957	56.8	+53,760	52.5
1992[a]	+31,730	50.7	+125,252	58.7	+55,733	53.2	+1,541	50.1
1996[a]	-13,005	49.7	+191,155	60.8	+53,675	52.9	+44,659	52.3

[a]Percentage shown excludes support for H. Ross Perot and other minor-party candidates.

Table 6.3. Percentage of vote, by party and margin, for attorney general elections, 1978–1994

Year	Republican candidate	Percentage of vote	Democratic candidate	Percentage of vote	Margin of victory
1978	Baker	44.0	White	55.2	252,632
1982	Meier	40.3	Mattox	59.6	584,110
1986	Barrera	47.2	Mattox	51.6	146,053
1990	Brown	45.2	Morales	51.9	255,604
1994	Wittig	43.4	Morales	53.7	371,749

election by coming up short in all four categories of counties, although barely losing the Big 6 group.[3] In 1986, Clements bounced back to win a vigorously contested primary and then oust Governor Mark White by carrying all four categories of counties, including a 105,729 plurality from the more rural counties which had been a thorn in the side of previous Republican gubernatorial candidates.

Ann Richards's fortunes were similar, as she won a close election in 1990 by amassing a large plurality in the base of GOP support of the Big 6 counties while losing the traditional Democratic area of rural Texas. By 1994, the tables were turned and Richards failed to gain re-election as George W. Bush carried all four categories of counties. It was apparent by the 1986 election that the category of Small Town counties had turned from a source of votes for Democratic candidates for governor to a predominantly Republican base. Likewise, the twenty-nine counties categorized as Suburban were becoming the most significant contributor of GOP votes for governor.

The shift toward two-party competition can be viewed not only in the five contests for governor but also in the campaigns for attorney general, one of the more important statewide constitutional offices (table 6.3). While the Democratic candidate was successful in each of the five elections from 1978 to 1994, the GOP became an increasingly competitive force, mounting serious challengers with well-financed campaigns. In 1978, Mark White defeated James A. Baker with 55.2 percent of the total vote while Jim Mattox won with 59.6 percent in 1982. For the last three elections the successful candidate won each time with less than 55 percent of the vote as Mattox was held to 51.6 percent by Roy Barrera Jr. in 1986 and Dan Morales was elected in 1990 with 51.9 percent and re-elected with 53.7 percent of the vote in 1994. Clearly, Democrats continued to hold this key statewide office but found themselves needing to launch expensive campaigns to do so.

Republican candidates were competitive in a few other statewide positions beginning in 1988, running some close losing campaigns and winning the offices of state treasurer and agriculture commissioner. Members of the Railroad Commission of Texas are elected for staggered six-year terms in partisan elections. Republicans picked up one of the three railroad commission seats in 1988, another in 1992, and two in 1994. After the 1994 election all three commissioners were Republicans.

A look at the two highest courts of appeal in Texas indicates the changing dynamics of party competition during the period from 1978 to 1996. The importance of these positions in determining the direction of Texas public policy outcomes is balanced by their relative obscurity. It is safe to say that many voters are unfamiliar with the individual performances and qualifications of candidates for these two courts and vote on the basis of party affiliation. Both courts comprise nine individuals, each chosen for staggered six-year terms in partisan elections. Both courts were entirely Democratic in 1978, but their partisan composition changed over time such that there were five Republicans and four Democrats on the Texas Supreme Court and a six-to-three Democratic majority on the Texas Court of Criminal Appeals in 1996.

In the 1978 general election Republicans fielded no candidates for either statewide court. When a vacancy took place on the supreme court, Governor Clements appointed Will Garwood, son of a previous distinguished supreme court justice. Garwood lost his campaign for election in 1980, falling 22,580 votes short with 49.7 percent of the vote. Through the early 1980s the GOP ran sporadic campaigns for the supreme court, but only one candidate for any court of criminal appeals position.[4] Beginning in 1986 Republicans nominated candidates for most positions available on the supreme court, but not until 1990 did they contest most positions on the court of criminal appeals. The party was successful in winning seven elections to the supreme court: two positions each in 1988 and 1990, one in 1992, and two in 1994. Six other candidates received over 45 percent of the vote in losing efforts.[5]

While the Republicans won only three seats on the court of criminal appeals during the latter part of this period, they provided serious competition beginning in 1988. Eight losing candidates achieved more than 45 percent of the vote from 1984 to 1992, with only one falling just short with 43.9 percent of the total vote.[6] Although all four candidates in 1990 and all three in 1992 reached this level of competitiveness, only one, Lawrence Meyers, was elected. Testifying to the growing competitiveness of down-ballot races, of the six statewide judicial positions on the ballot in 1992, only one was elected with more than 55 percent of the vote (56.8%). Two years later the GOP candidates for the supreme court won, with slightly over 56 percent, while the party's two candidates for the court of criminal appeals each won with 54 percent of the vote.

In terms of Texas's representation in Congress, it is evident that neither party was dominant in elections for the statewide office of senator. From 1978 to 1993, Texas had one Democratic and one Republican United States senator, as had been the situation since 1961. When Lloyd Bentsen accepted an appointment as secretary of the treasury in the Clinton administration in 1993, Governor Ann Richards appointed former congressman Bob Krueger to serve until a special election could be completed. That resulted in several candidates filing in a special election in which Krueger ended up ninety-nine votes behind then state treasurer Kay Bailey Hutchison. In the runoff Krueger lost overwhelmingly. From 1993 forward, Texas has been represented in the Senate by two Republicans. While both the initial Senate campaign of this period and the final campaign were both within the range of competitiveness, the intervening contests for both the Democrat Bentsen and the Republican Phil Gramm produced victories just beyond the 55 percent range.[7] Hutchison's 1993 victory can be seen as the beginning of a transition away from two-party competition and toward Republican dominance in statewide politics.

Legislative Contests

After the 1978 election the Texas delegation to the U.S. House of Representatives included four Republicans and twenty Democrats. By the conclusion of the 1996 election, there were thirteen Republicans and seventeen Democrats in the much larger delegation as the state gained six new seats after the 1980 and 1990 census counts were released. Whereas the Republicans frequently contested less than half the districts from 1960 to 1976, they fielded candidates in more than two-thirds of the state's congressional districts in every election from 1978 to 1996 except one. Cumulatively, Republicans ran in 78.8 percent of all the possible congressional contests in the latter period, and their candidates reached a competitive level of 55 percent or more of the vote in 48.8 percent of the elections they contested.[8] For the first time in the twentieth century, many Democratic representatives had to consider the possibility of not only a primary challenge but also a concerted effort in November from a serious Republican candidate. This became increasingly the situation by the middle of the 1990s.

A similar development was occurring with elections to the Texas legislature. In the 1978 general election the Republican Party fielded candidates in 68 of the 150 house districts (45.3%) and contested six of the sixteen senate districts then up for election (37.5%).[9] Among the sixty-eight candidates for the house, twenty-two won election, nine lost with more than 45 percent of the vote, and thirty-seven obtained less than the competitive minimum.[10] Only one of the six senate candidates, incumbent Betty Andujar, was elected and was also the only candidate to receive more than 45 percent of the vote.

By the time of the 1994 election and the last years of the two-party interlude, the GOP was running house candidates in 88 of the 150 districts (58.7%) and for twenty-two of the thirty-one senate seats (71.0%). In that general election sixty-two Republican candidates were elected to the house, an additional five obtained more than 45 percent of the vote in a losing effort, and twenty-one candidates lost with less than 45 percent of the vote. For the senate elections Republicans captured fourteen seats, lost two with more than 45 percent of the vote, and had six candidates obtain less than the competitive minimum. From contesting less than half the legislative districts in 1978, the party was now fielding candidates in a majority of districts. Moreover, the percentage of competitive campaigns had increased dramatically, with more than 75 percent of all GOP legislative candidates receiving in excess of 45 percent of the vote.

When the 1979 regular session of the legislature convened in Austin there were four Republicans among the twenty-seven senators, and 22 of the 126 members of the Texas House of Representatives had been elected under the GOP label. By the end of the two-party period the party had obtained a slim majority in the senate and was within striking distance of control in the house. While the growth of Republican representation in the house came from all four categories of counties, the most dramatic increases took place in the Suburban and Other Metro categories.

Beginning in 1978 and on through the 1996 elections at the end of this period, the GOP won 42 percent of the house seats from the Big 6 counties, ranging from nineteen to thirty-six members.[11] Until the 1996 election, when the GOP came close to a majority in the house, it was the Big 6 counties that always provided a majority of Republican state representatives. Suburban representation increased from one lone Republican in 1979 to 25 percent of these delegations in 1983 and a majority from 1985 forward. A similar but less dramatic rate of growth occurred among

Table 6.4. Democrats and Republicans in the Texas House of Representatives, by county type, in 1979 and 1997

County type	1979		1997	
	D	R	D	R
Big 6	51	19	39	33
Suburban	12	1	8	14
Other Metro	29	2	15	16
Small Town	34	2	17	8

counties in the Other Metro category, which had only two Republican members in 1979 but provided roughly a dozen each session from 1985 to 1995 to reach a majority (sixteen of thirty-one) in 1997. Representation from the Small Town grouping of counties varied from one to three throughout most of the period but reached a high of eight (32%) after the 1996 election (table 6.4).

By the end of the two-party interlude, in terms of state legislative elections, Republicans were clearly a competitive force in the major metropolitan counties, dominant in the suburbs surrounding the Big 6 counties, and holding a majority of districts from the remaining urban counties. The strongest Democratic representation continued to come from the more rural counties, where Republicans comprised less than a third of the house delegations. All this would change as the state approached the twenty-first century.

District Judicial Elections

The change in the extent of party competition can be seen in the contests for one group of low-profile elected positions, namely the justices of the state's courts of appeals. Texas is divided into fourteen appellate court districts to which appeals are made from the various state district courts. There are a total of eighty justices on the courts of appeals with a varying number in each appellate district, all of whom are elected for staggered six-year terms in partisan elections. Given the traditional dominance of the Democratic Party it is not surprising that at the beginning of the two-party interlude these positions were almost totally held by Democrats.[12] With the election of a Republican governor in 1978, a small number of

GOP attorneys were given interim appointments to fill vacancies until the next general election, most of whom were then defeated by Democratic candidates. Only near the end of the first Clements administration did some Republicans begin to appear among the ranks of appeals court justices.

From 1982 to 1986, a total of thirteen Republicans were elected to the eighty positions on the courts of appeals. By the end of the two-party interlude, the situation was quite different. In the general elections from 1992 to 1996 there were one hundred contests for the appeals court positions.[13] Republican candidates won fifty-one elections (twenty-three of which were unopposed positions), were competitive in another eleven, and ran noncompetitive races in five more races. The remaining thirty-three positions comprised situations where Democratic candidates were unopposed.[14] As an indication of the lesser importance placed on partisanship for these judicial positions, a majority (fifty-six) during this period of time were filled with no opposition from the other party. The small number of noncompetitive contests implies that candidates sought this office only when the possibility of election seemed realistic. The end result from these one hundred relatively low profile district contests is that in the mid-1990s, the election performance of the two parties was split fifty-one to forty-nine.

County Competition

While Republicans had achieved parity in these district elections by the end of the current period, the situation was quite different for county-level elections. With 254 counties in the state there are a total of approximately five thousand elected county positions. The commissioners court serves as the legislative and executive leadership of county government; it consists of a county judge elected by all voters and four commissioners selected from districts within the county. The number of other county elective offices varies greatly, partly reflective of the population of a county.

Given the total number of county elective positions in the state, the Democratic domination at the start of this period was overwhelming. In 1978, the GOP held only eighty-seven county offices of any type, although even this small number was an increase from fifty-three in 1974 and sixty-seven in 1976.[15] Republicans had greater success in winning county offices related to the judicial system, such as sheriff, constable, and justice of the peace. Two years later, with the Reagan coattails, the overall total of county elective officials had expanded to 166. Of these, fifty served

Table 6.5. Percentage of Republicans and Democrats elected to commissioners courts, by county type, 1980

County type	Republican	Democratic
Big 6	23.3	76.7
Suburban	8.3	91.7
Other Metro	9.5	90.5
Small Town	2.2	97.8

on the commissioners court, including eleven as county judge. Nevertheless, only 47 of the state's 254 counties had a Republican elected to any county office, representing four Big 6, eleven Suburban, ten Other Metro, and twenty-two Small Town counties. As had been the case with presidential and other statewide campaigns, the GOP performed best in the Big 6 counties of the state and was only beginning to make small inroads into the Democratic Party's dominance of local elections in the Suburban and Other Metro groupings of counties (table 6.5).

Some observers maintain that the Democratic Party was organizationally unprepared for the challenge from Republicans because of its long-standing control of county courthouses.[16] After the loss of the Governor's Mansion in 1978 and the Reagan victory two years later, the Democrats did fund a study of the political attitudes of voters in Republican-majority precincts in and around Dallas–Fort Worth, Houston, and San Antonio.[17] The study asked respondents to rank a number of issues on their importance to the voter and with which party they associated the issue. The findings reflected not only the current situation but also attitudes that would continue through the remainder of the twentieth century and into the next. In summarizing his findings the author noted, "There appears to be a consensus that the voters want less—less taxes, less government spending, less government intervention. Here, they classify the Democrats as primarily concerned with more of everything. . . . In short, Democrats are perceived to be taking the 'wrong' stands and are taking a disinterested approach to the concerns of this group of voters."[18] Moreover, most of these Republican-leaning voters in the major metropolitan areas perceived the Democratic Party as standing in opposition to the profit motive: "The issue 'Opposes large profits by any business or individual' ranked second among the most disagreed with statements and was also second in terms of the positions most closely identified with the Democratic party."[19]

Over the next decade the Republicans would continue to increase their support among the electorate of the Big 6 counties and their suburbs.

Throughout the 1980s the number of Republicans elected to county offices continued to grow exponentially, rising to 287 in 1984, 410 in 1986, and 547 in 1990.[20] Republican success was most evident in the Big 6 counties. By 1990, the GOP held 102 of the 127 elective offices in Dallas County and a majority in Harris County, both counties being led by a GOP county judge.[21] Tarrant County had a Republican majority on the commissioners court along with several other GOP county officials. As Tarrant County moved more in the Republican direction at the end of the 1980s, eight Democratic judges switched parties and filed for re-election as Republicans. They were joined by the four-term district attorney and a former congressman who filed for county judge.[22] In all, the GOP held a majority on the commissioners court in 21 of the 254 counties. By 1993, it was estimated that nearly one thousand county officials were Republican.[23] One year later, in the 1994 elections, forty-seven of forty-eight judges elected in Harris County were Republican.[24]

In the 198 counties classified as Small Town, however, the Democratic Party continued its dominance of courthouses. Much of the party's continued success in these communities may have been due to tradition and personal relationships. Writing in the early 1980s one observer concluded that "a great many of those who have remained loyal to the Democratic party have done so out of inertia. Tradition has been Democratic, and small town voters take longer to break with tradition. One reason for this is no doubt personal contact and friendship between the voters and the Democratic candidates."[25] This Democratic tradition reinforced the predicament confronting efforts to expand Republican support: in such an environment it was difficult to recruit electable candidates to the GOP ticket; the shortage of viable candidates meant continued Democratic domination of county elections.[26]

By the end of the two-party interlude Republicans had made progress in electing their candidates to district and county offices throughout much of the Big 6, Suburban, and Other Metro categories of counties. In these same counties the party had increased its representation in the Texas House and was beginning to reach parity in congressional elections. Already they controlled the two U.S. Senate positions and the Governor's Mansion, as well as reaching a majority in the Texas Senate. Although the 198 counties categorized as Small Town remained strongly Democratic it was clear by the end of the 1996 elections that Texas was moving in the direction of becoming a one-party dominant state.

Party Identification

One additional means of measuring party competition is to compare the number of individuals affiliated with the two major parties. Since Texas residents do not enroll in a political party when they register to vote, party affiliation can only be loosely defined and established. One useful measure is the self-identification provided in response to a public opinion survey. Another way to indicate the extent of party identification among the electorate is to review exit polls taken on election day. These results, however, reflect only the views of those who participated in a specific election. To measure the views of the broader electorate, table 6.6 indicates responses obtained at times other than election day and is not limited to likely or actual voters in an election.[27]

During this period of time there was a precipitous decline in the percentage of Texans who identified themselves as Democrats. In the 1950s and 1960s roughly two-thirds of Texans chose this designation. As late as 1974, 59 percent of all registered voters called themselves Democrats. From 1978 forward, less than half were so labeled, meaning that a statewide candidate could no longer rely on Democratic Party loyalty as a path to sure victory. Over this period Democratic support fell from half the electorate to less than three in ten registered voters.

This decline in Democratic loyalty led to an initial growth in those not associating themselves with either major political party. Independents comprised roughly 25 to 28 percent of the electorate in the 1950s and 1960s.[28] By the early 1980s, this component grew to well over 40 percent of the electorate only to slide back to the 30 percent range in the 1990s. Such movement appears to support the conclusion that voters moving away from the Democratic Party were not willing to automatically adhere to another party's label. The independent status for some became a way station on the road to Republican identification by the late 1980s and 1990s. As Jewell and Morehouse noted, this movement was prevalent in a number of Southern states. "Because southern voters had little reason or opportunity to vote a straight Republican ticket or to vote in a Republican primary, they were more likely to begin thinking of themselves as independents than as Republicans. . . . Over a period of years, as conservative voters began to vote more consistently for Republican candidates and sometimes participate in Republican primaries, they began to think of themselves as Republicans."[29] The data seem to indicate that this was clearly the case in Texas as it entered a period of two-party competition.

With the election of Bill Clements in 1978, Republican identification

Table 6.6. Party identification as percentage of total
electorate, 1978–1996

Year	Party identification		
	Democrat	Independent	Republican
1978	48	37	14
1980	43	39	18
1982	44	36	18
1984	33	43	24
1986	33	40	27
1988	31	37	28
1991	31	31	32
1994	28	33	29
1996	29	41	30

began a slow, consistent growth through the 1980s, peaking at roughly one-third of the electorate in 1991. This time period mirrors the presidencies of Ronald Reagan and George H. W. Bush. By the end of the two-party period Texas had rough parity among Democratic and Republican identifiers, with a very slight GOP edge.

There are various ways of looking at how this change took place. Certainly the election of Bill Clements made it more acceptable for conservative Texans to identify with the Republican Party. The governor's power of appointment to numerous state boards and commissions provided an avenue for expanding the number of visible Republicans in communities across the state. Also, he could appoint attorneys to newly created or vacated judicial positions, thereby enhancing the Republican presence in the legal community. No longer was Republican identification a path to obscurity and exclusion. Now the electorate could see that party members held relatively high state positions.

The Clements win was followed by the Reagan landslide over Jimmy Carter in 1980, returning the White House to Republican control. Reagan's personal appeal, especially to younger Texas voters, cannot be overlooked as a factor in increasing Republican identification. His eight years would be followed by the presidency of Texan George H. W. Bush, reflecting the increased importance of Texas to Republican success and resulting in increased voter attachment to the party. Reagan was able to attract many first-time voters to the Republican Party, both younger voters and evangelical Christians who had previously not participated in the electoral process.

Party Change and Ideological Consistency

An additional component of the changing partisan attachments was the conversion of existing members of the Texas electorate. Thus, a number of Texas Democrats moved first to independent status before converting to the Republican Party. During this time several prominent Democratic officeholders also changed parties, including Congressman Phil Gramm, former congressman Kent Hance, and a handful of state legislators. These conversions certainly contributed to the acceptability of the Republican label. Survey data from the period tend to support this conclusion. By 1985 the Texas Poll was reporting that of those voters who reported their original party identification as Democratic, only 63 percent retained that allegiance with 17 percent having become independent and 20 percent now classifying themselves as Republicans.[30] Nearly the same percentages were found one year later in the 1986 Texas Poll.[31]

A survey by the University of Houston Public Affairs Research Center in 1986 yielded similar results. As the authors of this study concluded, "The Republican Party has been the big winner among those who have switched their party attachment. Forty-three percent of the current Republicans claim that they were once Democrats, while only nine percent of the Democrats claim they were once Republicans. The Democrats also seem to be moving into the ranks of the Independents—perhaps a temporary stopping point before making a complete switch."[32] Since the Democratic Party had been the overwhelming affiliation of Texans up to the late 1970s, it is not surprising that they experienced the most defections. What is significant, however, is the extent to which this occurred. Prior to the two-party interlude, the Democratic Party in Texas was the proverbial "big tent," serving as a useful and friendly home to nearly all elements of society. Decisions on who would serve in public office were settled in the Democratic primary. Before 1978, "the Democratic Party was a home to liberals, conservatives, reactionaries, union members, minorities, business people, and trial lawyers. It was a party that brought together enough diverse interests that it was dominant."[33]

The data also indicate the importance of ideology in changing party identification. Among self-described liberals in 1986, the overwhelming majority retained their initial Democratic association. Of the original Democrats, 81 percent of liberals remained affiliated with the party, a percentage that drops to 63 percent among conservatives and 65 percent among moderates.[34] Democrats who became Republicans were two times more likely to call themselves conservatives. Comparing survey results from 1984–1985 with those obtained in 1993–1994, the authors of one study concluded that there had been an ideological sifting of the electorate, with fewer liberals in the Republican Party and fewer conservatives in the Democratic Party. Liberals in the GOP fell from 19 percent to 13 percent, while conservatives dropped from 28 percent of self-described Democrats to 20 percent in 1994. For both ideological groups the percentage of independents was up.[35]

There appeared to be no significant ideological change in the Texas electorate; rather, the electorate increasingly came to see the Republican Party as being consistent with the political ideology they already had.[36] As the Texas parties began running candidates more clearly distinguishable on ideology and more consistently in line with their national parties' programmatic goals, the result was a gradual increase in those who called themselves Republican and a concomitant decline in Democratic identifiers.[37]

Population Movement

Traditionally it has been maintained that migration of Republican-leaning voters into Texas contributed greatly to the rise in party identification. This view was challenged by Harold W. Stanley in a review of Southern party changes published in 1988, wherein he concluded that "native southern whites have accounted for the largest share of the changes" in party affiliation.[38] While Stanley's conclusions may be correct for the South as a region, when the discussion is limited to Texas the results clearly show the importance of in-migration to the growth in Republican identification.

Texas has experienced rapid growth, from fewer than 10 million residents in 1960 to more than 25 million as of the 2010 census. Much of this growth came from individuals moving into Texas from other states. In the two-party period being discussed here, roughly 60 percent of the state's population was native born, 23 percent were long-term residents, and 17 percent were newcomers residing in the state less than ten years.[39] Newcomers during the 1970s and 1980s were frequently from states with competitive Republican constituencies. Many of these newcomers had been relocated by their employers and moved to middle- and upper-middle-class suburban communities in the state's major metropolitan areas.[40] In relation to longevity of residence, the partisan identifications of the three

Table 6.7. Party identification by length of residency, 1985

	Percentage identifying with party		
Residence status	Republican	Independent	Democrat
Recent arrivals	41	35	24
Long-term residents	34	35	32
Native Texans	28	32	40

Source: Tedin and Murray, "The Dynamics of Candidate Choice in a State Election," 238.

groups are striking, with the newcomers and native Texans being polar opposites, and the long-term residents being evenly divided in their party support (table 6.7).[41]

Similar survey data covering the period from 1985 to 1993 showed little variation in the partisan distribution, with newcomer Republican identification ranging from 38 to 44 percent, long-term resident support for the GOP from 30 to 34 percent, and native Texans identifying with the party at 28 to 29 percent. Likewise, Democratic support ranged from 21 to 27 percent among newcomers, 29 to 34 percent for long-term residents, and 32 to 40 percent among native Texans.[42] A Texas Poll conducted in 1985 indicated that less than half of all Republicans surveyed had lived in Texas their entire lives, as contrasted with more than two-thirds of the Democrats. Twenty-two percent of the Republicans had lived in the state less than ten years, 18 percent of the independents were new to the state, and only 9 percent of the Democrats were newcomers.[43] Clearly, migration was adding to the Republican numbers in Texas in the period of the 1970s and 1980s.[44]

Data for political activists also show a high percentage of converts and newcomers to the state. A 1984 survey of Republican activists indicated that 41 percent had previously been Democrats.[45] Likewise, a national study of state party convention delegates for 1984 concluded that throughout the South party switching was taking place overwhelmingly into the Republican Party. These individuals tended to have little past involvement in party politics and were frequently those who had not lived for a long time in the South.[46] In a 1991 study of Texas political activists, Republicans were better represented among those under 40 and from 40 to 49 years of age, while Democrats were more likely to be over 60 years old.[47] Of the delegates to the 1994 Republican state convention, "over half of these delegates had never attended a political convention before."[48]

Migration can have both a direct and an indirect impact on partisan affiliation and voting behavior. First, it can influence the existing balance by introducing a wave of new voters into the electorate. In so doing it can help create a critical mass of party members that allows the minor party to become more competitive. In turn, this new competition may free up the partisan loyalties of the existing electorate and cause some to change party identification. When there are few if any GOP local and district candidates, voters who wish to influence the selection of such officials will vote in the Democratic primary and consider themselves Democrats. This combined impact of migration was evident in a study of Denton County, a suburban county that experienced a tripling of its population from 1960 to 1980. While the party division changed little in the rural northwest of the county and in the city of Denton, the expansion of the electorate in the growing southeast section of the county turned it into a Republican stronghold. This was especially true in a planned development called The Colony, where over two-thirds of the residents were non-native Texans, over 80 percent of whom had moved to the state since 1970.[49]

The Generational Factor

While the conversion of existing voters and the migration of individuals to Texas both contributed to the growth in Republican identification, a third factor was the entry of new participants into the electorate. The major contributor here consisted of younger Texans who were attracted to the Republican Party mainly because of the appeal of individuals such as Barry Goldwater, John Tower, and Ronald Reagan. Various public opinion surveys during the two-party interlude indicate that the youngest age category was the most Republican and least Democratic in Texas. Those in this previously youngest group, many now aged 30 to 44, retained their Republican identification into the 1990s. Thus, the Republican leanings of the 18- to 29-year-olds ranged from 40 percent in 1990 to a low of 34 percent in 1994. At the same time, the 30- to 44-year-old age group increased its Republican support from a low of 27 percent in 1986 to 35 percent in 1994. Table 6.8 indicates the changes in each age group from 1986 to 1994 (keep in mind that many of these individuals moved from one category to another over the nine-year period).

Among middle-aged (forty-five to sixty-one) voters there was little in-

Table 6.8. Percentage identifying with party, by age category, 1986–1994

Year	Republican	Democratic	Independent
		18-29 years old	
1986	37	27	36
1990	40	22	31
1991	38	26	36
1994	34	27	39
		30-44 years old	
1986	27	31	42
1990	34	27	33
1991	34	31	36
1994	35	30	35
		45-61 years old	
1986	23	41	36
1990	30	35	31
1991	35	36	29
1994	28	33	39
		62 years or older	
1986	21	48	31
1990	17	50	28
1991	28	45	27
1994	25	44	31

Source: Data for 1986 from Vedlitz, Dyer, and Hill, "The Changing Voter," in *The South's New Politics*, ed. Robert H. Swansbrough and David M. Brodsky, 46; 1990 from Moakley, *Party Realignment and State Politics*, 80; 1991 from Gibson and Robison, *Government and Politics in the Lone Star State*, 1st ed., 212; 1994 from Gibson and Robison, *Government and Politics in the Lone Star State*, 2nd ed., 173.

crease in Republican support, although the rate of increase varied widely during this period. There was, however, a significant decline in Democratic identification as the number of independents grew to 39 percent of this age group. This appears to be the population segment that took the half-way path of calling themselves independents as they lost their identification with the Democratic Party but did not as yet call themselves Republicans.

Those voters aged sixty-two and over were least inclined to be Republican but did experience a slight shift from Democratic to independent, although they remained the most strongly Democratic voter group. As early as 1986, the authors of a study on Texas voters could conclude that "the percentage of Republicans increases and the percentage of Democrats decreases as we move from older to younger categories."[50] Ten years later the same authors were projecting that "as the younger Republican voters age, they will likely continue to be Republican, and thus replace older Democratic voters."[51] This replacement was taking place by the end of the two-party interlude and would continue into the next stage, a return to one-party dominance of Texas politics.

In the two-party interlude most of the younger voters entered the electorate during the presidencies of Jimmy Carter and Ronald Reagan, a factor that appears to have contributed to their party identification. One measure of the younger voter support for the Republican Party can be seen in voter perceptions of the Reagan presidency. In a 1986 survey of Texas voters, those viewing Reagan's job performance as excellent or good reached its highest level among voters aged thirty to forty-four, at 71 percent, followed by younger voters (67%), middle-aged (65%), and least positive (59%) among those sixty-two and over.[52]

From a broader perspective, an informative panel study of Southern Whites who were high school seniors in 1965 and their parents highlighted the changes and continuities occurring in partisan identification. The high school students in the panel study were interviewed in 1965 and then again in 1973, 1982, and 1997. Beginning with a partisan division of 57 percent Democratic to only 26 percent Republican while in high school, this cohort of Southern whites had become 57 percent Republican to 39 percent Democratic by 1997, when they had reached their late forties. At the same time, there was no evidence of changing partisanship among the parents. The parents' Democratic support remained over 60 percent and Republican allegiance never exceeded 25 percent. Speaking of the parents, one writer concluded that "apparently these respondents were too old to have their partisanship affected by this period of substantial party system change."[53] Considering the path followed by this group of early baby boomers, who had moved firmly in the Republican direction, "it is now the case that an historic event has occurred: for the first time in southern politics a generation of Republican parents is now transferring their Republican identification to the next generation of southern voters."[54]

This change in partisanship was most evident among younger Anglo voters, as the following section will indicate. While discussing the South as a region, Seth C. McKee concluded that "younger voters were driving the increase in Republican identification among southern whites."[55] Writing in 2008, Hayes and McKee summarized the contrasts among age cohorts: "The Democratic Party's most loyal age cohort is the pre-civil rights generation: those over the age of 65. At the same time, young voters are the most reliably Republican group, a discrepancy that will provide a GOP skew in the distribution of party identification in the Southern electorate as time wears on."[56] This discussion of Southern White baby boomers and party identification provides the context for viewing race and ethnicity as they impacted party identification in Texas during this period of time.

Ethnicity, Race, and Partisan Identification

Throughout the two-party interlude race and ethnicity became more important factors in defining and differentiating party support. The most dramatic changes occurred in the composition of the Texas Democratic Party. These changes can be seen clearly in a comparison of survey results for Hispanic, Anglo, and Black Texans from 1984 to 1994 (table 6.9).[57]

In 1984 Democrats continued their lead in party identification among Anglo voters with 33 percent of the Texas electorate, although those declaring themselves independent as well as the Republican identifiers were closing in on the party's traditional dominance. By the 1990s, less than one-fourth of the Anglo electorate viewed themselves as Democrats while Republican became the most frequent response. The percentage of independents grew slightly but remained around one-third. The situation was quite different with Hispanic and Black voters. While the Democratic Party retained a strong lead over both Republicans and independents, their level of support fell, especially among Hispanics. Republicans increased their support slightly among Hispanics, but their level of identification remained negligible in the Black community.

Viewed from the perspective of party composition, Anglos became

Table 6.9. Percentage identifying with party, by ethnicity and race, 1984–1994

Year	Republican	Democrat	Independent
		Anglo[a]	
1984	26	33	30
1991	40	24	31
1994	37	24	34
		Hispanic	
1984	7	48	26
1991	14	45	31
1994	15	33	32
		Black	
1984	7	72	17
1991	6	67	24
1994	2	59	32

Source: Data from the 1984 and 1994 Texas Poll, in *Texas Poll Report* 11, no. 3 (Fall 1994): 5. Data for 1991 from *Texas Poll Report* 8, no. 3 (Fall 1991): 4.
[a] "Anglo" comprises those responding as White, non-Hispanic.

a smaller element in the Democratic constituency while the Republican identifiers remained more than 90 percent Anglo. As the researchers at the *Texas Poll* concluded, "In 1984, 70 percent of the at-large membership of the Democratic Party in Texas was Anglo, 30 percent minority—split nearly evenly between Blacks and Hispanics. But in 1994, only 57 percent of the Democratic Party is Anglo. The other—nearly half—of the party is minority (still split between the two major minority populations in Texas: 19 percent Black and 20 percent Hispanic)."[58] By 1994, roughly 4 percent of the Republican identifiers were Hispanic, 2 percent were Black, and 2 percent were Other. Those classifying themselves as independent were also heavily Anglo, although the percentage of Black and Hispanic voters so identifying themselves had risen to roughly one in three.

While there were significant changes in the ethnic and racial composition of Democratic identifiers during this period, a study of party activists completed in 1991 indicated that an overwhelming majority of those involved in both the Democratic and Republican Parties were Anglo. Nearly 90 percent of Democratic county chairmen and over 80 percent of county executive committee members were Anglo, while over 90 percent of both categories of Republican Party leaders were Anglo. Blacks and Hispanics were underrepresented in the local leadership of both parties.[59]

Primary Participation

An additional measure of party competition is the level of participation in each political party's primary. Over the period from 1978 to 1996 primary participation in Texas went from more than 90 percent Democratic to virtual parity. This change came about as increasing numbers of Republicans began to compete seriously for more district and county offices. When the Democratic Party dominated these local offices many Texans voted in that party's primary to be able to choose officials rather than out of partisan loyalty or any desire to be involved in the party process. As the November elections became the arena of final choice where decisions on who obtains public office are made, many of these voters were no longer motivated to vote in the primary.

In a 1980 review of Southern primary participation, Malcolm Jewell noted that "the growth of two-party competition in the South is likely to be accompanied by declines in Democratic primary turnout without a commensurate growth in the Republican primary."[60] It was only as Republicans became at least a competitive force locally, if not dominant, that many of these individuals began to participate in the GOP primary. Thus, when one party controls most of the county and district offices, that party's primary becomes the arena of final choice, and those voters who are interested in selecting local officials value participating in that primary.

As discussed earlier, up to the 1960s more Texans voted in the Democratic primary in nonpresidential years than took part in the November general election. Throughout the period of two-party competition, the Democratic Party continued to be the vehicle for election of most county and district officials, especially in the vast majority of the state's more rural counties as well as the outer suburbs of the Big 6 counties. Thus, the Democratic Party held primary elections in all 254 counties every election year through the end of the two-party period. Republican organizational efforts were less successful, but by the end of the period, in 1996,

Table 6.10. Number and percentage of primary votes, by party, 1978–1996

| | Democratic Party | | Republican Party | |
Year	Total votes	Percentage of total	Total votes	Percentage of total
1978	1,812,896	92.0	158,403	8.0
1980	1,377,354[a]	72.3	526,769[a]	27.7
1982	1,318,663	83.2	265,851	16.8
1984	1,463,449[a]	81.3	336,814	18.7
1986	1,093,887	66.8	543,172	33.2
1988	1,767,045[a]	63.5	1,014,956[a]	36.5
1990	1,487,260	63.5	855,231	36.5
1992	1,483,047[a]	65.0	797,856	35.0
1994	1,036,907	65.0	557,340	35.0
1996	921,256	47.5	1,019,803[a]	52.5

[a]Year in which presidential nominating contest in party occurred.

they had reached parity. From a start of only 186 counties holding a GOP primary in 1978, every county provided an opportunity for voters to take part in the 1996 Republican presidential primary. Beginning with a low of 158,403 votes in 1978, the Republicans obtained a high in 1996, with over 1 million votes. That final year of the two-party period saw the GOP exceed the Democrats in primary turnout for the first time, and it was the first time since World War II that the Democratic primary attracted the participation of fewer than 1 million Texas voters. It was also the last year in which the Democratic Party was able to organize and conduct a primary in all 254 counties (table 6.10).

During the first phase of this period (1978–1984) the partisan breakdown of primary participants varied greatly depending on the top-of-the-ticket contests. Beginning in 1986 and continuing for the next decade a stable pattern of roughly two Democratic voters for every one GOP primary voter existed. The 1996 primary, with the Democratic president seeking a second term and the Republicans hosting a competitive nomination battle, presents the first time with more voters taking part in the GOP primary.[61]

As the number of individuals casting votes in the Republican primary grew, the geographical distribution of the votes expanded also. Tradition-

Table 6.11. Percentage of Republican primary votes, by county type, 1978–1996

Year	County type			
	Big 6	Suburban	Other Metro	Small Town
1978	66.8	7.5	17.7	8.0
1986	50.5	15.7	20.3	13.6
1996	45.3	21.5	18.9	14.3

ally the Big 6 counties were the source of most Republican votes and, as in the past, these counties provided more than two of every three votes from 1978 to 1982. For the next five primaries these counties were home to slightly more than half of the Republican electorate, falling to little more than 45 percent in 1994 and 1996. Thus, after contributing a majority of GOP primary votes every year previously, the Big 6 began to exert less influence starting in 1994, a trend that continues to the present. Meanwhile, all three other county groups provided a higher percentage of the GOP electorate in nearly every election from 1978 to 1996.

It was the counties in the Suburban and Small Town categories that became ever more important in Republican primaries. From 7.5 percent of the total vote in 1978, counties surrounding the Big 6 counties contributed 21.5 percent in 1996. Small Town counties produced only 8 percent of the 1978 GOP primary totals, a percentage that increased to 14.3 percent in 1996. Both of these county groups would continue to be relatively more important in Republican primaries into the present. Counties in the Other Metro category increased their contribution from 17.7 percent to 18.9 percent but basically ranged in most years from one in seven to one in five of all votes cast in the Republican primary (table 6.11).

By the end of the two-party interlude, the Republican Party had reached parity with the Democratic Party in terms of primary participants. The base of Republican support, however, had shifted away from the Big 6 counties and was now dispersed among all four categories of counties. In some of these counties, the final choice for state legislative and county offices had begun to move from the November general election to the Republican primary—mirroring the pattern that had existed for nearly a century, only now in a different political party.

A closer look at the 1996 primary turnout for the two parties shows an interesting pattern in various counties where one-party domination of local contests contributed to heavy participation in that party's primary. In contrast to the pre-1960 pattern, it is not a single party that is dominant everywhere; rather, the Democrats are the overwhelming primary choice in some counties while the Republicans have reached a similar level of dominance in other counties. Among the Big 6 counties more than two-thirds of all primary votes were cast at Republican polling places in Dallas, Tarrant, and Harris Counties at a time when the GOP controlled the county judge and commissioners court as well as most other county offices. At the same time, over 76 percent of voters in El Paso, where few Republicans held any county office, took part in the Democratic primary.

Republican voters cast 71.2 percent of all primary votes in the Suburban category of counties. In these twenty-nine counties, eleven continued their Democratic domination, five of them with a more than two-to-one advantage in turnout. These eleven Democratic-dominant counties tended to be the outer suburbs or ex-urban areas such as Kaufman and Wise Counties outside Dallas–Fort Worth; Chambers, Liberty, San Jacinto, Waller, and Galveston on the outer fringes of the Houston metropolitan area; Bastrop and Caldwell south of Austin; and Atascosa and Wilson to the south of San Antonio. In only two of these counties (Galveston, with 54.3% Democratic primary votes, and Wilson with 58.0%) was there anything approaching parity in party participation.

A similar situation existed in the eighteen Republican-majority counties, with the GOP turnout exceeding two-thirds of all voters in fifteen counties and only two with less than 60 percent Republican. Here one can see the growing Republican dominance of the close-in suburbs around the Big 6 counties, led by Collin (90.2% Republican primary participation), Denton (87.5%), and Rockwall (90.7%) outside Dallas–Fort Worth; Montgomery (90.9%) to the north of Houston; Williamson (86.3%) north of Austin; and Kendall (94.3%), Comal (89.9%), and Guadalupe (84.0%), three close-in suburbs north of San Antonio. With the GOP's newly established control of most county and district offices, these counties had begun the move back to one-party dominance in primary participation.

As was the situation with the suburbs, there is a clear demarcation among the Other Metro grouping of counties. Fourteen of the twenty-one counties had a majority of Republican primary voters, and in twelve of these the GOP had over 65 percent of the vote, ranging as high as 91.2 percent in Midland, 88.0 percent in Randall, and 83.9 percent in Lubbock, all in West Texas. At the other end, six counties had more than two-thirds of their voters take part in the Democratic primary, led by Webb (95.5%) and Hidalgo (85.7%) Counties. The seven counties with Democratic majorities on primary day comprised five with sizable minority populations (Cameron, Hidalgo, Webb, Nueces, and Jefferson) and two with a high proportion of elderly voters (Bowie and Grayson). While the last two and Nueces would soon trend Republican, the remaining four would remain Democratic-dominant areas into the twenty-first century.

As had been the case for over a century, the Democratic Party remained comfortably in control of most counties in the Small Town category. Over 70 percent of those who participated in the 1996 primary election did so at a Democratic polling place. These 198 counties accounted for 40.0 percent of the Democratic primary electorate, far and away the largest component, even though they were home to only 20.9 percent of the state's registered voters.[62] Clearly in these counties the Democratic Party's domination of local offices continued into the late 1990s and helped to ensure a sizable turnout in the party's primary. As the period of two-party competition came to an end, there was little to predict the transformation that would occur in the twenty-first century among these mostly rural counties.

Straight-Ticket Voting

Texas voters have an option in general elections that is not available to most voters in the United States—they can support all the candidates of a political party by simply casting one straight-ticket vote. Straight-ticket voting is basically an issue of branding or establishing an identifiable label for a group of candidates. The motivation for straight-ticket voting may be philosophy or political ideology, emotional attachment to a party, or family influence and historical practice.[63]

Given the Democratic Party's dominance of Texas politics until the latter part of the twentieth century, the typical straight-ticket voter was the proverbial "yellow-dog Democrat"—one who would vote for a yellow dog as long as it was running on the Democratic ticket. Although there is little specific data available, a safe assumption is that up to the last years of the two-party interlude, more straight-ticket votes were Democratic than Republican.[64] The impact of Democratic straight-ticket voting is claimed by one writer to have been a significant factor in the defeat of the Republican statewide candidates in 1982, including incumbent governor William Clements.[65]

Table 6.12. Percentage and raw vote margin for straight-ticket votes in Big 6 counties and three Suburban counties, 1996

	Straight-ticket percentage of total votes cast in county	Party obtaining majority of straight-ticket votes	Percentage of straight-ticket votes	Raw vote margin from straight-ticket votes
Big Six counties				
Dallas	52.8	D	51.8	10,862
Tarrant	49.8	R	53.5	14,275
Harris	48.2	D	51.3	10,802
Bexar	50.9	D	57.1	26,079
Travis	35.9	D	59.2	15,986
El Paso	48.5	D	75.4	33,976
Three Suburban counties				
Collin	39.3	R	75.3	26,335
Denton	47.6	R	70.3	21,501
Montgomery	38.5	R	74.9	14,798

Beginning in the 1990s, however, an increase in the number of Republican straight-ticket votes can be noticed in several of the state's more populous counties. This increase was occurring at the same time that the percentage of straight-ticket votes overall was increasing. One example of this changing relationship was the situation in Dallas County. In 1990, only 36.1 percent of all votes cast were straight ticket, and Democratic votes comprised 57.7 percent of the two-party straight-ticket votes. Two years later the percentage of straight-ticket votes had increased to 38.2 percent, but the Democratic share dropped to 52.7 percent. By the 1996 election at the end of the two-party interlude, 52.8 percent of all votes in Dallas County were straight ticket, and the Democratic percentage had dropped to 51.8 percent for a lead of only 10,862 votes countywide. Similar increases in straight-ticket voting can be seen in Collin and Tarrant Counties outside Dallas during this time frame.[66]

By the end of the two-party interlude Republican straight-ticket votes in key growing suburbs were overcoming the traditional Democratic straight-ticket leads in Dallas and Harris Counties. Table 6.12 shows the impact of straight-ticket votes in selected counties in the 1996 election.

Clearly, what had occurred by the end of this period is the development in certain areas of the state of a viable Republican Party fielding a sufficient number and quality of candidates to attract the straight-ticket support of a sizable element of the Texas electorate. Moreover, Republicans had become sufficiently dominant in at least the three populous Suburban counties of Collin, Denton, and Montgomery that they were receiving nearly three out of every four straight-ticket votes and in sufficient numbers that the Democratic lead in the Big 6 counties depended solely on the party's overwhelming margin in El Paso.[67] While the data available is limited, it does appear that two-party competition had developed among straight-ticket voters in the Big 6 counties, while at least some of the suburbs were moving strongly toward a one-party dominant direction.

Just as primary participation can be seen as a measure of party identification and support, so too can voting a straight ticket for all candidates of a specific political party. Likewise, an increase in the number of primary voters, as well as the extent of straight-ticket voting, can be an indication of the ability of a political party to nominate candidates for most elected positions. The number of primary participants and straight-ticket voters appears to increase as a party becomes the dominant force in a jurisdiction. As the two-party interlude came to an end, this was the case with at least some of the major Suburban counties outside Dallas and Houston.

The Two-Party Interlude Concludes

For nearly twenty years Texas experienced a period of two-party competition. This interlude would end by 1996, however, as the gradual growth of Republican influence reached a tipping point. In that year's primary elections, for the first time more Texans participated in the Republican than the Democratic primary. This reversal of voting history would serve as a precursor for the results of the general election. In November the Democratic Party would come up short in all ten statewide contests and lose its majority in the Texas Senate. From that point forward Republican candidates have won every contest for all twenty-nine statewide elective offices and carried the state for the GOP presidential candidate. It would not be until the present century, however, that the GOP would achieve a majority in the Texas House of Representatives and the state's congressional delegation, at least partially due to successful Democratic gerrymanders of previous years.

Why did Texas not remain a two-party state once it had reached this stage of party competition? Several factors can be identified leading to the decline of the Democratic Party and the growing dominance of the Republican Party from 1996 forward. Surveys indicate that the electorate has remained ideologically consistent, with the overwhelming majority regarding themselves as conservative. At the same time the national political parties have become more ideologically polarized, with the GOP becoming more clearly conservative and the Democratic Party more liberal. This clarification of the parties on ideological grounds has led to the Texas Democratic Party no longer being viewed as an all-inclusive political force. The expansion of the Republican organization and candidate recruitment combined with the weakness of the Democratic organization allowed the GOP to reach into not only the Other Metro and Suburban categories of counties but eventually into the more rural areas of the state referred to as Small Town counties. The appeal of George W. Bush, evident in his defeat of a popular incumbent Democratic governor and his appearance on Texas ballots over ten years, helped to solidify the party's image and base of support.

By the late 1990s, the Texas electorate had effectively passed through a period of two-party competition and was once again entering a period of one-party dominance. This new phase, however, would not be as all-encompassing and comprehensive as the nearly one hundred years of Democratic dominance. For one, Texas was now a much more diverse place in terms of population composition, economics, and potential electorate. Each party retained pockets of strong partisans throughout the state and the provisions of the Federal Voting Rights Act, especially its pre-clearance requirement, would ensure that the Democratic Party would be able to elect a considerable segment of the Texas legislature, the congressional delegation, and county commissioners courts.[68] With the close of the two-party interlude, the stage was set for a new period of one-party dominance.

CHAPTER 7

The Era of Republican Dominance

In retrospect, the year 1996 can be seen as a turning point in the transformation of Texas politics. True, the Democratic Party still controlled most statewide offices and had a majority in the congressional delegation and the Texas legislature. But the tea leaves foretold a different future. It was a year of three important and historic firsts in terms of party competition. That spring, more Texans voted in the Republican than the Democratic primary election. Then in the November general election Republican candidates won all ten statewide contests. Finally, the GOP gained a majority in the Texas Senate. For a while the Democratic Party would continue to have more officeholders but the political winds were now moving in a different direction.

Beginning in the mid-1990s Texas had once again returned to a period of one-party dominance of its electoral process. This new era, however, is unlike the era of Democratic dominance, since there remain pockets of heavy support for the minority party where it continues to dominate local politics. The overriding force in state politics remains conservative in its outlook and ideology, as it was for most of the earlier one-party era, but this time it is the Republican Party that is dominant. While nearly 50 percent of the state's electorate perceive themselves as conservative, the two parties have taken on clear ideological perspectives in the minds of many voters. In a 2008 survey conducted by the University of Texas at Austin and the *Texas Tribune*, when asked to associate the two parties with an ideological perspective, 70 percent of those interviewed saw the Democratic Party as liberal while 68 percent described the Republican Party as conservative.[1] These perceptions have contributed to the growth in support for Republican candidates in the twenty-first century.

Table 7.1. Best Democratic candidates' performance in statewide elections, 1996–2012

Year	Number of Democratic candidates/ positions on ballot	Office sought	Top Democrat's percentage of two- party vote	Shortfall
1996	9/10	President	47.3	–276,484
1998	13/14	Comptroller	49.7	–20,223
2000	4/10	Court of criminal appeals	43.9	–721,388
2002	16/16	Lieutenant governor	47.1	–259,594
2004	4/8	Railroad commission	47.5	–1,018,765
2006	10/16	Justice, supreme court	46.8	–257,703
2008	8/9	Justice, supreme court	47.3	–400,874
2010	10/13	Governor	43.5	–631,086
2012	5/10	Justice, supreme court	43.8	–907,623

Winning Elections

Consider the contests for statewide electoral offices. Since 1994 no Democratic candidate has carried the state for either state office or the presidency. From the late 1990s forward all twenty-nine statewide elective offices have been held by Republicans. Beginning in 1996 Democrats have run candidates for only 79 of the 106 statewide contests on the ballot, slightly less than 75 percent of the positions to be filled.[2] Only one of these seventy-nine candidates, running for state comptroller in 1998, came close to winning, receiving 49.7 percent of the two-party vote while losing by 20,223 votes.[3] In the nine election years starting in 1996 the Democratic Party's best showing did not reach as high as 44 percent of the two-party vote on three occasions, including 2012, when its best-performing candidate, running for the state supreme court, obtained only 43.8 percent of the vote (table 7.1).

Of the seventy-nine statewide Democratic candidates since 1996, only fourteen reached the level of competitiveness by receiving at least 45 percent of the two-party vote. Three of these competitive races were run by incumbents who failed to gain re-election and one was by a judicial candidate who subsequently changed parties and was elected to the court of criminal appeals as a Republican. A number of the Democratic candidates ran statewide more than once during this period. Two attorneys, David Van Os and J. R. Molina, each ran statewide in four of the nine elections, with only Molina once reaching the level of competitiveness.

It is interesting to note that only twice, in 1996 and again in 2010, was the best Democratic showing delivered by its candidate at the top of the ticket. Four of the best-performing candidates were seeking one of the eighteen low-profile statewide judicial offices. Writing as early as 2003, one prominent textbook on Texas politics claimed, "In contemporary Texas, Republican candidates are close to holding an advantage that Democrats held up through the 1960s: When the voter knows little about the candidates, they tend to pick the Republican."[4] Given that the best-performing Democratic candidates were often running for the low-profile offices of Texas Supreme Court and the Texas railroad commission, the lack of knowledge about a candidate may have not been a factor in choosing which candidate to support. While the gap between the best-performing Democratic candidate and worst-performing Republican candidate has varied significantly, the results of 2010 and 2012 do not show any statewide trend toward the Democrats.

Presidential Campaigns

In each presidential election since 1980 the Republican candidate has received a higher percentage of the vote in Texas than his overall national performance. From a low of 52.9 percent of the two-party vote in 1996 for Robert Dole, George W. Bush received over 60 percent in each of his two campaigns, while both John McCain and Mitt Romney obtained above the competitive measure of 55 percent.[5] What has changed during the period from 1996 forward is the distribution of the vote for president within the state. From 1960 to 1992 the GOP presidential candidate carried the Big 6 counties in every election save for the Johnson landslide of 1964.[6] Beginning with the 1996 presidential election the Big 6 counties have produced the lowest percentage of the vote for the Republican candidate in all five elections, although Bush did carry them in his two campaigns. While both the Suburban and Other Metro counties have become more solidly Republican, it is in the Small Town counties that the most dramatic change has occurred. Since 2000, it is this category that has produced the highest percentage of the vote for the Republican presidential candidate (table 7.2).

The contest between Gerald Ford and Jimmy Carter provides a point of reference as it was the last one to occur during the period of two-tiered competition, when Republicans were competitive but Democrats won most federal elections in the state. A Republican presence was developing in the major urban areas of Texas, but in most of the remaining 248 counties the Democratic Party remained supreme. Ford built up a lead in these Big 6 counties sufficient to overcome Carter's advantage in the Suburban and Other Metro counties, but could not make up his 157,918 shortfall in the Small Town counties. Twenty years later Clinton's lead in the Big 6 counties was wiped out by Dole's performance in all three other county categories. This new pattern, with Democratic majorities in the Big 6 counties outweighed by Republican leads elsewhere, would reoccur in 2008 and 2012.

The parties each won three of the Big 6 counties in both 1976 and 1996. By 2008 and 2012, the Republican candidate could carry only Tarrant County.[7] The trend was in the other direction in the Suburban counties around the Big 6, however. Carter bested Ford in nineteen of these twenty-nine counties in 1976, but Dole won twenty-four to Clinton's five in 1996. In each of the last four elections the GOP candidate for president has carried all twenty-nine counties in the Suburban category.

The twenty-one counties classified as Other Metro were split eleven to ten for Ford, but twenty years later they went fifteen to six for Dole over the incumbent Democratic president. Most of these counties had been consistently voting Republican since the initial Reagan victory. Nueces County, with a Hispanic-majority population, is an interesting conversion to the Republican column, previously having voted for the GOP candidate only in the landslides of 1972 and 1984. For the past four elections, however, the majority of its votes has gone to the Republican presidential candidate.[8] Beginning in 2000 the Democratic candidate has never carried more than the four Other Metro counties of Cameron, Hidalgo, Jefferson, and Webb, all of which have majority-minority populations.

The most dramatic change has taken place among the Small Town group of counties, which have increased their support for Republican presidential candidates consistently in every election since 1996. Given the disparity in population and voter turnout among these 198 counties, only the larger ones (those with a participation rate of 7,500 voters or more in the 2012 election) are analyzed here.[9] These fifty-seven counties

Table 7.2. Republican vote for president by county category, 1976–2012

	County category				
	Big 6		Suburban		
Year	Percentage voting Republican	Vote margin	Percentage voting Republican	Vote margin	
1976	51.8	+68,824	47.0	−26,368	
1996	49.7	−13,005	60.8	+191,155	
2000	55.2	+290,982	69.2	+466,044	
2004	53.6	+239,130	68.9	+605,134	
2008	44.8	−365,074	63.9	+512,955	
2012	47.4	−186,557	67.5	+666,535	

were traditionally the base of the Democratic Party of Texas, and in 1976 fifty of them gave a majority of their votes to Jimmy Carter. By 1996, the movement toward two-party competition had begun to reach these counties and Dole carried thirty-five of them. Since 2000, a reversal in party fortunes has taken place, with Democratic candidates never able to carry more than five of these fifty-seven counties.[10]

Gubernatorial Elections

As previously discussed, Republican presidential candidates were competitive in Texas from as early as the 1950s, although such competitiveness had been mostly limited to the Big 6 counties and the few traditional Republican Hill Country and Panhandle counties. During the two-party interlude this competitiveness extended into other areas of the state, due greatly to the appeal of Ronald Reagan and the attraction of Texas resident George H. W. Bush. It was only in the two-party interlude that Republicans began winning gubernatorial races and ran competitive races for some statewide positions, eventually winning a few of them. What differentiates the current period of one-party dominance is the ability of Republican candidates to win all statewide elective offices and extend their base of support into new categories of counties.

Just as Bill Clements introduced a period of two-party competition by

County category					
Other Metro		Small Town		Statewide	
Percentage voting Republican	Vote margin	Percentage voting Republican	Vote margin	Percentage voting Republican	Vote margin
49.1	-13,557	41.3	-157,918	48.4	-129,019
52.9	+53,675	52.3	+44,659	52.7	+276,484
62.2	+261,152	65.6	+347,715	60.9	+1,365,893
64.8	+365,549	69.5	+486,400	61.5	+1,694,213
58.6	+220,080	71.5	+580,734	55.9	+950,695
59.4	+233,503	72.7	+548,238	58.0	+1,261,719

winning over those he called the "Texas ticket-splitters," so another gubernatorial candidate would usher in the era of Republican domination
that would begin in 1996 and continue to the present. To start this process in motion, the party needed to win the 1994 gubernatorial election.
Ann Richards had returned the governor's office to Democratic control
in 1990. Writing in 1994 before the gubernatorial election, Sue Tolleson-
Rinehart and Jeanie R. Stanley maintained that Richards was in a strong
position for re-election.

> Many observers, even among Republicans, believe that she will have a
> second term. She is likely to face only token opposition, if that, in the
> Democratic primary. In a refreshing change from the constant money
> worries she faced in the 1990 campaign, her 1994 campaign begins with
> a war chest of some three million dollars even before the reelection cam-
> paign is seriously under way. Her likely Republican opponents are only
> now exploring the viability of their candidacies and know that they will
> face a popular incumbent.[11]

Richards had won in 1990 by just under one hundred thousand votes, and
the Republicans had a further setback two years later when Bill Clinton
defeated George H. W. Bush, giving Democrats control of both the Governor's Mansion and the White House.

After Kay Bailey Hutchison won the special election for the United States Senate in 1993, George W. Bush determined that he would seek the governorship and believed he could defeat Richards. There were many skeptics among Republican politicos. As Peter and Rochelle Schweizer noted in their portrait of the Bush family, "Many believed that W's campaign was a fool's quest. Ann Richards was riding high in the polls. Her approval numbers in the summer of 1993 were 63 percent, and it wasn't as if W had much experience in being a candidate."[12] There were doubts even among longtime friends and Bush's mother. "Barbara wasn't the only Bush family friend who thought Richards was unbeatable. Nearly all those closest to George W told him to wait four years until she was out of office to challenge someone less popular."[13] As Bush explains, "My mother told me I couldn't beat Ann Richards, then was a little put out with me when I gleefully shared her opinion with the world."[14]

According to political consultant George Shipley, long a major player in Democratic politics, Governor Richards started out with a twenty-point advantage on Bush and was well liked in the state.[15] While Bush was able to keep any other serious candidates from seeking the Republican nomination, Richards, as the sitting governor, ended up losing three counties and barely winning several others in the Democratic primary against the "token opposition" of unknown candidate Gary Espinosa.[16] After the primary, Bush emphasized building a campaign presence and organization in all 254 counties, with visits to a number of rural counties throughout the summer coupled with media appearances in urbanized areas throughout the state. By September, political observers realized that this would be the toughest political fight of Richards's career.[17]

When the votes were counted in November, Bush had bested Richards by more than 330,000 votes. As longtime Richards friend Jan Reid concluded, "The outcome was not preordained. Ann blew that election all on her own, and a man who was a decent sort and a very good politician was propelled toward occupying the White House."[18] Once elected, Bush devoted himself to building relationships and a record that would result in the strengthening of the Texas Republican Party's image, outreach, and organization. Those efforts would allow the party to establish a lasting winning record two years into the Bush governorship.

George W. Bush's victory in 1994, with 53.8 percent of the two-party vote, was a breakthrough in all four categories of counties. His largest lead and best percentage came from the ever-growing electorate in the Suburban category of counties, closely followed by his performance in the Other Metro areas, where he had devoted much of his campaigning throughout the summer months. Bush carried four of the Big 6 counties, twenty-seven of the twenty-nine Suburban counties, sixteen of the twenty-one Other Metro counties, and forty-three of the fifty-seven larger Small Town counties. Richards was left with Travis and El Paso Counties, along with a base in five traditionally Democratic Other Metro counties. The end result was a 334,066 margin in upsetting the incumbent governor.

Four years later, Bush rolled to re-election by a margin of 1,385,229 votes over Garry Mauro, then completing sixteen years as state land commissioner. Bush carried 240 of the state's 254 counties, leaving Mauro with a 385-vote victory in Webb County and even smaller leads in thirteen of the Small Town counties. The Bush landslide brought Republicans to all the other statewide executive positions for the first time in the state's history (table 7.3).

Several notable changes can be seen by looking at Bill Clements's performance in the 1978 election, the Bush performance in 1994, and the three victories by Rick Perry in this century. Due to the landslide nature of the 1998 election it is not considered here. All three GOP candidates were able to obtain a small majority from the Big 6 counties, but by the last two elections the Democratic candidate had gained a slight lead in that category. Both Bush in 1994 and Perry in 2002 were able to carry four of the Big 6 counties, but this slipped to three for Perry in 2006 and only Tarrant County in 2010. From serving as a base of Republican support in the twentieth century, these major urban centers now provide the Democratic Party with a high level of support.

The counterbalance to the more recent Republican deficits in the Big 6 counties has come from the suburbs surrounding them, in many cases from Republicans who previously lived in one of the Big 6 counties. As the suburbs grew they became an ever-increasing base for the Republican candidates, producing the largest raw vote lead as well as over 60 percent of the votes cast. While Clements was able to win only eleven of the twenty-nine Suburban counties in 1978, Bush captured all but two in 1994. Since then, all twenty-nine have voted Republican except for one dissent in 2006 from Bastrop County in an election involving four gubernatorial candidates.

Although the transformation is not as dramatic, similar changes have occurred in the Other Metro category of counties scattered throughout the state. Clements carried only ten of the twenty-one counties in his first election, while Bush pushed it to sixteen in his initial victory. In the two most recent gubernatorial elections, however, Rick Perry received a

Table 7.3. Republican vote for governor, by county category, selected years

	County category				
	Big 6		Suburban		
Year	Percentage voting Republican	Vote margin	Percentage voting Republican	Vote margin	
1978	52.4	+50,523	50.9	+4,511	
1994	51.3	+52,089	59.9	+146,114	
2002	53.9	+154,751	69.8	+349,073	
2006	49.4	-17,174	63.6	+180,070	
2010	47.7	-96,297	64.7	+337,720	

majority in eighteen of the twenty-one counties, leaving his Democratic opponent with only the party's traditional base of Hidalgo and Webb Counties, along with the slightly less reliable Cameron and Jefferson Counties.[19]

Table 7.4 shows the transformation that has occurred in six of these Other Metro counties from the beginning of the two-party interlude to the present. These counties were solidly Democratic in gubernatorial elections through the early part of the 1980s; it was the Bush election of 1994 that turned them into areas of consistent Republican support. In the current period of one-party dominance, only once did one of these counties provide a Democratic majority in the race for governor when Perry lost Nueces County by 850 votes out of nearly 69,000 cast in the 2002 election.

Perhaps the most dramatic turnaround, however, took place in the Small Town counties of the state. This was the area that provided the margin of victory for many past Democratic candidates in those few early campaigns where the Republican candidate was competitive. By cutting his losses in these mainly rural counties to less than fifty thousand votes in 1978, Bill Clements was able to squeeze out a victory. By 1994 Bush was able to produce a majority in this category and Republican candidates have built up substantial net margins ever since. Of the fifty-seven highest turnout counties in this category, Clements carried only ten in his first campaign. In 1994, Bush carried forty-three of the fifty-seven, and

| County category | | | | | |
| Other Metro | | Small Town | | Statewide | |
Percentage voting Republican	Vote margin	Percentage voting Republican	Vote margin	Percentage voting Republican	Vote margin
51.2	+10,622	45.6	-48,777	50.4	+16,879
58.4	+51,959	54.8	+83,904	53.8	+334,066
57.6	+106,098	62.4	+202,871	59.1	+812,793
61.7	+112,867	62.5	+130,692	56.7	+406,455
59.5	+141,772	65.3	+247,891	56.5	+631,086

Table 7.4. Party of gubernatorial candidate winning selected counties, 1978–2010

| County | Winner's party affiliation | | | | | | | | |
	1978	1982	1986	1990	1994	1998	2002	2006	2010
Bell	D	D	R	R	R	R	R	R	R
Bowie	D	D	D	D	R	R	R	R	R
Grayson	D	D	R	D	R	R	R	R	R
McLennan	D	D	R	D	R	R	R	R	R
Nueces	D	D	D	D	D	R	D[a]	R	R
Wichita	D	D	R	D	R	R	R	R	R

[a] In 2002, Perry lost Nueces by 850 votes out of 69,000 cast.

since then the Republican candidate has never failed to carry at least fifty of these counties.

In retrospect, the most critical election in turning the state to one-party dominance again was the contest for lieutenant governor in 1998. George W. Bush was completing four years as a popular officeholder and seeking a second term as governor, but even then thoughts were developing about a possible presidential campaign. Were he to run and be elected to the White House, Bush would be turning over the Governor's Mansion to his lieutenant governor. According to some observers of that year's election, "Most voters realized that the winner of the lieutenant-governor's race would succeed Bush as governor in midterm if Bush were promoted to the White House."[20] Moreover, the office of lieutenant governor has long been considered by many political observers to be more powerful than governor because the lieutenant governor has the ability to preside over, dominate, and set the agenda for the Texas Senate. Bush had developed an effective working and personal relationship with his lieutenant governor, Democrat Bob Bullock, but Bullock was in poor health and decided not to seek another term. Whoever would be elected in 1998 could possibly become governor by January 2001 and, in fact, that was what happened.

The Democrats nominated state comptroller John Sharp as their candidate for lieutenant governor. Sharp had held statewide office for the previous twelve years, four on the railroad commission and eight as comptroller. Previously he had served in both the Texas Senate and the Texas House of Representatives and was perceived as a well-respected moderate acceptable to nearly all elements in the Democratic Party. The Republicans nominated agriculture commissioner Rick Perry, first elected to that office in 1990. Perry had been a Democratic state representative for six years prior to changing parties and being elected to his statewide position. One of the earliest polls showed that Sharp had a six-point lead over Perry, but nearly all surveys indicated that a sizable portion of the electorate was undecided.[21]

The Sharp-Perry contest was exceedingly tight and divided the loyalties of many of the major political lobbies in Austin, who had longstanding relationships with both candidates. For Governor Bush, the contest was seen as a test of his ability to help elect other candidates and build his party, factors that could be important in building credentials to seek the presidential nomination. Bush's key advisor, Karl Rove, recognized the importance of this campaign to Bush and his political future. "The argument that sending Bush to the White House would leave Texas in Democratic hands would not keep Bush from the GOP presidential nod, but it would be a nuisance, giving people an excuse to back someone else. Electing Perry was a goal to which we devoted a lot of money, energy, and attention, including the only two Texas fund-raisers former president George H. W. Bush did in Texas that election."[22] With the election approaching and early voting about to begin, a sizable portion of the likely electorate remained undecided between the two state officeholders. As late as mid-October, the Texas Poll showed Sharp and Perry tied at 37 percent among likely voters, with more than 20 percent still unable to make a choice.[23]

With Bush heading for a landslide re-election and the race for the second slot as tight as it appeared, the governor's supporters shifted some of their efforts to helping Perry score a victory. According to Bush's key campaign strategist, "We stepped up phone bank efforts to identify households that supported Bush but were undecided in the lieutenant governor's race so the Perry campaign could focus on these persuadable voters. Households backing Bush and Perry got an all-out push to turn out via absentee or early voting or on Election Day, while voters backing Bush and Sharp got dropped from the turnout efforts."[24] When the votes were counted, Perry had managed to beat Sharp by fewer than sixty-eight thousand votes out of more than 3.7 million cast. It may have been a squeaker of a win but it set Rick Perry on the path to becoming the longest-serving governor in Texas history.

Four years later, the Democrats once again called upon Sharp to run for lieutenant governor as part of their "tri-ethnic" slate for the three top statewide elective positions.[25] Sharp lost that contest also and in 2008 announced that he would be a candidate for the United States Senate; however, in 2011 he was named chancellor of the Texas A&M University system.[26]

The Sharp-Perry contest in some ways was a portent of the future and in other ways the last hurrah for the Democratic Party in statewide contests. The two candidates each carried three of the Big 6 counties, but Sharp built a lead of 18,628 votes out of this category of counties. By the next decade, Democratic candidates would begin to turn the Big 6 into their own significant base of votes, a flip from the years when this category was strongest for the Republican Party. Sharp was one of the last statewide Democrats to break even in the Other Metro category and lead among the Small Town counties, where he built his largest net advantage of 29,452 votes. His campaign lost the Suburban counties by 114,361 votes, but he did carry ten of the twenty-nine in this category, better than any future Democratic candidate would do. Among the fifty-seven larger Small Town counties, the traditional Democratic loyalty produced majorities for Sharp in thirty-five, making it a turning point election for this group of counties. In the end no one individual better epitomizes the difficulties for the Democratic Party in winning statewide contests. Even a well-respected and experienced political leader such as John Sharp could not overcome the growing tide of Republican votes in either 1998 or 2002.[27]

Throughout the 1990s, the Republican Party had been building a stable of candidates, effectively using lower-profile statewide offices to develop winning campaigns starting with Rick Perry and Kay Hutchison in 1990, followed by John Cornyn, Greg Abbott, Susan Combs, and David Dewhurst, all of whom began in one statewide low-profile position and used that experience to move on to a higher office. Interestingly, the first statewide elective office for both Cornyn and Abbott was serving on the Texas Supreme Court.

Legislative Contests

Throughout the twentieth century the Democratic Party retained a majority in the Texas congressional delegation even as the Republicans began receiving a majority of the overall votes cast in these elections. As the Republican vote grew during the two-party interlude, the Democrats pushed through the Texas legislature what has been called "an unabashed Democratic gerrymander" and "the shrewdest gerrymander of the 1990s."[28] As Earl and Merle Black summarized the situation, "Holding the governorship and both chambers of the legislature, Texas Democrats completely controlled the redistricting process in 1991. As they had done in the past, Democrats protected their incumbents and consigned the Republicans to a few utterly safe seats."[29] With Texas gaining three new seats, Democrats were able to re-elect all their incumbents and add new additional congressmen.

The success of the Democrats' redistricting efforts in 1991 can be seen by comparing the thirty congressional districts. While each district had roughly equal population numbers, these totals included those under eighteen years of age, noncitizens, and individuals otherwise ineligible to vote. Despite the misnomer of "one man, one vote," the plan did not equalize voter registration totals or the number of likely voters. What it did was pack high-turnout Republican voting precincts in as few congressional districts as possible. The disparity in turnout ranged from only

Table 7.5. Republican performance in congressional elections, 1994–2002

Year	Percentage of votes for Republican candidate	Percentage of seats won by Republicans	Total seats won by Republicans
1994	57.0	36.7	11
1996	54.1	43.3	13
1998	53.9	43.3	13
2000	51.2	43.3	13
2002	54.9	46.9	15

98,673 voters in the new Congressional District 29 to 264,653 participants in Congressional District 21. In the 1992 election the nine districts won by GOP candidates had an average turnout of 218,154 voters as contrasted with 174,240 voters in the twenty-one Democratic-won districts, a difference of 43,914 votes. For the remainder of the twentieth century GOP candidates obtained a majority of congressional votes statewide but won fewer than half the seats (table 7.5).[30]

While the vote for Republican congressional candidates continued to exceed the Democratic totals, and the party was winning every statewide contest as early as 1996, Democratic members of Congress continued to be re-elected up to and including the 2002 election. Only when reapportionment based on the 2000 census took effect did the GOP pick up two more seats, but it still remained a minority in the delegation of thirty-two House members.

The redistricting battle after the 2000 census was intense and multifaceted. The Texas delegation increased from thirty to thirty-two members starting with the election of 2002. With a Democratic majority in the state house and a Republican state senate and governor, no plan was adopted and the decision was left to the federal courts. As Steve Bickerstaff explains the situation, "Democratic lawyers in 2001 expected that a court-driven plan was likely to be more favorable to Democrats than any plan that could pass the legislature and avoid veto by Republican governor Perry. . . . A redistricting plan preserving the core of existing districts was exactly what the Democrats wanted."[31] As Seth McKee and Daron Shaw noted, "Because the court-ordered plan for the 2002 elections had a strong incumbency bias, it protected several at-risk Anglo Democrats who would otherwise have faced potential defeat."[32] Realizing that the electorate had been moving in a Republican direction, the Democratic Party strategy was to preserve as many of their current officeholders as possible, an objective that would be aided by keeping the districts as close to existing lines as possible. This would produce an electorate familiar with the incumbent legislator and enhance the advantages of incumbency.

Redistricting of the state legislature was accomplished in 2001, however, and when the 2002 election was held under the new lines the GOP picked up sixteen additional state house seats to produce its first majority since the 1870s. The newly Republican legislature took up the task of drawing new congressional lines to replace those put in place by the federal courts. The drawn-out battle to approve these plans, including walk-outs by Democratic members of both the house and senate to prevent a quorum, put Texas in the national news. Republicans maintained, according to Steve Bickerstaff, that they should be able to undo the 1991 Democratic gerrymander as a matter of fairness.[33] Democrats tried everything possible to stop the Republicans from passing a new redistricting plan but in the end were unsuccessful and the 2004 elections took place under a new map.[34]

Given the provisions of the Voting Rights Act and previous judicial decisions requiring the protection of all majority-minority districts, the Republicans were limited in how they could draw the thirty-two district lines. Thus, their efforts did not change the overall racial and ethnic makeup of the congressional districts.[35] Nor was there much change in the presidential voting history of the new districts. The GOP strategy focused on protecting GOP incumbents but then redrawing the districts of Anglo Democrats. Their objective was to create districts that would divide the existing constituencies of these Democratic congressmen, adding a high percentage of new and preferably Republican-leaning voters, and thus taking away the advantages of incumbency. As McKee and Shaw noted, "By greatly reducing the constituencies of these Anglo Democrats, the bond of incumbency is weakened because so many 'new' voters have little familiarity with these members and less incentive to vote for them."[36]

Roughly 60 percent of the Anglo Democrats' constituents were new, as contrasted with under 20 percent for minority Democratic congressmen and 40 percent for GOP incumbents. Absent the advantage of incumbency as a voting cue, the belief was that much of the electorate would rely on party labels in voting for a congressman. These Democrats were faced with the choice of running in districts where they were little known,

Table 7.6. Republican performance in congressional elections, 2004–2012

Year	Percentage of votes for Republican candidate	Percentage of seats won by Republicans	Total seats won by Republicans
2004	59.7	65.6	21
2006	53.4	59.4	19
2008	58.5	62.5	20
2010	67.8	71.9	23
2012	60.0	66.7	24

changing political parties, or retiring. The end result was that one Democratic incumbent decided to retire, another switched parties, one was paired with and lost to a Republican incumbent, three were defeated by GOP challengers, and two Anglo Democrats won re-election. After the 2004 election the Democratic congressional delegation comprised five Hispanics, three African Americans, and three Anglos, one of whom represented a majority-minority district.[37]

Operating under a Republican-approved redistricting plan, the party's candidates won nearly 60 percent of the votes cast for Congress in 2004 and Republicans won 65 percent of the districts. For the first time since 1871 the GOP held a majority of the Texas delegation to the U.S. House of Representatives. Over the next four elections their numbers would vary slightly but the party would always retain a majority of the congressional seats (table 7.6).

In 2012 the federal judiciary again played a role in congressional redistricting as the state gained four additional seats. The interim map approved by a federal court ended up adding two Republicans and two Democrats to the delegation, but the Democrats also defeated one Republican incumbent to bring their numbers to twelve and the Republicans to twenty-four. In the 2013 session, the legislature made minor modifications to the court-drawn "interim map" and the federal court intervening in the case allowed the plan to be in place for the 2014 elections.[38] As has been the case with each recent redistricting, lawsuits to the plan remain pending. However, this time it is the Republicans who have the majority of incumbent congressmen they wish to protect.

A similar situation existed with the changes occurring during the two-party interlude in terms of partisan representation in the Texas legislature. To understand these changes it is useful to begin with the redistricting that took place after the 1990 census. As former state representative Sherri Greenberg has noted, "Redistricting in Texas always has been, and always will be, political and partisan. The political and partisan question is one of degree."[39] However, despite the objectives of the mapmakers, any redistricting plan will be impacted over time by variations in voter turnout, national and statewide trends, population movement, the quality of the candidates, and the presence of incumbency or open seats. These factors all contributed to wide swings in partisanship that took place in the Texas House elections from 2002 to 2010. Efforts at redistricting are also influenced by the provisions and requirements of the Voting Rights Act as well as the Texas constitutional requirement that counties may not be divided into more than one house district, unless of course the county population entitles it to more than one house member.

When the Texas legislature took up the task of redrawing state senate and house districts in 1991, the governor and lieutenant governor were Democrats and the party had a majority of ninety-two to fifty-eight in the house and twenty-two to nine in the senate. While the party was able to pass a plan that benefited the party and it was signed by Governor Ann Richards, this was not the end of the process. A number of lawsuits were filed challenging these redistricting plans and, once again, federal courts played an essential role in the final determination of district lines. "Ultimately, the state of Texas held the 1992 Texas House and Senate elections in districts that the court redrew and substantially changed. As a result of court actions, the state held the 1994 house and senate elections in districts redrawn by the Legislature in 1992 with significant changes in the senate districts. After additional court actions, the Legislature made changes in the 1997 regular session to the Texas House and Senate districts for the 1998 elections."[40] Despite all these modifications and maneuverings, the Democrats were able to retain control of the house and, as Brian K. Arbour and Seth C. McKee observed, "This advantage held throughout the decade of the 1990s. While Republicans came to dominate statewide elections, the Democrats continued to hold onto their advantage in the Texas House throughout the decade, maintaining a 78 to 72 majority after the 2000 elections."[41] Nevertheless, the GOP continued to eat into the Democratic lead, picking up fourteen additional seats during the ten-year span. The court actions, however, did impact the partisan bal-

Table 7.7. Number of Democrats and Republicans in the Texas legislature, 1991–2001

Year	Texas Senate		Texas House of Representatives		Year	Texas Senate		Texas House of Representatives	
	R	D	R	D		R	D	R	D
1991	9	22	58	92	1997	16	15	69	81
1993	13	18	58	92	1999	16	15	72	78
1995	14	17	63	87	2001	16	15	72	78

ance in the senate more dramatically and by the middle of the decade the Republicans had a razor-thin sixteen-to-fifteen lead (table 7.7).

Although Texan George W. Bush carried the state with nearly 60 percent and Kay Bailey Hutchison was re-elected to the senate with 65 percent of the vote in 2000, the Democratic Party held on to control of the Texas House of Representatives. Democratic speaker Pete Laney, a moderate-conservative from a rural district in West Texas, supported a redistricting plan designed to protect incumbents, preserve rural legislative districts, and ensure a continued Democratic majority. As has been noted, "In 2001 the House, which had a slight majority of Democrats, passed a redistricting plan that would have favored a number of Democratic incumbents."[42] In fact, one subsequent detailed analysis indicated that this plan would have retained a majority of Texas House seats for the Democrats.[43] Laney's redistricting plan passed the house in a vote of seventy-five to sixty-eight before being stymied in the Republican-majority senate, where it was never brought up for a vote.

The long-range importance of keeping the Laney plan from passing the senate cannot be overemphasized as it had implications not only for the Texas legislature itself but also for the nation's capital. "If the Democratic plan had been passed, Pete Laney would have remained Speaker, and hence Texas Republicans could not have pursued their successful effort to redraw the congressional map for the 2004 U.S. House elections. . . . By not passing the Laney House plan, the Republican-controlled Texas Senate ensured that Texas House redistricting would be left to the Legislative Redistricting Board. There, Republicans could use their majority to pass a plan favorable to them."[44] That is indeed what happened next. With no legislative agreement, the issue was referred to the Legislative Redistricting Board (LRB), comprised of four Republican officeholders (lieutenant governor, attorney general, comptroller, and land commissioner) and Speaker Laney. When they met, the LRB "drew plans that distinctly favored Republicans. Several groups sued, as was expected, and state and federal courts ultimately approved the constitutionality of the plans."[45] In so doing, however, "the judges made only minor changes to the plan passed by the Legislative Redistricting Board. The data show that the impact of the Court plan was similar, but slightly less favorable to the Republicans, than the LRB plan."[46] Nevertheless, as one former house member indicated, "The new Texas House and Senate districts devised by the LRB helped change the balance of political party power in the Texas House from Democratic to Republican."[47]

When the results of the 2002 election were in, the GOP had its first majority in the Texas House since 1873, winning eighty-eight districts to the Democrats' sixty-two. Six Democratic house members and one Republican were defeated while several others retired, sought other offices, or simply chose not to seek re-election. Both parties focused their attention on winnable races as the Democrats left forty districts uncontested. Of the sixty-two Democrats who took office, forty-three had no Republican opponent on the general election ballot, while six others won with less than 55 percent of the total vote. Despite being reduced in numbers, these legislative candidates performed better than the party's top-of-the-ticket candidates; senatorial nominee Ron Kirk carried only fifty-two legislative districts and the party's gubernatorial candidate won even fewer.

In the contest for the thirty-one redrawn state senate districts, each party left nine districts uncontested and the Republicans picked up three additional seats. Only one incumbent Democrat, David Cain, was defeated as the GOP also won two open seats. From 2003 forward the Republicans would continue to hold a minimum of nineteen seats in the thirty-one-member Texas Senate, a number just short of a critical two-thirds majority. But it was in the Texas House that the most dramatic changes occurred, in terms of both overall numbers and the distribution of members throughout the state.

While the GOP kept control of the Texas House throughout the redistricting cycle covering elections from 2002 to 2010, it experienced a roller-coaster of support. In the 2002 elections the party secured eighty-eight districts, only to drop to a slim seventy-six to seventy-four majority after the 2008 elections and then bounce back to win ninety-nine districts in 2010. After the election, three Democratic incumbents switched parties to produce an all-time Republican high of 102 members, the largest partisan split in the Texas House since 1984. Clearly the variations in numbers elected indicate that sometimes the best-laid partisan plans can be impacted by unforeseen events. When the Republicans fell from eighty-eight to seventy-six districts, some commentators maintained that the party had stretched its supporters too thinly across too many districts. These individuals were silent, however, after the Republicans bounced back strongly just two years later.

With a controlling majority in the house and a sizable lead in the senate, the GOP was able to pass a redistricting bill in 2011 that preserved the party's strong majority in both chambers. The inevitable court cases resulted in some minor changes in the district lines by a federal court in San Antonio, but the overall partisan split appeared to be likely. "When the consultants loaded the court-drawn maps into their computers, they found that ninety-five house districts held a majority of Republicans, while fifty-five contained a majority of Democrats. Once the dust from the election settled early Wednesday morning unsurprisingly the results in the Texas House were ninety-five Republicans to fifty-five Democrats."[48] Interestingly enough, the Democratic Party's legislative representation nearly mirrors the statewide level of support for President Obama in the same election. While Obama won 41.4 percent of the state's total vote, the Democratic Party held 36 percent of the Texas house districts and 38 percent of the state senate seats.

In the Texas Senate, only six of the nineteen successful Republican senate candidates had a Democratic opponent while eight of the twelve Democratic senators were opposed by the GOP. With less than half of the senate contested, only one race was close. That election was won by an incumbent Democrat with 51 percent of the vote.[49]

In drawing the house districts it was apparent that they had been constructed to maximize support for each party. Of the fifty-five Democrats elected to the house, thirty-four had no Republican opponent. Yet, of those twenty-one with opposition, in only four instances did the GOP candidate exceed 45 percent of the vote. In the ninety-five districts won by a Republican candidate, only thirty-one had a Democratic opponent and of these only five losing candidates received over 45 percent of the vote. Therefore, out of 150 legislative districts, only nine (6%) fell within the standard level of competitiveness.

The changing dynamics of house elections can be seen in the 2012 primary contests. Of the eighty-five districts with Democratic candidates,

Table 7.8. Party presence in the Texas House of Representatives, by county category, 1993–2013

	County category							
	Big 6		Sub-urban		Other Metro		Small Town	
Year	R	D	R	D	R	D	R	D
1993	32	40	13	9	12	19	1	24
1995	33	39	15	7	12	19	3	22
1997	33	39	14	8	16	15	8	17
1999	32	40	16	6	16	15	8	17
2001	32	40	16	6	16	15	8	17
2003	40	33	21	4	16	16	11	9
2005	38	35	22	3	17	15	11	9
2007	32	41	22	3	16	16	11	9
2009	26	47	21	4	17	15	12	8
2011	37	36	23	2	24	8	18	2
2013	29	40	30	2	21	10	15	3

only twenty had primary contests and of these only nine were won with less than 55 percent of the vote, including four that ended up in runoff elections when no single candidate obtained a majority in the primary. Contrast these totals with what occurred in the 116 districts with Republican candidates. More than half these districts (sixty) had a primary contest, with twenty-two won by less than 55 percent of the vote, including thirteen that went to runoff elections. Just as the Democratic primary was the arena of final choice for more than one hundred years, so it appears that at least in some areas of the state, legislative elections are once again being settled in primary contests, but this time in the Republican Party.

Finally, it is informative to view the geographical changes in representation that have taken place in the four categories of counties over the past twenty years (table 7.8). While the Big 6 counties have varied greatly in their partisan breakdown, with the Democrats ranging from a low of thirty-three to a high of forty-seven members, the party is currently at the same number (forty) as in 1993. On the other hand, counties classified as Suburban have become a graveyard for Democratic candidates, as the party's representation declined from nine of twenty-two in 1993 to only two of thirty-two in 2013. The Other Metro counties have moved from a Democratic lead of nineteen to twelve in 1993 to fall as low as twenty-four to eight after the 2010 elections and now stand at ten of twenty-one. Eight of the ten Democratic members representing this category are from the Democratic strongholds of Cameron, Hidalgo, and Webb Counties, along with lone members from Jefferson and Nueces Counties. No category epitomizes the decline of Democratic dominance more than the 198 Small Town counties. Traditionally the home of Democratic courthouse political leaders, twenty years ago all but one state representative in this category were Democrats. The party's legislative representation declined from twenty-four to three as the GOP won more rural and ex-urban districts.

Whether one views the state's delegation in Congress or in the two chambers of the Texas legislature it is apparent that the Republican Party has become the dominant force over the period from 1996 to the present. Given the traditional advantages of incumbency and the development of a broader farm team of candidates, combined with the dominance of the party in more areas of the state where the primary has become the arena of final choice, it is likely that the Republican Party will continue to dominate legislative elections for the present. Absent the election of a Democratic governor or an aggressive intervention by federal courts after the 2020 census, the Republican state legislative majority will once again control redistricting for an additional decade and is likely to draw district lines to its partisan advantage.

District Judicial Elections

The Texas judicial branch has also seen significant partisan change, due not only to the election of Republican candidates but also to the presence of a Republican governor since 1995. Many of those now serving on the state's courts first came to office by appointment to complete unexpired terms and as initial appointments to newly created district courts.[50] As previously noted, all eighteen members of the Texas Supreme Court and the Texas Court of Criminal Appeals have been Republican since the last Democrat to serve on the supreme court resigned in 1998.

A somewhat less dramatic change has taken place on the state's intermediate appellate courts and the more than four hundred state trial courts. From 1992 to 1996, the end of the two-party interlude, the fourteen courts of appeals districts experienced one hundred elections to complete unexpired terms or elect members to regular six-year terms. During this period the two parties contested evenly, with Republicans winning fifty-one justices and Democrats winning forty-nine. Indicative of the still-prevailing Democratic historical bias, however, thirty-three of these forty-nine Democratic justices were unopposed compared to twenty-three of the fifty-one Republicans without a Democratic opponent. Fast-forward to the period from 2008 to 2012, and there were seventy-five Republican victories but only seventeen successful Democratic campaigns for courts of appeal. Thirty-three Republican, but only five Democratic, justices were unopposed in this recent period.

The partisan divide is less apparent for state district courts, many of which are located within one county while others have a multicounty jurisdiction. As of 2012, there were 250 Republican district judges and 191 Democratic, each elected for a four-year term of office. Where partisanship appears to be most relevant in the choice of district judges is in the Big 6 counties. The large number of judgeships to be filled frequently means that the electorate has little knowledge of the individual candidates, resulting in a greater reliance on party affiliation. It is also in these Big 6 counties where the Republican Party made its initial election breakthroughs, but also where the Democratic Party has recently made a comeback in competitiveness.

Perhaps the most dramatic partisan changes took place in Dallas County, once a banner county for the GOP: "Since 1994, Republicans had captured all the courthouse races in the state's four largest counties. . . . In 2006, Dallas County turned back to the Democrats; their candidates won every contested county race that year, ousting a series of long-term incumbents. The 2006 Dallas results reflect the changing demographics of an ever more diverse county and the pro-Democratic national wave."[51] From 1996 to 2004, only two Democratic candidates were elected as district judges in Dallas County compared with twenty-two successful Republicans. In 2006, only five Republican district judges whose terms were up for election remained in office, due most likely to the fact that they were unopposed on election day. Not a single district judgeship in Dallas County has been won by a Republican since that time. Nevertheless, the margins of victory for the Democratic candidates have been slim. In the 2006 landslide, the Democratic vote ranged from 50.7 percent to 54.2 percent of the vote over twenty-three contests. Four years later, the closest Democratic victory came with 50.35 percent of the vote, and the widest margin resulted from receiving 53.3 percent of the vote among the seventeen contested races.

Bexar County Republicans were able to win thirty-four district judge contests from 1996 to 2004 compared to twenty-two victories for Democratic candidates. In 2006 and 2008, however, Democrats captured sixteen judgeships to ten for the Republicans. Then, in 2010, while their fellow Democrats were winning every race in Dallas County, Bexar County Democrats lost eleven district judgeship elections, retaining only five unopposed incumbents. By 2012, the partisan tide had shifted again as eleven Democrats won election and the GOP retained one district judgeship on the ballot. As in Dallas County, however, all of the contests were close, ranging from 51.1 percent to 56.0 percent for the Democrats and a razor-thin 50.5 percent for the lone successful Republican candidate.

The shift in Harris County was delayed by one election cycle; this delay was associated with the successful Democratic presidential campaigns of 2008 and 2012. From 1996 to 2006, one lone Democrat was elected as a district judge in Harris County compared to 185 successful GOP campaigns, although 120 of those were unopposed candidacies. Then in 2008, Democrats won twenty-two judgeships to four Republican victories. The roles were reversed in the gubernatorial election year of 2010 when the Republicans captured all thirty-six district judgeships on the ballot. Attempting to repeat their efforts of two years earlier the Democratic Party ran attorneys for all thirty-six positions, but only seven were able to obtain more than 45 percent of the vote. In 2012, the two parties were once again competitive as the GOP captured nine judgeships to fourteen for the Democrats.

The remaining three Big 6 counties exemplify the movement to one-party dominance in various regions of the state. Not a single Republican has won a district judgeship in El Paso County during the current period. Four individuals were appointed district judges in Travis County and subsequently ran for election as Republicans. Only one was elected in 2000 and 2004, but four years later and again in 2012 this individual was re-elected as a Democrat. The situation in Tarrant County is the reverse, where Democrats have not won a single district judgeship and contested only 8 of the 102 positions on the ballot from 1996 to 2012, never receiving as much as 45 percent of the vote.

In terms of district judicial offices, Texas Republicans have elected the overwhelming majority of justices on the state's courts of appeals, with most now retaining office unopposed. Since the courts of appeals districts are multi-county, Democratic areas in Dallas, Austin, and San Antonio are frequently outvoted by Republicans in the surrounding counties. The partisan division of the state's approximately 450 district courts is much closer, due mainly to Democratic success in the Big 6 counties, whose territory encompasses a sizable number of state district courts, as well as in the stronger Democratic areas of the Rio Grande Valley and the border counties.

County Competition

County government was one of the last areas to experience partisan transformation in most sections of the state. While the Republican Party made major inroads into the Big 6 counties of Bexar, Dallas, Harris, and Tarrant during the two-party interlude and started winning more county offices in most Suburban counties, Democrats continued to hold control in most Other Metro and Small Town counties throughout the 1990s. By 1996, slightly less than one thousand county offices of all types were held by Republicans, approaching 20 percent of all elected county officials.[52] This total grew exponentially in the following years, rising to 1,608 in 2004, when 37 percent of county judges and 36 percent of county commissioners were Republican.[53] By 2008, the number of Republican county officials had risen to 2,241 and, after the 2012 elections, had reached 3,012.[54]

While this number is impressive, it is also inclusive of a wide range of offices and positions. Some smaller counties have only one justice of the peace, while Harris County elects sixteen. The office of county treasurer has been abolished in some counties but is still filled by election in others. The county court system may provide for a wide disparity in the number of elective positions. Moreover, as one author observed shortly after the beginning of the twenty-first century, "Democrats may win far more offices than the GOP but many of these victories occur in small, low-population, rural counties."[55] Indeed, it was the more rural counties where the Democratic Party traditionally organized around control of the county courthouse and its local officeholders (table 7.9).

Meanwhile, during the first part of the George W. Bush presidency, Republicans were a major player in most Big 6 county elections, although with the Democratic surge nationally in 2006, most of these Big 6 counties moved in a more Democratic direction. While the two parties remained competitive in Harris County, only Tarrant among the Big 6 continued as a Republican stronghold. From holding four of the six county

Table 7.9. Republican county officeholders, 1978–2012

Year	Number of officeholders	Year	Number of officeholders
1978	87	2008	2,241
1996	938	2012	3,012
2004	1,608		

judge positions in the 1990s, the Republicans were left with only Tarrant and Harris Counties by 2013. Similar losses were experienced in other county elective offices.

At the end of the twentieth century, the Republican Party was slowly becoming a competitive force in more of the Other Metro counties while continuing to expand its influence in the Suburban category of counties. Among the Other Metro counties, Republicans were already the dominant party in Gregg and Smith Counties in East Texas as well as Lubbock, Midland, Ector, Potter, Randall, and Taylor Counties in West Texas. By the twenty-first century they had added Bell and McLennan in Central Texas along with Tom Green County in West Texas. Still others would be added to the list in following elections. Meanwhile, Democrats maintained their strong dominance in Cameron, Hidalgo, Jefferson, and Webb Counties.

It was in the grouping of Small Town counties, however, where a dramatic shift in partisanship was taking place. Until recently, rural Democrats were able to retain control of the political environment longer than more urbanized partisans, partly due to their candidates' conformity with local mores and attitudes. As David Lublin noted, "Rural Democrats slowed the ability of Republicans to attract voters based on social issues through the adoption of highly conservative positions on social issues. In most parts of the rural South, there is usually little gap between Democratic and Republican partisans or local officials on social issues because the liberal position is highly unpopular and would be political suicide for the ambitious politician—even one who merely desires to continue to hold office."[56] By holding positions popular with the local electorate, even when they were at odds with the stands of the national party, these local Democrats could hold onto office and retain a presence for their party in the Small Town counties.

Throughout the second half of the twentieth century, the Democratic base in rural Texas was the Depression generation and the minority communities. According to one Democratic strategist, as late as the 1990s people born before 1929 were still active as leaders in their community. Born into a one-party environment, these civic leaders were dedicated Democrats.[57] In small communities, the politically active individuals realized that local electoral success depended on being a Democrat. With few local Republicans and often none in public office, the minority party had difficulty attracting capable candidates, let alone electing them to office. As has been noted, "Decisions by political elites play an especially vital role in local and state legislative contests because the party label that a high-quality candidate selects may determine the outcome of the election. . . . The ability to attract elites to its banner is thus a crucial component of a party's success."[58] The Democrats had a continuous flow of talent. In such an environment, "even when both parties could attract candidates, the Democrats were more likely to recruit candidates with experience in running a campaign and holding office."[59]

By the late 1980s and into the 1990s, the Depression generation was retreating from civic involvement or beginning to die off. At this time a younger generation was becoming prominent in local affairs and was more enamored of the Republican Party, attracted to a large extent by the Reagan presidency. Among many voters social, rather than economic, issues became more important.[60] Meanwhile, "voters from the Solid South generation have joined the heavenly electorate in ever larger numbers as time has passed, so the share of southern white voters with strong long-term ties to the Democrats has shrunk."[61]

One early example of this transition among Small Town counties was Hansford, in the far north of the Texas Panhandle, bordering Oklahoma. After a long history of electing Democratic candidates to county office, Hansford set off on a new path in 1998, becoming the only one of 254 counties to not hold a Democratic primary. Without a primary election no Democratic candidates could be nominated for local offices and, thus, all the elected officials in Hansford County from that point forward have been Republicans. As county clerk Kim Vera explained, "Over the last eight to 10 years it has become predominantly Republican. Everybody has switched to Republican. I've worked here for 20 years and when I started, the county was predominantly Democrat."[62] Thus, from 1998 to the present, Hansford County voters have not had the opportunity to participate in a Democratic primary election and, therefore, do not have any input into the selection of national, state, or district Democratic candidates.[63]

The partisan transformation experienced in Hansford County has spread to other counties across the state. In East Texas, Sabine County witnessed four county officials, including the county judge, sheriff, and one county commissioner, switch to the GOP in 2011. Two years later, in August 2013, six more Democratic officeholders switched to the Republican Party, giving the party five of the six top county offices. Referring to the neighboring county of Newton, Republican state representative Wayne Christian said, "Every one switched to the Republican party last summer, less than a year ago. And here goes Sabine county, and it's just a trend."[64] Another Republican state representative from East Texas, Bryan Hughes, noted that "Wood county was one of the first. . . . The last Democrat retired, so the Democrats have all retired or switched parties by now."[65]

Similar changes were occurring in Panola County, where three elected officeholders changed parties in 2011.[66] Further west, in Coke County, the county judge, the sheriff, and two county commissioners were among seven elected officials who switched parties.[67] In Throckmorton, all elected Democratic county officials converted to the Republican Party. After holding only a Democratic primary from 2006 to 2010, the county conducted only a Republican one in 2012.[68]

Many of the political elites in Small Town counties could see the handwriting on the election wall. In the 2010 election more than 105 Democratic county officials, including 16 incumbent county judges, lost their re-election bids. As one candidate who lost, Lavaca county judge Ronald Leck, noted, "Our county, up until this election, anything above county judge had gone Republican. Counties in Texas have slowly rolled more and more Republican. I didn't realize I was going to get caught in the flip, but I did."[69] After the 2010 election, Republicans held 115 county judges in the state's 254 counties, including 2 from Big 6 counties, 27 of the 29 in the Suburban category of counties, 17 of 21 in the Other Metro category, and 69 in the 198 Small Town counties of the state.[70]

The 2012 election was a mixed blessing for both political parties. While the Democratic Party was re-electing the president and picking up additional seats in both houses of Congress and the Texas House, Republicans continued to add to their numbers in county offices across the state. This success can be seen in the partisan breakdown for the most important positions in county government: county judge, sheriff, and the four com-

Table 7.10. County officials by county type and party, 2013

County type	County judge		Commis- sioners		Sheriff	
	R	D	R	D	R	D
Big 6 (n = 6)	2	4	10	14	2	4
Suburban (n = 29)	27	2	98	18	27	2
Other Metro (n = 21)	17	4	55	29	16	5
Small Town (n = 57)[a]	46	11	165	63	45	12

[a] Totals for fifty-seven counties with 7,500 or more votes cast in 2012.

missioners elected from districts. Unless unexpired terms need to be filled, the county judge and commissioners from precincts 2 and 4 are elected in gubernatorial years, while the sheriff and commissioners from precincts 1 and 3 are on the ballot in presidential years.

As of 2013, Republicans held most of the county judges in both Suburban and Other Metro counties but not in the Big 6 or the Small Town grouping of counties, although they are dominant in the more populous of the smaller counties. They have had a similar level of success in electing sheriffs and are only slightly less dominant among county commissioners in each of these categories of counties.

Among the Big 6 counties, Republicans retain a majority on the commissioners court in Harris and Tarrant Counties, while the Democrats have a four-to-one lead in Bexar, Dallas, El Paso, and Travis Counties. From being a stronghold for the GOP in the 1980s and 1990s, these six counties—especially Dallas County—have been shifting more Democratic in local elections over the past four election cycles (table 7.10).

County courthouses in the Suburban grouping are now overwhelmingly controlled by Republicans. In seventeen counties the GOP holds every seat on the commissioners court as well as the office of sheriff. Only three counties (San Jacinto, Caldwell, and Atascosa) have a Democratic majority, while only San Jacinto and Atascosa have a Democrat in the county judge's office. The Republican domination can be seen clearly in the statistics: 93.1 percent of all county judges and sheriffs along with 84.5 percent of all county commissioners from these twenty-nine Suburban counties.

The Other Metro category of counties can be subdivided into a subset of four strongly Democratic counties and seventeen predominantly Republican ones. While Cameron has a Republican county judge and Jefferson two GOP county commissioners, the other key officials in these counties, as well as all those in Hidalgo and Webb Counties, are Democrats. In the remaining subset, five counties have only Republicans on the commissioners court and in an additional eight counties the partisan split is four to one Republican. Even including the subset of heavily Democratic counties, the GOP holds 81.0 percent of all county judges, 76.2 percent of all sheriffs, and 64.3 percent of the county commissioners.

In the fifty-seven larger counties in the Small Town category (where a minimum of 7,500 votes were cast in the 2012 general election), the change in partisanship is clear. Whereas these counties were initially the slowest in moving away from total Democratic domination, the last few election cycles have brought about a transformation of local politics. In twenty-four of these counties, the county judge and all four commissioners are Republican. These twenty-four are also part of the forty-five counties with a Republican sheriff. Only Cass, Maverick, and Starr Counties have an all-Democratic commissioners court, although Cass has a Republican sheriff. In addition, another nine counties have a Democratic majority on the commissioners court. Republicans now control 80.7 percent of the county judge offices, 72.4 percent of all county commissioners, and 78.9 percent of the sheriffs in these fifty-seven counties, once a stronghold of the Democratic Party. While data for the remaining 141 less populated counties is not available, it is likely that the partisan division of these offices would be similar.[71]

Once limited to few county courthouses, the transformation of Texas politics is now evident in these arenas of local government. From less than one thousand county officials at the end of the two-party interlude, Texas Republicans now claim over three thousand, including over two-thirds of the county commissioners in the 113 most populous counties, which comprise nearly 24 million of the state's approximately 25 million residents.

With GOP total control of the statewide offices, more than two-thirds of the Texas congressional delegation, over 60 percent of the state legislature, the vast majority of state judicial offices, and a two-thirds majority in the county governments serving over 95 percent of the state, the transformation of Texas politics to a one-party dominant state is apparent when one looks only at the partisan composition of the state's elected officeholders.

Party Identification

There is one dimension of party competition where the Democratic Party has remained roughly equal to the Republican Party even while losing most contests on election day. When individuals are asked with which political party they most closely identify, in the period since 1996 to the present, the two parties frequently end up even. In the Texas Poll of 1997, some 30 percent of respondents labeled themselves Democrats while 31 percent chose Republican. From a compilation of all its surveys in 2011 involving a combined Texas sample of 22,473 respondents, Gallup reported party identification as being 43.3 percent Republican and 36.8 percent Democratic, incorporating in party totals all independents who leaned toward one party.[72] However, in the three surveys conducted in 2012 by the University of Texas at Austin and the *Texas Tribune* newsletter, where a higher percentage of independents was found, both parties' support stood at 32 percent. Other polls in the interim had the GOP in the lead by as much as 42 percent to 26 percent, while still others had the Democrats preferred by a margin of 35 percent to 30 percent.[73]

Although the results varied, the number of self-described independents normally ranged from 25 percent to 30 percent of all respondents. When these individuals were then asked whether they leaned toward one of the major parties, the Republican lead was substantial. In the six surveys conducted by the University of Texas at Austin and the *Texas Tribune* in 2011 and 2012, approximately 8 percent of all independent respondents leaned Democratic while roughly 15 percent thought of themselves as independents who leaned Republican. It is the support of this segment of the electorate that has provided the margin of victory for many Republican candidates. Many of these individuals may be on the path to modifying their traditional party identification, viewing independent status as a way station on the road to partisan change.

One clear conclusion from the data on party identification is that, unlike the previous period of one-party dominance, the minority party retains a significant level of support among the Texas electorate. Neither party can claim the loyalty, in terms of personal labeling, of much more than one-third of all Texas voters. In such an environment, the voting decisions of those who call themselves independent become a determining factor. The current Republican dominance in elections depends largely on winning over a significant portion of these voters who describe themselves as independent. This should provide a ray of hope for Texas Democrats. Should they be able to win over the support of these non-attached voters with an appealing candidate, the possibility of returning to a period of two-party competition would be enhanced. Unfortunately for the Democrats, at the current time most of these independents lean more in the GOP's direction.

Primary Participation

The extent of voter participation in each political party's primary can be seen as one further measure of party competition and an indication of the transformation of politics in many areas of Texas over the past fifty years. Since the Democratic Party tended to control nearly all elections in the state up until 1960, it is not surprising that more individuals took part in the Democratic primary than voted in the November general election. All across the state, with very few local exceptions, the Democratic primary was the arena of final choice for the selection of public officials. When one political party tends to dominate this process, voters who wish to participate in choosing their local public officials must vote in that party's primary. According to one Texas political commentator, "Local races—particularly in the less-populated areas of the state—are often the main attraction for voters. A voter might actually know the candidate for district attorney. Presidential candidates, who seldom stray from major airports, seem like TV characters by comparison."[74] As Texas politics has been transformed over the past half-century, this arena of final choice has shifted in many counties from the Democratic to the Republican primary.

Moreover, voting in a primary election can be viewed as one means of affiliating with a political party. When an individual takes part in a primary in Texas, a voter registration card is stamped with that party's name and the voter becomes ineligible to participate in any precinct caucus, convention, or runoff primary of another party during that election cycle. Primary elections have traditionally been party undertakings throughout Texas and in most counties are even today conducted by the political party and not by local government officials. Without individuals willing to conduct an election for a political party in each county, no primary can be held. Thus, not every voter in the state may have the opportunity to vote in a party's primary. While both major parties held primary elections in all 254 counties in 1996, this was the only year in which this occurred. The number of counties not conducting a Republican primary has varied from five to twenty-five since 1996, while the number without a Democratic primary has ranged from one to thirteen.

Table 7.11 Counties not conducting party primaries, 1996–2012

Year	Republican	Democratic	Year	Republican	Democratic
1996	0	0	2006	16	5
1998	0	1	2008	25	3
2000	6	1	2010	11	8
2002	5	3	2012	5	13
2004	10	4			

Of the thirty counties that, at one time or another since 1996, did not hold a Republican primary, as well as the fifteen counties without a Democratic primary during that time, all were among the 141 smallest counties except one.[75] In the earlier periods of party competition, the Texas Democratic Party was able to conduct a primary in every county, whereas the number without a Republican primary ranged from a low of seven to a high of eighty-six. While the number of counties and the number of voters participating in each party's primary have varied, some interesting transformations have occurred in the strongholds of party support and the partisan division in various counties (table 7.11).

The last primary to occur before the two-party interlude took place in 1978. More than nine of every ten votes were cast in the Democratic primary. Democratic voters outnumbered Republicans in all Big 6 and Suburban counties, while only Midland County among the Other Metro category of counties had slightly more Republican voters. Significant changes in partisan participation took place from the beginning to the end of the two-party interlude. In both 1996 and 2012, the Republican Party attracted more voters in the vast majority of the Big 6, Suburban, and Other Metro counties. In fact, 1996 was the first time in the state's history when more Texans voted in the Republican primary. Nevertheless, comparing voter participation in these three primaries over a span of thirty-four years suggests some conclusions as to the nature of the transformation of Texas politics (table 7.12).

Clearly, before the beginning of the period of two-party competition, the Democratic primary was the essential preliminary in selecting many local officials as well as nominating the party's candidates for the general election—candidates who were expected to, and almost always did, win. Those who voted in the Republican primary in nearly every county were true believers in the party willing to forego taking part in the selection of local government officials. The year 1978 was perhaps the last occasion,

Table 7.12. Voter participation in three primary elections, 1978, 1996, and 2012

County type	1978			1996			2012		
	R	D	Democratic percentage of all primary votes	R	D	Democratic percentage of all votes	R	D	Democratic percentage of all votes
Big 6	105,841	604,743	85.1	462,063	273,398	37.2	443,034	287,153	39.3
Suburban	11,852	215,011	94.8	218,844	88,492	28.8	399,166	57,939	12.7
Other Metro	27,970	369,703	93.0	193,106	190,894	49.7	246,455	135,609	35.5
Small Town	12,740	623,439	98.0	145,790	368,472	71.7	360,822	109,463	23.3
TOTAL	158,403	1,812,896		1,019,803	921,256		1,449,477	590,164	

Table 7.13. Composition of primary electorate by county category

County type	Percentage of total Republican primary vote from county category			Percentage of total Democratic primary vote from county category		
	1978	1996	2012	1978	1996	2012
Big 6	66.8	45.3	30.6	33.4	29.7	48.7
Suburban	7.5	21.5	27.5	11.9	9.6	9.8
Other Metro	17.7	18.9	17.0	20.4	20.7	23.0
Small Town	8.0	14.3	24.9	34.4	40.0	18.5

however, when the Democratic primary was the arena of final choice in many parts of the state. By the end of the two-party interlude in 1996, the Republican primary was attracting more voters, and by the 2012 primary it was obtaining roughly seven out of every ten primary votes.

In addition to changes in the raw numbers voting in each primary, the two parties' constituencies have changed. No longer do voters in the Big 6 counties control the outcome of a Republican primary. At the same time, the Big 6 electorate now casts nearly half of all Democratic primary votes. In terms of partisan realignment, it is the more rural counties that have undergone the most dramatic shift. From casting over one-third of all votes in the 1978 Democratic primary, these counties now provide fewer than one in five Democratic primary votes. At the same time, the Republican Party has drawn more of its support from this Small Town grouping of counties, going from less than one in ten to one in four votes in the Republican primary (table 7.13).

Although the number of Republican primary voters in the Big 6 counties expanded greatly from 1978 to 1996, the electorate in the last two primaries was relatively stable. In both 1996 and 2012 more voters took part in the GOP primary, with a similar ratio each time. While roughly the same number of voters participated each year, Republican numbers are down while Democratic participation is up. What did change, however, was the relative importance of these Big 6 voters in each party's primary. These voters now play a much more important part in determining the statewide nominees of the Democratic Party and have less critical roles to play in selecting the Republican Party's statewide candidates. Such a change in the distribution of each party's primary electorate can have an impact on the type of candidates nominated for statewide office.

Among the twenty-nine counties in the Suburban category there has been a dramatic shift over the three elections. All of these counties cast more votes in the 1978 Democratic primary but, by the 2012 primary, more voters chose to take part in the Republican primary in all twenty-nine counties. Eighteen of these counties, most of which had provided more than 90 percent of their votes to the Democratic primary in 1978, switched to casting more votes in the Republican primary of 1996 and again in 2012. Rockwall County outside Dallas, Montgomery County to the north of Houston, and Kendall County northwest of San Antonio provide the clearest examples of this shift. More than 95 percent of all primary votes in Rockwall County in 1978 were Democratic but only 9.3 percent in 1996 and 7.2 percent in 2012. For Montgomery County the Democratic share of the primary vote fell from 94.3 percent to 9.1 percent in 1996 and down to 5.2 percent in 2012. Kendall was the least Democratic of this category with 71.2 percent of the total vote in 1978, a percentage that dropped to 5.7 percent in 1996 and down to 4.2 percent in the most recent primary.

What has occurred in these and several other counties is that the arena of final choice for the selection of county and district officials has shifted from the Democratic primary to the Republican. By 1996, most of these county officials were Republican, and any serious competition to their continued holding of public office was more likely to take place in the primary. Sixteen years later the transformation of local politics was almost total and complete. Of these eighteen counties, only three (Hays, Hunt, and Fort Bend) had a Democrat serving as county judge, sheriff, or as one of the four county commissioners. In the other fifteen, the GOP had control of the policy-making branch of county government as well as having elected most, if not all, county elective officials (table 7.14).

In the remaining eleven counties in this category the Democratic primary retained the participation of most primary voters in 1996, but these also converted to a Republican majority in the 2012 primary. In five of these counties, the two parties remain competitive, with the Democratic primary attracting from as few as 21.7 percent to as high as 41.6 percent of all primary voters. In four others, less than 10 percent of all voters chose the Democratic primary in 2012 even though it had been the dominant environment in both 1978 and 1996. The relationship between primary participation and partisan dominance of county elections can be seen in

Table 7.14. Democratic percentage of primary vote in Suburban counties, 1978, 1996, and 2012

County	Democratic percentage of primary vote			Republicans in top six county offices, 2013
	1978	1996	2012	
	Trending Republican by 1996			
Bandera	100.0	10.2	4.5	6
Medina	100.0	35.1	11.4	6
Ellis	97.7	23.2	10.8	6
Hays	97.7	43.2	26.5	5
Hunt	97.6	47.2	7.3	5
Johnson	97.6	32.1	7.9	6
Parker	97.0	32.4	6.1	6
Williamson	96.9	19.7	12.8	6
Guadalupe	96.0	16.0	12.3	6
Brazoria	95.9	21.4	12.7	6
Rockwall	95.6	9.3	7.2	6
Austin	95.6	26.6	5.7	6
Montgomery	94.3	9.1	5.2	6
Denton	89.6	12.5	9.8	6
Fort Bend	87.0	24.1	21.2	4
Comal	82.9	10.1	4.5	6
Collin	82.5	9.8	10.3	6
Kendall	71.2	5.7	4.2	6
	Trending Republican by 2012			
Chambers	100.0	78.1	7.0	4
Liberty	100.0	68.6	8.0	6
San Jacinto	100.0	83.3	39.4	3
Wilson	100.0	58.0	15.9	3
Atascosa	99.7	65.3	41.6	3
Bastrop	99.0	63.7	35.6	5
Waller	98.9	67.5	21.7	5
Caldwell	98.1	65.8	41.6	2
Kaufman	98.0	62.1	9.5	6
Wise	97.3	65.8	6.0	5
Galveston	95.7	54.3	18.9	5

most instances also. Both Caldwell and Atascosa had the highest percentage of Democratic primary voters and also the largest number of office-holders in the key county positions. As in Wilson, San Jacinto, and Chambers Counties, the return to one-party dominance of local elections had not occurred in these counties as of 2012.

The partisan transformation and the return to one-party dominance is most apparent in three counties. Liberty County did not even have a Republican primary in 1978, and eighteen years later the Democratic primary was still receiving 68.6 percent of all primary voters. Fast-forward to 2012 and the Democratic percentage had shrunk to 8.0 percent. For Wise County, the Democratic proportion fell from 97.3 percent to 65.8 percent to 6.0 percent, and for Kaufman County the relevant percentages are 98.0 percent down to 62.1 percent and to only 9.5 percent in the most recent primary election measured here.

While the shift in these counties took longer to develop, it appears that in some of them the Republican Party has replaced the Democratic Party as the preferred affiliation for those who seek local elective office. Kaufman and Liberty have a Republican sheriff and all-Republican commissioners courts. Yet among this category of counties the transformation is not complete; Atascosa, Caldwell, and San Jacinto Counties still have a Democratic majority on their commissioners courts. These outer suburbs of Austin, Houston, and San Antonio remain the most Democratic of the Suburban category.

Among the Other Metro counties, a similar transformation has occurred (table 7.15). Although all of these counties except Midland provided the vast majority of their votes to the Democratic primary in 1978, thirteen of the twenty had shifted to a majority of Republican primary voters by 1996, with only one of them having a Democratic participation rate above 15 percent in the 2012 primary. Taylor County, home to the city of Abilene, was the most Democratic of these dozen counties in 1978, with 97.4 percent of all votes cast. By 1996, Democratic primary voters comprised only 21.2 percent of the total. In 2012, the level of Democratic participation had dropped to 6.6 percent. It is no surprise, then, that Taylor County had a Republican county judge, sheriff, and all four county commissioners after the 2012 election.

Three other counties in this category continued a Democratic dominance in 1996 but provided a majority of their votes to the Republican primary in 2012. While Nueces remained competitive with 41.5 percent of its primary voters choosing the Democratic primary, in Grayson County the level of participation dropped to 7.8 percent and in Bowie

Table 7.15. Democratic percentage of primary vote in Other Metro counties

County	Democratic percentage of primary vote			Republicans in top six county offices, 2013
	1978	1996	2012	2013
Trending Republican by 1996				
Taylor	97.4	21.2	6.6	6
Victoria	97.3	34.5	24.2	4
Bell	97.2	31.4	12.6	6
Brazos	96.8	23.3	8.2	5
McLennan	96.4	48.2	10.2	5
Ector	96.4	21.6	8.2	5
Gregg	94.4	20.2	11.6	5
Smith	93.1	19.2	7.6	5
Wichita	92.8	47.2	11.7	4
Tom Green	91.9	34.8	10.5	6
Potter	90.1	22.3	14.5	4
Lubbock	87.3	16.1	13.3	5
Randall	78.2	12.0	4.8	6
Midland	47.8	8.8	4.7	5
Trending Republican by 2012				
Bowie	98.6	79.6	18.2	4
Grayson	97.5	55.6	7.8	6
Nueces	94.3	68.4	41.5	4
Remaining Democratic				
Webb	99.7	95.5	94.7	0
Jefferson	97.3	76.5	55.5	2
Cameron	96.4	78.4	80.2	1
Hidalgo	96.3	85.7	87.4	0

County it fell off to 18.2 percent. Grayson County had an all-Republican commissioners court while the GOP had a majority on the policy-making body of county government in both Bowie and Nueces Counties. Of the seventeen counties with a majority of Republican voters in the 2012 primary, none had fewer than four of the six top county officials elected as Republicans. Nevertheless, four counties remained heavily Democratic on primary day in all three elections cited. They were the three Mexican-border counties of Cameron, Hidalgo, and Webb, along with Jefferson County on the Louisiana border. Only a few local officials in these counties were elected as Republicans.

Of the fifty-seven counties in the Small Town grouping with a minimum of 7,500 residents voting in the 2012 general election, not a single one had more Republican than Democratic primary voters in 1978. Eight of these counties provided no opportunity to vote in the GOP primary, while thirty-three of them had less than 2 percent selecting a Republican primary ballot. In fact, only two of the fifty-seven counties were less than 90 percent Democratic, both in the traditionally Republican German Hill Country.

Eighteen years later the Republican Party had gained a majority of primary voters in nine of fifty-seven counties. In both Kerr and Gillespie, the two least Democratic counties in 1978, the percentage of voters participating in the Democratic primary had fallen to 7.1 percent and 5.9 percent, respectively. By 2012 there were few Democratic primary voters left in these nine counties. Republicans now controlled county government to the extent that for the positions of county judge, sheriff, and county commissioner, only Llano and Wood Counties had a single Democratic commissioner each.

It took longer for most of the other counties to make the partisan transition. By 2012, only six of these fifty-seven counties had more Democratic than Republican primary voters. In sixteen of the counties that had been more Democratic in both 1978 and 1996, less than 10 percent of primary voters went Democratic. What these sixteen counties have in common is a county government that in almost all cases has been totally taken over by GOP officeholders. Only four Democrats were elected to key county positions, one each in four of these sixteen counties (table 7.16).

Less than 10 percent of all primary voters in these twenty-five counties chose to take part in the Democratic primary in 2012, an astounding reversal from their voting history as recently as 1978. What is apparent from these numbers is that county government has been transformed from Democratic to Republican in terms of partisan affiliation. Other than in

Table 7.16. Democratic percentage of primary vote, selected Small Town counties

County	Democratic percentage of primary vote			Republicans in top six county offices, 2013
	1978	1996	2012	
	Trending Republican by 1996			
Washington	99.0	30.3	5.3	6
Wood	98.7	43.0	4.0	5
Cooke	98.6	21.0	3.5	6
Erath	98.1	43.8	6.5	6
Hood	96.9	27.5	6.1	6
Llano	92.0	36.8	7.6	5
Hutchinson	89.9	16.8	3.8	6
Gillespie	73.3	5.9	5.3	6
Kerr	54.7	7.1	4.9	6
	Trending Republican by 2012			
Upshur	99.5	77.4	8.3	6
Hardin	99.2	76.7	7.3	6
Cherokee	99.0	70.9	8.5	5
Harrison	98.9	79.0	7.3	5
Brown	98.9	51.2	3.7	6
Hill	98.9	64.7	7.0	6
Lamar	98.8	85.4	8.2	6
Montague	98.7	81.2	3.9	6
Rusk	98.3	62.4	9.2	5
Palo Pinto	98.2	81.1	4.7	6
Burnet	98.0	64.8	6.9	6
Van Zandt	97.3	60.5	5.7	6
Nacogdoches	96.8	66.1	7.4	6
Coryell	96.5	56.3	6.9	6
Hale	95.6	75.2	8.4	5
Colorado	95.5	76.1	7.5	6

Table 7.17. Straight-ticket voting in Texas, 1998–2012

Year	Straight tickets as percentage of total votes	Republican percentage of straight-ticket votes
1998	47.6	52.7
2000	49.0	51.0
2002	49.6	52.0
2004	55.6	57.0
2006	45.0	51.3
2008	57.6	50.3
2010	59.2	58.1
2012	61.4	55.9

Kerr, Llano, and Nacogdoches Counties, all the key elected county officials in each of the other twenty-five mainly rural counties were Democrats in 1978.[76] By 2012, of the 150 most important county offices in these twenty-five counties, a total of six Democrats held office. While this partisan change has not occurred in every county, it is apparent that movement has taken place in a substantial number of the larger counties in the Small Town category. As the arena of final choice for county officials moved from the Democratic to the Republican primary, voters in these counties have also made the transition to participate in the primary of the now-dominant party.

This transformation of county politics is present not only in these Small Town counties but also in most Suburban and Other Metro counties, where the level of voter participation in the Republican primary has increased over time as the party's control of key county offices has taken place. This relationship between county politics and primary participation appears to indicate that in many areas of the state, Texas has returned to a time of one-party dominance.

Straight-Ticket Voting

One final measure of party competition consists of the composition and extent of straight-ticket voting in Texas general elections (table 7.17). Prior to the beginning of the present period of one-party dominance, the Democratic Party could rely on a substantial number of straight-ticket voters to give their candidates a cushion in any head-to-head contest with a viable Republican opponent. From 1978 to 1996, as the Republican Party began winning more elections, the balance between the two parties in terms of straight-ticket voters began to shift. As noted in chapter 6, between 1978 and 1996 it appears that two-party competition developed among straight-ticket voters in the Big 6 counties, while at least some of the suburbs around these Big 6 counties were moving strongly in a one-party direction. However, since 1998 and the return to one-party dominance, it is the Republicans who have obtained the support of a majority of straight-ticket voters statewide because they have been able to extend their support to a wider range of Other Metro and Small Town counties.[77]

A breakdown of the performance of the electorate into the four categories of counties indicates that some changes have occurred during the period from 1998 to 2012 (table 7.18). As a group, the Big 6 counties have vacillated in party support among straight-ticket voters, three times providing a net advantage for the Republicans and three times for the Democrats since 2002. El Paso and Travis have provided a Democratic cushion in all six elections and have a history of voting Democratic. Dallas, one of the bastions of a revived Republican Party beginning in the 1950s, has shifted dramatically to the Democratic Party in recent elections. With a nearly even split in straight-ticket votes in 2000, the Democratic percentage went as high as 60 percent in 2008 and stood at roughly 59 percent in 2012. Meanwhile, its neighboring Big 6 county, Tarrant, has provided a Republican advantage each time, and in the most recent election 58.3 percent of its straight-ticket votes were Republican. Both Bexar and Harris Counties have given each party a majority on three occasions. In 2012, the Democratic advantage from Harris County was only 2,644 out of 809,554 straight-ticket votes.

Only one of the twenty-nine Suburban counties (Caldwell) provided more Democratic than Republican straight-ticket votes in 2012. The limited data available from past elections shows that since 2002, Bastrop, Hays, Fort Bend, and Galveston have on occasion given the Democrats an advantage, but none did so in 2012, and they appear to be trending more Republican each year. In nine of the twenty-nine counties more than 80 percent of all straight-ticket votes were Republican in the last election.[78] One of the more populous counties in this category, Montgomery, has given roughly eight of ten straight-ticket votes to the Republican Party in each election since 1998, with percentages ranging from 79.2 percent to 85.5 percent. Clearly, this category of counties has become a critical base in a statewide Republican majority, providing a solid foundation for all of the party's candidates.

Table 7.18. Straight-ticket voting, by county category, 2012

County category	Republican	Democratic	Republican vote margin	Percentage Republican of straight-ticket votes	Percentage straight-ticket of all votes cast	Total votes
Big 6 (n = 6)	1,088,224	1,241,372	-153,148	46.7	64.5	3,612,487
Suburban (n = 29)	825,667	371,053	+454,614	69.0	61.5	1,944,707
Other Metro (n = 21)	404,361	329,511	+79,850	55.5	57.3	1,271,536
Small Town (n = 56)[a]	294,505	123,846	+170,659	70.4	53.3	785,181
Total 112 counties	2,612,757	2,060,782	+551,975	55.9	61.4	7,613,911
Remaining 142 counties[b]	—	—	—	—	—	379,940

[a]The 56 small-town counties included here each had a minimum of 7,500 votes cast in the 2012 election and provided over two-thirds of the votes cast in the 198 small-town counties. No data was available from Jim Wells County, which also had a minimum of 7,500 voters in 2012.
[b]Data was not collected for the remaining 142 smaller counties, which provided 4.8 percent of all votes cast in the 2012 election.

Five of the twenty-one Other Metro counties provided more Democratic than Republican straight-ticket votes in 2012. These are the traditionally strong Democratic counties of Cameron, Hidalgo, and Webb in the Rio Grande Valley, plus Jefferson and Nueces Counties. Interestingly, Nueces County has one of the lower rates of straight-ticket voting (45.6%) and in 2010 had slightly more Republican straight-ticket votes (53.0%).

Beginning in 2006, Randall County has consistently produced a minimum of eight Republican to two Democratic straight-ticket votes, reaching its highest proportion of 89 percent Republican in 2010. The most heavily Republican straight-ticket areas in 2012 were Randall (87.0%), Midland (81.1%), Tom Green (78.7%), Taylor (78.2%), and Ector (74.0%) Counties, all of which are located in West Texas and have been heavily Republican in their straight-ticket votes since 1998.

Historically, most of the state's more rural counties were the home to "yellow dog Democrats," but if the fifty-six larger Small Town counties are reflective of the remainder, then it appears that the dog has changed its colors. While fewer of these voters cast a straight-ticket in 2012 than did residents in the more urbanized areas of the state, those that did were strongly Republican in their party support, providing the highest GOP percentage of over 70 percent of all straight-ticket votes cast. Of the fifty-six counties for which data could be obtained, only six (Bee, Kleberg, Maverick, Starr, Uvalde, and Val Verde) cast more Democratic than Republican straight-ticket votes in November 2012.[79] In nineteen of the fifty-six counties more than three of every four straight-ticket votes were Republican. The most heavily Republican Small Town counties were scattered around the state from Van Zandt (87.6%) in the northeast to Hutchinson (87.5%) in the Panhandle and Montague (86.0%) in Central Texas, as well as Brown (86.6%), Cooke (85.8%), Erath (85.5%), and Hood (85.7%), where at least seventeen out of every twenty straight-ticket votes were Republican.

In recent years some Republican state senators and party leaders in Dallas County have advocated either totally abolishing the straight-ticket voting option on Texas ballots or limiting its application to certain public offices. Viewing the data reflected here raises questions as to why this should be done. As Peck Young, onetime Democratic strategist, has noted, "Why would the Republicans want to do away with straight-ticket voting? It's been doing them enormous good. The truth is, the Democrats should have been complaining about it. Doing away with it is, I think, a bad thing, because it ignores modern politics. Modern politics is about modern advertising."[80]

According to Young, politics today is basically an issue of branding. As the two political parties have become more clearly differentiated on overall ideology as well as on specific policy stands, the decision to vote for all of a party's candidates becomes more logical for many voters. This becomes especially true in more populous counties, where as many as fifty or more public offices are filled in any one election. In such a situation, very few voters will be familiar with the names, let alone the policy stands and public records, of many candidates seeking their votes.[81] From his own anecdotal experiences Young is convinced that there is a logic to straight-ticket voting for many people. As he explained, "Some of the people who vote straight ticket most reliably—I found in one study I did for a client—were literally guys who work for NASA. They weren't voting straight ticket out of ignorance—that was the brand they were in favor of as Republicans."[82]

The overall importance of straight-ticket voting in the transformation of Texas into a one-party Republican dominant state can be exaggerated, however. While more Texans are voting straight ticket and more of those votes are going to the slate of Republican candidates, the overall total of such votes is not determinant in statewide elections. Even without straight-ticket voting, virtually all Republican statewide candidates since 1996 would have won. It is the Republican candidates' advantage among "swing," or non-straight-ticket, voters that has contributed to the party's current success. In the most recent presidential contest, Mitt Romney began with nearly 56 percent of the straight-ticket votes for a lead over Barack Obama of 551,975 votes. However, among swing voters, Romney's lead grew by 708,687 additional votes since he obtained 61.0 percent of the two-party votes cast by these individuals. Even in the contest for governor in 2010, which was a closer race, Rick Perry received 52.8 percent of swing votes in his contest with Bill White, which would have secured his re-election without the nearly six in ten straight-ticket votes cast for the Republican ticket.

The results from the 2012 election show that more Texans are casting straight-ticket votes, especially in the more urbanized areas of the state. Further, these straight-ticket voters are more Republican than Democratic and in the most recent election provided the GOP slate of candidates with more than a half-million-vote cushion over their Democratic opponents. Geographically, straight-ticket voters are most strongly Republican in the Small Town counties, followed closely by the suburbs around the Big 6 counties. It is in these suburbs that the Republican Party was able to build its largest base of straight-ticket support, overcoming a recent Democratic advantage in the Big 6 counties. There is nothing in the recent results analyzed here to indicate either that there is likely to be any significant decline in straight-ticket voting or that the Republican advantage, however slight, will not continue to provide a base of support for its slate of candidates.

Regardless of the measure of party competition employed—elections from president to county commissioner, party identification, primary participation, or straight-ticket voting—it is evident that since 1996 Texas has been a one-party dominant state. Among the types of counties, the Republican surge has been greatest in the Suburban and Small Town categories but with sizable gains also in the Other Metro category. Only among the Big 6 counties has the Democratic Party staged a comeback to competitiveness or even dominance. Overall, Texas is now a Republican-dominant state with pockets of strong Democratic support.

CHAPTER 8

The Future of Texas Politics

Texas politics has undergone a major transformation over the past fifty years from one-party Democratic to two-party competitive and, most recently, to one-party Republican. By the beginning of the twenty-first century Texas Republicans had become the majority party regardless of the measure of party competition employed. As writer Erica Grieder recently noted, "The greatest advantage that Texas Republicans currently enjoy . . . is that Texans really haven't had a problem with their policies. The evidence is that people keep voting for them."[1] Given the various stages of party competition since the admittance of Texas as a state in 1845, the relevant question remaining is whether this Republican dominance will continue into the future.

Trending Democratic?

While the Democrats made only slight gains in the 2012 election, some long-term trends appear to give the party hope for future success. Generational trends that for long had moved in a Republican direction may now be shifting toward the Democrats. As late as 2004, survey data showed Democratic support strongest among voters over age sixty, with Republican support highest among voters from thirty to fifty-nine.[2] More recent surveys, however, show that as these Republicans move into older subsets they are being replaced by younger cohorts of more Democratic voters. In a 2011 survey inquiring as to primary voting intent, the only cohort more likely to vote in the Democratic primary comprised those aged eighteen to twenty-nine. Only 28.9 percent of these younger voters indicated a likelihood to vote in the Republican primary compared to 67.2 percent of voters sixty-five and over.[3]

It appears that many of the Reagan-attracted baby boomers are now approaching senior-citizen status. While they will continue to participate at a high level, their numbers will begin to decline over time, creating for the Republicans the generational impact previously experienced by the Democratic Party. Meanwhile, younger voters are entering the electorate during the administration of a Democratic president who has appealed to many of their age group.

Democrats can also take hope in the fruits of Republican success possibly being bitter. With its overall success in electing individuals to public office, the Republican Party has created a clogged candidate pipeline that could result in potentially divisive primaries and weakened general election candidates. This occurred with state comptroller Carole Strayhorn challenging Governor Rick Perry as an independent in 2006 and Senator Kay Bailey Hutchison opposing him in the 2010 primary. More recently, several statewide officeholders have expressed interest in seeking higher office, much to the chagrin of current incumbents who may desire re-election.[4] Such internal competition may provide an opening for a strong Democratic challenger who could break the GOP hold on statewide offices. Such an event, some Democrats maintain, would be a tipping point to open up opportunities for victory in other statewide positions, sweeping away the argument of Republican invincibility.

Similar situations of competition within the Republican Party could develop at the county and legislative levels in various areas of the state. Where one party is dominant, potential candidates may determine they have a greater opportunity for nomination in the Democratic Party with the possibility of an outsider victory in November. Having too extensive a farm team of candidates at one level of government, while normally an asset, may become a detriment when insufficient opportunities for advancement are available. The end result may be divisive and expensive primaries where supporters of the losing candidate defect to the Democratic candidate in the general election.[5]

Divisiveness in the majority party may come not only from individual candidate ambition but also from ideological and policy differences. Much has been written as to the "religious right" influence in the Republican Party as well as the more recent impact of the "tea party" movement.[6] Together, these two elements have contributed to an increase in primary contests for legislative nominations as well as challenges to the Republican speaker of the Texas House of Representatives. The conflicts between social issues voters and business-oriented Republicans may provide an opportunity for Democratic victories.

Democrats also look to the Big 6 counties for the possibility of building a majority. Along with traditional Democratic dominance of El Paso and Travis Counties, the last several elections have turned Dallas County into a Democratic stronghold where Democrats now control four of five positions on the commissioners court and nearly all other county offices. Where Dallas had been a source of net votes for Republican candidates from the 1960s forward, starting with the 2006 election it has provided a lead for top-of-the-ticket Democratic candidates as high as 110,000 votes in the last two presidential elections.

After recent Democratic gains in Bexar and Harris Counties, Tarrant County is left as the only bastion of GOP support among the Big 6 counties. These urban voters also play a larger role in Democratic primaries, as the overall primary electorate has declined among the other three categories of counties. This can lead, however, to general election problems for the party's candidates. As one political consultant wryly noted, "Democratic primaries in Austin can be as humorless and judgmental as telling a bride that she doesn't deserve to wear white. We inflict purity tests on one another's partisan fidelity that Barack Obama couldn't pass. But in a city where every other car on MoPac Boulevard (Loop 1) has an Obama sticker, it's easy to forget that all Democrats in Texas aren't as liberal as we are."[7] It is from these Big 6 counties that nearly half of all Democratic primary votes come, impacting the type of candidate able to obtain a statewide nomination.

While the Democratic candidates are gaining support in the Big 6 counties, this is not a growing segment of the overall Texas electorate. Having been as high as 48 percent of the statewide vote in the latter part of the twentieth century, these Big 6 counties have been under 45 percent in each election since 2002. The Suburban counties, where Republican candidates dominate, constitute the one category increasing its share of the statewide vote, from less than 10 percent in 1960 to nearly 25 percent in 2012. Both the Other Metro and Small Town categories are declining as percentages of the total vote, but they are also becoming even more Republican.

Realizing the importance of Texas as the second largest provider of electoral votes, Democratic activists have launched "Battleground Texas" as a major effort to revitalize the party's fortunes in the state. Headed by Jeremy Bird, former national field director for the Obama re-election campaign, the effort plans to spend "tens of millions of dollars over several years" but began in February 2013 with a website and two mid-level staffers in Austin.[8] The new effort will attempt to expand the electorate and mobilize registered voters who have not participated in recent elections, focusing especially on Hispanics and African Americans.

Still other factors, however, indicate that Republican dominance is likely to continue into the near future. The election results from 2012 provided little indication of changes in overall partisan support. Writing a *New York Times* column emphasizing Democratic gains, Ross Ramsey admitted that "it is not the best situation, but it could have been a lot worse," concluding that "the Democrats' numbers are not great, but they are better than they were two years ago."[9] Two years ago, of course, refers to the election of 2010 when the GOP picked up a net of three additional congressional seats and twenty-three state house districts as well as seventeen county judges and numerous county commissioners. After mentioning the party's net gain of six state house seats in the 2012 election, Democratic consultant Jason Stanford humorously claimed that "Texas Democrats have been in the wilderness so long we could teach survival skills to Grizzly Adams."[10]

In the last nine elections since 1996, only 17.7 percent of the seventy-nine Democratic statewide candidates ran a competitive race where the losing candidate received at least 45 percent of the two-party vote. Most often, the party's best showing statewide was for a low-profile judicial position. The Republican dominance of the state legislature appears likely to continue, although the great variance in party support during the past decade indicates that redistricting is not always determinant. Nevertheless, in 2012 only 9 of the 150 house districts were competitive; five of these were won by Republicans. There were considerably fewer Democratic primary contests for state legislative nominations than Republican primaries, a situation normally associated with the relative chances of general election victory. While the Democrats have run some competitive judicial races and have won in certain areas of the state, the judicial branch overall has become overwhelmingly Republican, with many incumbents unopposed for re-election.

Apart from the Big 6 counties and a few other areas of the state, especially near the Mexican border, county government is becoming more solidly Republican. This is especially true in Suburban and Small Town counties, a situation evident not only in the number of elected officials but also in primary participation and straight-ticket voting. As more Texans have begun to cast a straight-ticket ballot, the Republican advantage has grown. With increased Republican success at the county level, the Democratic Party finds fewer Texans participating in their primary. What was once considered an improbability—the lack of a Democratic primary—is now occurring in more elections, with a total of thirteen counties providing no opportunity to nominate Democratic candidates in 2012. Even in those counties conducting a Democratic primary, participation is often minimal. In fourteen of the twenty-nine Suburban counties less than 10 percent of all primary voters took part in the Democratic Party nominating process. This minimal level also occurred in seven of the twenty-one Other Metro counties and twenty-five of the fifty-seven larger Small Town counties. With no primary, no Democratic candidates for county office can be nominated. With less than 10 percent participation, the party's candidate begins with only a small cadre of support. In such an environment the candidate recruitment difficulties that once confronted Republicans are now a challenge for Texas Democrats.

Ethnicity and Texas Politics

By the time of the 2010 census, Texas had become statistically a "majority-minority" state wherein Anglos comprised less than one-half the total population. Most often cited as a factor providing an opportunity for Democratic success is the growing number of Hispanics. Both Hispanics and Asian Americans are increasing their numbers and their overall percentage of the state's population.

That is not the situation, however, for African Americans, who in 2010 constituted nearly 3 million of the 25 million people living in Texas. Texas has always been distinct from the other Southern and ex-Confederate states in its racial and ethnic composition. As a former part of Mexico it has always had a large Hispanic population and a smaller percentage of African Americans than other Southern states. In 1920, roughly 16 percent of the state's population was African American. This proportion declined to 12.4 percent in 1960 and down to 11.8 percent in 2010. In political terms, at least since the passage of the Voting Rights Act in 1965, African Americans have been overwhelmingly Democratic. Despite this, three African Americans have been elected to statewide office in the last decade as Republicans, along with three state representatives and a handful of county officials in office as of 2013. Nevertheless, there is little indication of any likely political changes in African American voting behavior or party identification in the foreseeable future.

While the strong attachment of African Americans to the Democratic

Party has led to an enhanced role in that party's outlook and nominating process, it has also contributed to the movement of conservative Anglos to the GOP. Speaking of the entire South and not specifically Texas, one recent study concluded, "As Blacks moved into the Democratic party in significant numbers, conservative white Southerners were forced to seek another vehicle for their political ambitions and objectives."[11] With fewer avenues for political success due to increased competition from African Americans and liberal Anglos, more conservative Anglos shifted their partisan allegiance to an increasingly viable Republican Party. While this situation certainly was more prevalent in other parts of the South, its impact cannot be dismissed in certain areas of Texas.

Blacks in Texas appear to be less geographically concentrated today than in the past as many have moved from traditional African American neighborhoods to integrated suburbs and urban neighborhoods. Their representation in government at all levels has been aided by the application of the Voting Rights Act and court decisions preventing retrogression in the number of districts where minority communities are able to determine elections. While there are four African American Congressmen from Texas and two state senators, none represents a Black-majority district. Of the eighteen African Americans serving in the Texas House (roughly proportionate to the state's Black population), only two come from Black-majority districts, both located in Harris County; these are the only two congressional or state legislative districts in Texas with a Black-majority population.

The situation is quite different with Hispanics, however. Fifty years ago less than 20 percent of Texans were Hispanic. That percentage grew to 37.6 percent according to the 2010 census and continues to increase, with various projections as to the likely date when Texas will have a Hispanic majority. Of course, it is not solely in Texas that the Hispanic proportion of the population has been increasing. The political impact of this growing segment of the population has been the focus of much recent discussion. After the resounding defeat of Mitt Romney in the 2012 presidential election, political commentators from left and right placed much of the campaign's failure, and the party's long-term future, on its inability to attract more Hispanic support.[12] According to national exit polls, not including Texas voters, Romney polled only 27 percent of Hispanic votes, far below what had been obtained by Bush in his two elections and by McCain in his losing campaign of 2008.

In Texas, the party's performance among Hispanics appeared to have been slightly, but not significantly, better. Conflicting data is available from a pre-election survey that showed 42.3 percent of Hispanics in Texas backing Romney and an election eve poll indicating 29 percent support for the GOP candidate. While the latter survey had only 15 percent self-identified Republicans, others maintain that roughly 26 percent of Hispanics in Texas identify themselves as Republicans.[13] One post-election survey of Hispanics who voted in the 2012 election, conducted for the Republican Party of Texas, found 36 percent who recalled voting for Romney, a percentage consistent with the 37 percent of Hispanics supporting Romney in the Reuters/Ipsos exit poll of Texas voters. Meanwhile, in the 2012 election, Democrats succeeded in defeating one Hispanic Republican Congressman and two state representatives, while the overall number of Hispanic GOP officeholders increased from fifty-eight to seventy-eight.[14]

The response from many Texas Republicans has been one of outright alarm for the future. According to GOP state chairman Stephen Munisteri, "The key to Republican success in the future is to reach out to Hispanic, African American and Asian voters because the state is growing increasingly diverse. The failure to do that will result, in the not-too-distant future, in this turning from a Republican state to a swing state."[15] Similarly, Jacob Monty of the Hispanic Republicans of Texas maintains that "the future of the Republican Party lies in keeping Texas as a Republican state. And if we allow our numbers to slip in Texas, we run the risk of losing the firewall that keeps the Republican Party as a viable option."[16] To accomplish this, former state representative Aaron Peña maintains that the party must change focus: "Republicans say they share the same interest, and that's true, but Hispanics also know when someone's with us or against us, even when you don't mouth the words."[17] For Tatcho Mindiola, director of the Center for Mexican American Studies at the University of Houston, "They're going to have to reach out and do more than say that 'Hispanics have values that are similar to ours.' That's an old refrain, which apparently is not bearing any fruit with the Hispanic population."[18]

Conflicting data is available on the ideological and issues orientation of Hispanics. The prevailing view among Republicans is expressed by first-term U.S. Senator Ted Cruz, himself a Cuban American, who maintains, "The Hispanic community is profoundly conservative. The values that resonate in our community are faith, family, patriotism. The rate of military enlistment among Hispanics is higher than any other demographic. Hispanic men and women want to work. Want to provide for our kids. Want to stand on our own feet. Those are all conservative values."[19] But this view is challenged by some, who maintain that Hispanics are more in line with Democratic demographics. According to one writer, "Native born Hispanics who make up the vast majority of such voters in the U.S. have far higher rates of welfare use, single-parent households, and low tax liabilities—all factors that usually indicate a better fit with the Democratic party than with Republicans."[20] Gary M. Segura, a political scientist at Stanford associated with the Latino Decisions polling firm, maintains that "Latinos are systematically to the left of whites on an entire array of economic-policy matters."[21]

Even when a policy position is in alignment with a given group, policy may not move party orientation. After reviewing the results of a 2000 presidential election survey of Latino likely voters, Alvarez and Bedolla found that voter attitude on abortion had only a minimal impact on partisan support. They concluded, "Given that socially conservative Mexicans are generally understood to be the group most likely to move to the Republican party because of their attitudes toward abortion, these findings suggest it is unlikely that will happen in the near future."[22]

A much different portrait, however, is painted by the data from the 2008 National Annenberg Election Survey, as reported in a recent article by Marisa A. Abrajano and R. Michael Alvarez. Here, Hispanics were slightly more in favor of reducing taxes than Anglos and held positions similar to Anglos on the importance of balancing the budget through a reduction in spending. Hispanics were more supportive of trade agreements and allowing private investment of Social Security contributions, but also supported more federal spending on health insurance and additional efforts to reduce income inequality. Somewhat reflective of this disparity of issue positions, Hispanic Democrats and self-described independents had high proportions of respondents who did not think of themselves in ideological terms.[23] Moreover, fewer than one in five Democrats and independents described themselves as liberal: "Among those Hispanics who identify as Democrats, the plurality of respondents, 31 percent, do not consider their political ideology in terms of conservative and liberal. . . . Thus, while the conventional wisdom is that individuals who identify as Democrats typically think of themselves as liberals, this association is not borne out among Puerto Ricans and Mexicans who self-identify as Democrats."[24] The conclusion from this more recent analysis was that "the correlation between ideology and Democratic partisanship does not appear to be as strongly related as it is for the rest of the American electorate."[25]

What, then, about Texas, the growth of its Hispanic population, and the future of partisan politics in the state? Before theorizing on the future it is helpful to consider the present and how it may well impact what is to come. As of the 2010 census, the Texas Hispanic population was slightly over 9.5 million, of whom only 43.8 percent were eligible to vote, contrasted with 78.4 percent of all Anglos and 69.6 percent of African Americans. Of these eligible Hispanic voters, 32.3 percent were aged eighteen through twenty-nine, 27.1 percent had less than a high school diploma, and 27.9 percent had a household income of less than $30,000—all characteristics traditionally contributing to a low level of voter participation.[26]

Of the nearly 4.2 million eligible Hispanic voters, some 2.3 million were registered in 2010, a decline from the 2.4 million on the rolls in 2008.[27] Viewing the potential impact of the Hispanic vote on Texas elections, George P. Bush sees this as a long-term issue: "Much has been made of the fact that the state of Texas will be majority Hispanic in less than five years. The voting percentage among Latinos is not commensurate with those percentages. So electorally speaking, we have, as Hispanics, a long way to go before we're a significant prize in that respect."[28] In a post-election analysis Nina Perales, vice president of the Mexican American Legal Defense and Education Fund (MALDEF), responded to optimistic remarks by other speakers and downplayed any prediction of a sudden surge in Hispanic voting resulting in turning Texas in a Democratic direction. "I just wanted to throw cold water on everything you have all said. We're losing ground. We have more U.S. citizen Latinos turning 18 every day than are getting registered. The gap between eligible and registered in the Latino community is widening, not narrowing."[29]

A post-election analysis of the 2012 presidential election by the U.S. Census Bureau helps place the impact of Hispanic voters in Texas in perspective. Of the estimated 6,831,000 Hispanics aged eighteen and above, 71.2 percent were citizens. They comprised 30.3 percent of the state's total adult citizen population. However, of Hispanic citizens aged eighteen and above, only 54.4 percent were registered to vote and the percentage of Hispanic citizens who actually voted in the 2012 presidential election was 38.8 percent. This contrasts with 60.9 percent of White non-Hispanics and 63.1 percent of Blacks who voted in 2012. In overall numbers, the census bureau estimated that some 5,087,000 White non-Hispanics voted in Texas compared with 1,890,000 Hispanics and 1,352,000 Blacks. These estimations put into better perspective the challenge confronting Battleground Texas as it attempts to turn Texas blue in future elections.[30]

Not only are Hispanics younger and less likely to register, they are also less likely to vote once they become eligible to do so. Moreover, accord-

ing to one Democratic strategist, among the middle-aged, "a new generation of minorities is moving into the middle class and buying homes in
the suburbs because of the good schools."[31] When these Hispanic voters
move to a neighborhood where nearly all elected officials are Republican
and many of the decisions on who serves in public office are made in the
Republican primary, a question remains as to whether they will retain any
Democratic tendencies or join with their neighbors in voting in the GOP
primary and for Republican candidates in November.[32]

Recent elections also tend to diminish the odds of Hispanic voters
turning Texas Democratic. In May 2013, Karl Rove claimed in a speech
to the Georgia Republican State Convention that "in Texas we get 40 percent of the Latino vote on average." This led to further research by Politi-
Fact Texas as to its accuracy. After reviewing more than twelve poll results
from 2000 to 2012, they found "an average of 39 percent of the Hispanic
vote for Republicans at or near the top of the tickets. We also averaged the
poll showing for each election year, reaching an across-the-years average
of 40 percent." Limiting the measure to nonpresidential candidates also
resulted in an average of 40 percent.[33]

In a state that is approaching 40 percent Hispanic, the Democratic
presidential candidate did worse in 2012 than he did in 2008 as the Republican vote was nineteen points higher in Texas than the overall national
performance. Moreover, Republican statewide candidates have been winning a sizable number of counties possessing a Hispanic majority. Only
when the percentage of Hispanics in the county population reaches 70
percent do the Democrats have an advantage. Indeed, beyond such counties the Democratic candidates for president and governor have had little
success (table 8.1).

President Obama carried a total of 26 of the state's 254 counties in
2012. Of these, twenty-one had a Hispanic population of over 70 percent. The five other counties he won were Bexar (58.7% Hispanic), Dallas
(38.3%), Harris (40.8%), Jefferson (17.0%), and Travis (33.5%). Two
years earlier, Democratic gubernatorial candidate Bill White obtained a
majority in twenty-eight counties. He won the same twenty-one counties with a more than 70 percent Hispanic population and the four Big 6
counties of Bexar, Dallas, Harris, and Travis. White added Falls County
(20.8% Hispanic) by a margin of 86 votes, Foard County (14.0%) by
5 votes, and Trinity County (7.7%) by 149 votes.

A further breakdown of the primary turnout in 2012 would show
a clear division among these categories of counties, mainly indicating
the one-party nature of politics in much of the state. In only two of the

Table 8.1. Voting in majority-Hispanic counties,[a] 2010 and 2012

Percentage of Hispanics	Number of counties in category	Mean percentage of 2012 primary votes for Democrats	Range of percentages in category	Romney (2012)		Perry (2010)	
				Percentage of two-party vote	Counties carried	Percentage of two-party vote	Counties carried
≥90+	8	92.0	87.4-100	26.0	0	28.9	0
80-89	8	81.5	69.2-100	34.1	0	38.8	0
70-79	7	82.4	58.9-98.4	42.9	2	45.0	2
60-69	8	41.2	0.9-98.0	54.4	8	55.3	8
50-59	19	18.4	0.0-64.8	70.3	19	68.6	19

[a] Bexar County (58.47% Hispanic), which voted Democratic in both elections but had a majority of GOP primary voters in 2012, is excluded from this analysis because of its disproportionate impact on the other counties in calculating performance.

twenty-three counties with a more than 70 percent Hispanic population did the Republican primary draw as much as 30 percent of the total vote. Moreover, in four of these counties no GOP primary was held and in an additional twelve, Democrats attracted over 90 percent of all primary voters. Clearly, these are one-party areas of the state where the Democratic Party retains its appeal. All of these counties are located either along the Mexican border or in the Rio Grande Valley region of the state.

When one moves to the counties with 60 to 69 percent Hispanic populations, one finds a mixed bag of partisan results. Both Romney and Perry carried all eight of these counties. Yet the Democratic primary attracted a majority of voters in three of these counties, ranging as high as 98.0 percent in Crockett County, indicating a continuation of the "two-tiered" politics of an earlier era, with voters electing Democrats locally but voting for statewide Republican candidates. Conversely, less than 12 percent voted in the Democratic primary in another three counties, with a low of 0.9 percent in Reagan County, areas where the transition to consistent Republican support appears to have taken hold.

The nineteen counties, excluding Bexar, with a majority of Hispanics but less than 60 percent, show the ability of the Republicans to win in areas thought to be inhospitable to the party. Both Perry and Romney carried every one of these nineteen Hispanic-majority counties. In only two of the nineteen did the Democrats attract a majority of primary voters; in only six was their percentage above 15 percent of the total primary vote. Meanwhile, in three of these counties no one could be found to conduct a Democratic primary election. These results appear to indicate that, except for those areas where the Hispanic percentage of the total population exceeded 70 percent, Democratic statewide candidates had limited success. These Republican counties with a majority-Hispanic population are found in two areas of the state: in a band running just north of the more heavily Hispanic counties and in the Panhandle near the New Mexico border.

Most Hispanics in Texas, however, do not live in these overwhelmingly Hispanic counties. Only Bexar, Cameron, Ector, El Paso, Hidalgo, Nueces, and Webb Counties fall within the Big 6 or Other Metro categories, with Atascosa classified as a Suburban county. The remaining forty-three all are best described as Small Town counties. The overall impact of Hispanic voters in other areas of the state can be seen in a discussion of legislative representation throughout the state.

It is informative to view both Democratic and Hispanic representation in the congressional delegation and the Texas legislature. Despite the growth in the state's Hispanic population, they are a majority of the total population in only 9 of 36 congressional districts, 7 of 31 state senate districts, and 35 of the 150 Texas House districts (table 8.2). Since the 2012 election, Democrats have held all of these seats except one in the Texas House.[34] While Republicans have been virtually shut out from Hispanic-majority districts, a reverse situation is true for Democrats. None of the state's twelve Democratic members of Congress represents an Anglo-majority district, only two are from such districts in the Texas Senate, and four in the Texas House. In this manner the Democratic Party may have a similar problem of running the risk of being perceived as the minority party in more ways than one at a time when most legislative districts have an Anglo majority.

The Texas Democratic Party sees its future in building on the support it has in the Hispanic community, maintaining that as more in that community become active in the political process, the state will begin to turn Democratic. In 2012, the party selected its first Hispanic as state chairman, Gilberto Hinojosa, a former county judge in Cameron County on the Mexican border. According to the *Huffington Post Politics* writer Elise Foley, Hinojosa expressed optimism about challenging the state's Republican dominance: "Hinojosa said he thinks that can change, particularly if the Democratic party focuses more on the growing Latino population. Some of his hopes are pinned on Julián and Joaquín Castro, who have recently begun to be considered rising stars in the party. Julián Castro, the mayor of San Antonio, may run for Texas governor in 2014, and Hinojosa expects Joaquín Castro to challenge Cruz in 2018."[35] The Castro twins of San Antonio are the most frequently cited potential statewide candidates for the Democratic Party. Both graduates of Stanford University and Harvard Law School, Julián Castro is currently mayor of San Antonio while his brother Joaquín is a Congressman from the twentieth district of Texas. In 2012, Democrats thought they had a strong candidate for statewide office in retired general Ricardo Sanchez, but after announcing for the United States Senate he withdrew from the campaign in December 2011.[36]

Although there is no question but that the number of Hispanics will continue to grow and that their proportion of the electorate may increase, possibly providing additional support for the Democratic Party and its candidates, there is another aspect that receives little attention. As shown above, Republicans have been receiving low levels of support in counties with 70 percent or more Hispanic populations. What is less often discussed is the Democratic Party's problem with obtaining a competi-

Table 8.2. Ethnic composition and party affiliation of Texas legislative districts, 2013

Incumbent legislator	District composition			
	Hispanic majority	Black majority	Black/ Hispanic combined	Anglo[a] majority
U.S. congressional districts (n = 36)				
Hispanic Democrat	6	—	0	0
Black Democrat	1	—	3	0
Anglo Democrat	2	—	0	0
Hispanic Republican	0	—	0	1
Anglo Republican	0	—	0	23
Senate districts (n = 31)				
Hispanic Democrat	7	—	0	0
Black Democrat	0	—	2	0
Anglo Democrat	0	—	1	2
Anglo Republican	0	—	0	19
House districts (n = 150)				
Hispanic Democrat	29	0	0	0
Black Democrat	0	2	13	0
Anglo Democrat	4	0	1	4
Other Democrat	1	0	1	0
Hispanic Republican	1	0	0	2
Black Republican	0	0	0	3
Anglo Republican	0	0	3	85
Other Republican	0	0	0	1

[a] "Anglo" comprises those responding as White, non-Hispanic.

tive segment of the Anglo population. In many areas of the state heavily populated by Anglos, a dramatic shift has occurred toward the Republican Party. While many examples can be cited, this change among Anglo voters is most apparent in one Texas county: "In Comanche County, a central Texas county where the population splits 73–26 between whites and Hispanics, Obama lost by an 80–18 margin. Michael Dukakis carried the white but traditionally Democratic county by 10 points in 1988, and Democrats have lost ground there in every presidential election since 1992."[37] The dramatic shift in this county was not limited to presidential elections but can be seen also in other measures of party competition. As late as 1994, Ann Richards carried the county in her losing re-election contest with George W. Bush. In 2010, Rick Perry won Comanche County by nearly thirty points over his Democratic opponent. Moreover, consider what happened to primary turnout. In 1994, Democrats outvoted Republicans 2,347 to 167, receiving 93.4 percent of all primary votes. Eighteen years later, the reverse situation existed, with 1,947 votes in the Republican primary and only 165 (7.8%) in the Democratic primary.

Comparing counties that are more than 70 percent Hispanic and counties over 70 percent Anglo leads to the conclusion that the Texas Democratic Party may have a more serious deficit with Anglo voters than Republicans do with Hispanics. In the eight over 90 percent Hispanic counties, Romney received 26.0 percent of the vote and Perry obtained 28.9 percent. In the four over 90 percent Anglo counties, Obama garnered only 13.1 percent of the two-party vote and White received 25.4 percent in his race for governor. Move to the eight 80 to 89 percent Hispanic counties and you find the Republican candidates receiving 34.1 percent for president and 38.8 percent for governor, while in the thirty-six 80 to 90 percent Anglo counties the two Democratic candidates obtained only 25.5 percent and 28.9 percent. Among the nineteen 70 to 79 percent Hispanic counties, Romney gained 42.9 percent of the vote while Perry had 45.0 percent in his 2010 contest. However, among the forty-seven 70 to 79 percent Anglo counties, Obama fell back to only 20.1 percent of the vote and White declined to 27.8 percent. Overall, the Reuters/IPSOS exit poll indicated that statewide Romney obtained 37 percent support from Hispanic voters while Obama received votes from only 24 percent of Anglo Texans.[38] One conclusion that can be drawn from such data is that the Texas Democratic Party may have at least as serious a problem in garnering Anglo votes as the Republican Party of Texas has in winning Hispanic votes. As author Erica Grieder has noted about the prevailing Democratic perspective, "Their strategy for retaking a statewide office, any statewide office, remains the same: statistically dubious optimism with a dash of identity politics."[39]

Nevertheless, both parties appear to be focused on attracting more Hispanic voters to their side. While Texas Republicans are pleased with the election of Ted Cruz, the state's first Hispanic senator, they also confronted a loss of Hispanic legislators in 2012, leaving them with one congressman and three state representatives.[40] One group focused on expanding the base of Hispanic GOP public officials is the Hispanic Republicans of Texas, founded in 2010 by Juan Hernandez, George Antuna, and George P. Bush. Its objective is to recruit Hispanic candidates and help them win as Republicans. According to Hernandez, "All we do is find candidates, recruit them, find money for them, train them if they need it and then defend them once they are in office."[41] Bush, the grandson and nephew of two presidents and son of a governor, recently formed a campaign committee and announced he is a candidate in 2014 for the office of commissioner of the General Land Office.

Speaking of how Republicans can attract more Hispanic votes, George P. Bush said, "I don't necessarily agree with the idea that having a candidate of Hispanic origin, or someone who can speak Spanish, can automatically obtain these votes. Having said that, it's important tactically to have candidates that understand issues of the community."[42] One clear example of a non-Hispanic candidate who could obtain substantial Hispanic support was his uncle, George W. Bush, who received more than 40 percent of the Hispanic vote in his campaigns for governor and president. His appeal focused not solely on issue positions but also on being able to communicate with Hispanic voters through use of complimentary, inclusive rhetoric. As political consultant Todd Olsen noted,

> Bush knew his Spanish sucked, but he knew the families that were listening to him appreciated that he was trying, that he was genuine in that effort. When he stumbled, or sounded a bit like only George Bush could deliver the line, they laughed and said, "But you can see in his eyes, he's genuine in his delivery, and his request of us, which is, 'Trust me, I will lead, and will do so in a way that will honor what you're telling your children and grandchildren.'"[43]

As president, George W. Bush advocated immigration reform and an effort to acknowledge the presence of millions of undocumented residents, but much of the rhetoric from Republican elected officials and conservative commentators has been perceived as anti-immigrant and even anti-Hispanic. Although most often associated with GOP officials in other states, such comments and policy positions have negatively impacted the party's reach into the Hispanic community in Texas.

While the growth in Hispanic populations in many other states has been seen as a relatively new phenomenon, many Hispanic residents in Texas have deep roots in the state and are third- and fourth-generation Americans. Some come from families who settled in the area when it was part of Mexico. As Mark McKinnon noted, "Texans have a long history with Mexico and immigrants. And our politicians have generally recognized the great cultural and economic contributions that Hispanics make to American society, and so they welcome them with open arms and friendly policies."[44]

It is by reasserting such an approach and recruiting candidates who can relate to the Hispanic community that the Republicans can reclaim some of their lost support among Hispanics while retaining the overwhelming support they receive from Anglo voters. For the Democratic Party to recover its majority position in the state, it must undertake to register more Hispanics and turn them out on election day as well as increase their appeal to Anglo voters. Regardless of each party's success with the Hispanic electorate, however, Anglo voters will remain a majority of the actual, if not potential, electorate even if it is a minority of the state's overall population.

Ideological Perceptions

While many considerations come into play when people vote in a specific election contest or identify with a political party in more general terms, one important factor involves ideological self-identification.[45] Attempting to isolate the relative importance of various factors on voter decisions, studies have found that ideological self-description is an important element apart from both party identification and positions on issues.[46] In this sense, an orientation to a political outlook or philosophy gives people a "set of criteria for interpreting the world around them."[47] This distinction between ideological self-description and party identification has become less relevant in recent years with the movement of the two national political parties in more clearly, and opposite, ideological directions.

Analyzing data from the American National Election Studies for 1952 to 2004 as well as exit polls from the 2004 election, Alan Abramowitz and Kyle Saunders concluded that there is an increasing correlation between ideological self-description and party identification and that this is mainly due to the impact of ideology on party identification. "The impact of ideology on party identification was much stronger," they found, than that of social background variables such as religion, race, marital status, union membership, age, and education.[48] Further, they stated that "the increasing clarity of ideological differences between the parties during the Reagan and post-Reagan eras has made it easier for citizens to choose a party identification based on their ideological orientations."[49] Eric Wilk, in his review of recent election results, similarly concluded that "voters are becoming increasingly ideologically consistent and the last few years have witnessed a dramatic increase in the correlation between party identification and ideology."[50]

Sean Cunningham also focused on the relationship between ideology and party in Texas, identifying what he calls "cowboy conservatism" as the dominant ideological perspective in the state. According to Cunningham, the reason Democrats were able to dominate Texas politics until the 1970s was their ability to be viewed as the populist conservative party while Republicans were perceived as the party of Northern transplants and big business. "This perception fomented loyalty and loyalty evolved into tradition: Texans trusted the Democratic Party."[51] By the late 1960s, however, national concerns over a continuing war in Vietnam, urban unrest in cities across the country, and changing values began to break down this traditional Democratic loyalty. "As Texas became more industrialized, more suburban, more middle class, and more influential in shaping national political discourse, a majority of Texans began to lose confidence in the Democratic Party and increasingly questioned their partisan loyalties."[52]

What was occurring in the late 1960s and 1970s was not a change in ideology or self-perception but, rather, a change in the way Texans viewed the traditionally dominant party. It was in this manner that "Texans' understanding of the relationship between political ideology and partisan politics, and especially their understanding of what it meant to be conservative and what it meant to be liberal, was redefined."[53] John Connally's switch to the Republican Party in 1973 opened the door for more Texans to associate conservatism with the GOP, a change in perception that only accelerated with the Reagan campaigns of 1976 and 1980.

Perhaps the final blows to conservative attachments to the Democratic Party in Texas came in 1983 and 1984 with the fate of two conservative Democratic congressmen. When the leadership of the Democratic Party removed Phil Gramm from the House Budget Committee in early 1983, he resigned from Congress, switched parties, and was then elected back to the House as a Republican. One year later Gramm easily won the Republican nomination for the United States Senate and was elected in November to succeed John Tower. Meanwhile, Kent Hance also sought the Senate nomination and came in first in the Democratic primary but well short of a majority. He lost the subsequent runoff to a liberal Democrat by 1,345 votes and soon thereafter switched parties. It can be maintained that the Hance candidacy was the last clearly conservative effort to obtain a statewide Democratic Party nomination. Gramm, Hance, and many other conservatives would from that point forward fight their electoral battles under the banner of the Republican Party.

By the twenty-first century the Republican Party was clearly perceived as more conservative and the Democratic Party as more liberal. One clear example of this can be seen in a survey undertaken by the University of Texas at Austin and the *Texas Tribune* newsletter. When asked in May 2011 as to their likely voting intention for the 2012 primaries, of those who usually vote in such elections 91.1 percent of self-described liberals chose the Democratic primary while 91.7 percent of self-described conservatives said they would vote in the Republican primary.[54] From July 2008 to October 2012, fourteen voter surveys were conducted by the same joint effort, each time asking respondents for their ideological self-description. The average response over these surveys was liberal 20.4 percent, middle 29.3 percent, and conservative 49.5 percent.[55] These results are consistent with other surveys over recent years indicating a consistent conservative plurality approaching a majority.[56]

The political importance of this ideological self-description, with its relatively consistent conservative bias, has lasting implications for Texas politics. In the 2012 presidential election, 91 percent of self-identified liberals indicated they were likely to vote for Obama while 86 percent of conservatives said they were likely to vote for Romney.[57] This interaction of ideology, party identification, and candidate support raises the question as to which is more likely to change when cross-pressures mount. Recent Texas political history has shown that for many Texans ideology trumps partisanship; many conservatives turned from their traditional loyalty to the Democratic Party as it became perceived as a liberal political force.

With the growing Hispanic population, this possible conflict between ideology and partisanship becomes even more important. In the 2004 national exit poll, a minority of Hispanics described themselves as conservatives, but of these a large majority identified with the Republican Party.[58] Other national studies have shown a higher proportion of self-described liberals among Hispanics. Such was true in a study of exit polls from 1980 to 1988, where "Hispanics were more likely than Anglos to call themselves liberals and to identify with and vote for Democrats."[59] More recently, the 2011 National Survey of Latinos, conducted by the Pew Hispanic Center, found that 27 percent of all Hispanics who are United States citizens self-identify as liberals, compared to 21 percent of all adult U.S. citizens, while the percentage of conservatives among Hispanic citizens stood at 35 percent.[60]

The situation in Texas may be somewhat different, however. According to pollster Michael Baselice, 46 percent of Texas Hispanics say they are conservative, 36 percent self-describe as moderate, and 18 percent describe themselves as liberal—proportions that are very close to those of the state overall.[61]

Moving from self-identification to policy preferences, Texas Hispanics, regardless of party affiliation, hold to many policy views perceived as conservative. From a survey of 2008 Democratic primary voters, 43 percent of Hispanics were pro-life (or anti-abortion rights), 30 percent believed that environmental regulations hurt the economy, and 45 percent would favor a candidate opposed to gay marriage over one who supported it. Perhaps even more surprisingly, "fully 35 percent of Hispanics voting in the Texas Democratic primary opposed giving preventive health care to illegal immigrants because it could provide an 'incentive for illegals to have children here.'"[62]

Thus it appears that Texas remains a strongly, if not majority, conservative state, with roughly one in five adult Texans calling themselves liberal. The two political parties are clearly differentiated in terms of their ideological orientation. This has resulted in a move by many Anglo voters away from attachment to the Democratic Party and toward either independent or Republican identification. What remains to be seen is whether the sizable minority of Hispanics who call themselves conservative will retain their long-standing attachment to the Democratic Party or move to consolidate their ideological and partisan alignments. Certainly Democratic strategists are banking on Hispanic voters retaining their traditional party identification even though their self-identification and policy outlooks may be more similar to those of the Republican Party. The challenge for Republicans is to overcome the negative perceptions of their party held by many Hispanics and to expand their outreach efforts to potential candidates and officeholders. In such a situation, demographics may not be determinant as to whether one-party domination continues into the near future.

Five Decades of Continuity and Change

Since 1960 Texas has experienced both continuity and change in its political environment. The overall population of the state more than doubled, and its composition and geographical distribution have changed dramatically. Once mainly rural, Texas is now one of the most urban states in the nation, with suburban growth and rural decline. The economy described by V. O. Key at mid-twentieth century focused on oil, cattle, cotton, and banking; the Texas economy has now spread to a diversity of new areas, including high tech, health care, and transportation, while becoming the headquarters for several of the nation's major corporations. Despite all these changes, there remains a continuity of ideological perspective and public policy orientations. Just as they were in the 1960s, more Texans today are conservative than liberal or middle of the road. Texas today, as it was in 1960, is a one-party state—only the party names have changed.

Beginning in 1960 Texas entered a period of two-tiered politics that lasted for eighteen years. From 1978 to 1996, the state experienced an interlude of two-party competition, moving from Democratic dominance to a situation where Republicans were gaining strength. In 2014, the Lone Star State entered the eighteenth year of another period of one-party dominance, this time by the Republican Party. Despite the renewal of Democratic strength in most Big 6 counties and the continued growth of the state's Hispanic population, it appears that this current phase of Republican domination of Texas politics may well continue into the foreseeable future.

Notes

Chapter 1: Understanding Texas

1. V. O. Key Jr., *Southern Politics in State and Nation* (New York: Alfred A. Knopf, 1949), 254.

2. Two comprehensive overviews of Texas history are T. R. Fehrenbach, *Lone Star: A History of Texas and the Texans* (New York: Macmillan, 1968); and, more recently, Randolph Campbell, *Gone to Texas* (New York: Oxford University Press, 2012). For the period of independence, see William Ransom Hogan, *The Texas Republic: A Social and Economic History* (Austin: University of Texas Press, 1969); for more recent interpretations of various aspects of the state, see Walter Buenger and Arnoldo De Leon, eds., *Beyond Texas through Time: Breaking Away from Past Interpretations* (College Station: Texas A&M University Press, 2011). For two interesting and contrasting journalistic overviews of contemporary Texas, see Erica Grieder, *Big, Hot, Cheap, and Right: What America Can Learn from the Strange Genius of Texas* (New York: Public Affairs, 2013), and Gail Collins, *As Texas Goes: How the Lone Star State Hijacked the American Agenda* (New York: Liveright, 2012).

3. The Joint Congressional Resolution was approved by Congress on March 1, 1845, but Texas was not officially admitted as a state until President James Polk signed the resolution on December 29, 1845.

4. Michael Holmes, "Poll Shows Texans' Allegiance to State," *Austin American-Statesman*, July 24, 1997. In a survey of five hundred Texans, nearly one-fourth considered themselves Texans first and Americans second. Commented the pollster Frank Luntz, "I would argue that there's no state in the country that would have a higher state personal identification than Texas does." It must be noted, however, that some Radical Republicans in the constitutional convention of 1868 proposed creating a new state in West Texas, an idea that never took hold. Campbell, *Gone to Texas*, 278.

5. Collins, *As Texas Goes*, 13–14.

6. Bill Minutaglio, "Build the Great Wall of Texas," *Dallas Morning News*, June 14, 1985.

7. Terry Kliewer, "What Being Texan Is Really All About," *Houston Post*, March 1, 1991.

8. http://www.traveltex.com/, accessed March 24, 2013.

9. Two somewhat dated works by *New York Times* bureau chiefs provide informative overviews of our North American neighbors. See Alan Riding, *Distant Neighbors* (New York: Vantage Books, 2000), for a discussion of Mexico in the twentieth century, and Andrew H. Malcolm, *The Canadians* (New York: St. Martin's Griffin, 1991), for a readable overview on those living to our north.

10. Daniel Elazar, *American Federalism: A View from the States* (New York: Thomas Y. Crowell, 1966).

11. The original work by Keillor, *Lake Wobegon Days* (New York: Viking Penguin, 1985), was followed by a series of others featuring the various characters of this mythical village.

12. Data from the Roper Center appears in *Texas Almanac, 2004–2005* (Dallas: Dallas Morning News, 2003), 525–528.

13. *A Walk through the Twentieth Century with Bill Moyers: Marshall, Texas*, Public Broadcasting System, telecast on January 11, 1984.

14. Two sources on the political culture of South Texas are David Montejano, *Anglos and Mexicans in the Making of Texas, 1836–1986* (Austin: University of Texas Press, 1987), and Douglas E. Foley, *From Peonies to Politicos: Class and Ethnicity in a South Texas Town, 1900–1987* (Austin: University of Texas Press, 1988).

15. Quotation is from Michele Stanush, "Orphan Train," *Austin American-Statesman*, November 30, 1990. See also Stephen O'Connor, *Orphan Trains* (Chicago: University of Chicago Press, 2004).

16. "Business: Mad Eddie," *Time*, May 26, 1980. H. E. Chiles, chairman of the board of the Western Company of North America, was the spokesman for a series of sixty-second radio commercials in the late 1970s. Normally they began with an announcer asking, "What's got you mad today, Eddie?" followed by Chiles's complaints about the federal government or "the liberals." Chiles's popularity was reflected in the appearance of "I'm Mad Too, Eddie!" stickers on cars and trucks throughout Texas during the latter years of the Carter administration.

17. J. David Woodard, *The New Southern Politics* (Boulder: Lynne Rienner, 2006), 89, 94.

18. Gerald Posner, *Citizen Perot: His Life and Times* (New York: Random House, 1996); Patricia Benjamin, *The Perot Legacy: A New Political Path* (Lincoln, NE: iUniverse, 2007).

19. John Bainbridge, *The Super-Americans* (New York: Doubleday, 1961).

20. Michael E. Young, "In Texas' Population Boom, Little Loving Stays the Same," *Austin American-Statesman*, March 13, 2011.

21. "Fire Guts Town's Only Grocery," *Dallas Morning News*, September 26, 1989. Fortunately, as of 2013, there are now two grocery stores to serve the residents of Dell City.

22. Carlton Stowers, *Where Dreams Die Hard: A Small American Town and Its Six-Man Football Team* (Cambridge, MA: Da Capo, 2005). A list of some of the schools playing six-man football can be found at www.texassixmancoachesassocia tion.com, accessed August 16, 2011.

23. D. W. Meinig, *Imperial Texas: An Interpretive Essay in Cultural Geography*

(Austin: University of Texas Press, 1985). See also William C. Pool, *An Historical Atlas of Texas* (Austin: Encino, 1975).

24. Elmer H. Johnson, *The Natural Regions of Texas*, University of Texas Bulletin 3113 (1931), is out of print but discussed in Terry G. Jordan, *Texas: A Geography* (Boulder, CO: Westview, 1984).

25. www.traveltex.com, accessed August 16, 2011.

26. Houston County in East Texas is 26 percent African American according to the 2010 census. All census data are from www.census.gov. For one historical perspective, see Chandler Davidson, *Race and Class in Texas Politics* (Princeton, NJ: Princeton University Press, 1990).

27. Although fewer than 7 percent of the total, nearly 250,000 Asian Americans lived in Harris County as of the 2010 census, most within the city of Houston.

28. "Mexico Cross-Border Shopping," www.Mexico.us/travel/business/border/Mexico, accessed August 18, 2011. Large numbers of cars with Mexican tags can be seen daily in the parking lots of factory outlet malls as far north as San Marcos, thirty miles south of Austin. For the impact of drug violence on Juarez and the migration of residents to the safety of El Paso, see Will Weissert, "Ciudad Juarez Dies as Its Residents Flee," *Washington Times*, January 4, 2011.

29. For a valuable general overview with helpful maps of ethnic settlement, see Terry G. Jordan, "A Century and a Half of Ethnic Change in Texas: 1836–1986," *Southwestern Historical Quarterly* 89, no. 4 (1986): 389–421. A valuable source of information on the various ethnic influences on the state is the Institute of Texan Cultures, located in downtown San Antonio.

30. Andrew Rice, "Life on the Line," *New York Times*, July 31, 2011, compares and contrasts the neighboring cities of El Paso, Texas, and Ciudad Juarez, Chihuahua, noting the devastating impact of drug cartel violence on the latter city's residents.

31. The Pew Hispanic Center 2009 Demographic Profile of Hispanics in Texas reports that 88 percent of Hispanics in the state are of Mexican origin. Some 69 percent of all Hispanics in Texas are native-born Americans (http://pewhispanic.org/states/?stateid=TX, accessed September 6, 2011).

32. According to the 2010 census, the number of Texans identifying themselves as Hispanic was 9,460,921, a figure that is only slightly lower than the total number of residents in Texas counted in the 1960 census: 9,579,677.

33. For an interesting view of the differences in dialect and use of language throughout Texas, see E. Digby Atwood, *The Regional Vocabulary of Texas* (Austin: University of Texas Press, 1962).

34. Policies and patterns of discrimination against Mexicans in twentieth-century Texas are reviewed in Arnoldo De Leon, *They Called Them Greasers* (Austin: University of Texas Press, 1983).

35. The history of this influence on the political system is described in Dudley Lynch, *Duke of Duval* (Waco: Texian Press, 1978), and Evan Anders, *Boss Rule in South Texas* (Austin: University of Texas Press, 1982).

36. Carl H. Moneyhon, *Republicanism in Reconstruction Texas* (Austin: University of Texas Press, 1980), 194. For the period from the end of the Civil War to the beginning of the twentieth century, see Merline Pitre, *Through Many Dangers, Toils and Snares: Black Leadership in Texas, 1868–1900* (Austin: Eakin Press, 1985).

37. The quote is from Karl and Betty Wehmeyer, "Freethinkers on the Frontier," *Austin American-Statesman* (*Onward* magazine), February 17, 1987. The incident is discussed also in Campbell, *Gone to Texas*, 265.

38. For a discussion of politics in the traditionally German counties, see James R. Soukup, Clifton McCleskey, and Harry Holloway, *Party and Factional Division in Texas* (Austin: University of Texas Press, 1964), 36–40.

39. Fredericksburg, home to Admiral Chester Nimitz, is the site of the National Museum of the Pacific War, originally housed in the Nimitz Steamboat Hotel.

40. Robert L. Skrabanek, *We're Czechs* (College Station: Texas A&M University Press, 1989).

41. www.spjst.org, accessed August 27, 2011. Unfortunately, West is more recently known as the site of a massive fertilizer plant explosion in April 2013, resulting in the deaths of fifteen and the destruction of much property in the community. Brian Formby, "Investigators Blame Ammonium Nitrate in Massive West Explosion," *Dallas Morning News*, May 6, 2013.

42. Robert Plocheck, "Czech Food, Music Add to State's Culture," *Texas Almanac, 2000–2001* (Dallas: Dallas Morning News, 1999), 504–506. Virginia B. Wood, "We Gotcha Kolache," *Texas Monthly*, November 1998.

43. T. Lindsay Baker, *The First Polish Americans: Silesian Settlements in Texas* (College Station: Texas A&M University Press, 1979).

44. www.city-data.com/states/Texas-Ethnicgroups.html and castroville.com /alsatian-language.htm, accessed August 20, 2011.

45. www.Texaswendish.org, accessed August 20, 2011.

46. For a discussion of these ethnic groups in Texas, see Ellen Sweets, "From Surviving to Thriving: Vietnamese in Texas," *Texas Co-op Power*, February 2010, http://www.texascooppower.com/texas-stories/people/from-surviving-to-thriving-vietnamese-in-texas, accessed March 24, 2013; Louis B. Parks, "Houston Most Ethnically Diverse City in United States, Study Finds," *Asia Society Texas*, May 23, 2012, http://asiasociety.org/texas/houston-most-ethnically-diverse-city -united-states-study-finds, accessed May 24, 2013.

47. Surprising as it may be to some, New York was the most heavily populated state in 1960, followed by California, Pennsylvania, Illinois, and Ohio. By 1970, Texas had moved just slightly ahead of Illinois and Ohio, into fourth place. It was not until after the 1990 census that Texas surpassed New York to become the second most populous state.

48. D'Ann Petersen and Laila Assanie, "The Changing Face of Texas: Population, Projections and Implications," Federal Reserve Bank of Dallas, October 2005.

49. Ibid.

50. "Texas Population and Components of Change," Real Estate Center at Texas A&M University, http://recenter.tamu.edu/data/pop/pops/st48.asp, accessed August 23, 2011. See also E. J. McMahon and Robert Scardamalia, "Empire State's Half-Century Exodus: A Population Migration Overview," *Research Bulletin* 6, no. 1 (August 2011), Empire Center for New York State Policy, Albany, NY.

51. Joel Kotkin, "The Next Big Boom Towns in the U.S.," *Forbes*, July 6, 2011.

52. Ibid.

Chapter 2: Dividing the State

1. A clear example of this geographical spread across political boundaries is the city of Dallas, whose limits extend beyond Dallas County into Collin, Denton, Kaufman, and Rockwall Counties.

2. As of 2010, Collin County had a population of 782,341, while Hidalgo County had 774,769.

3. The spread of cities into more than one county makes the assignment of a city to a county less than precise. Grand Prairie actually spreads into Tarrant County, while the city of Carrollton flows into Collin, Denton, and Dallas Counties. For present purposes, a city is associated with the county in which most of its territory is currently located.

4. A classic fictional depiction of mid-twentieth-century Austin is Billy Lee Brammer, *The Gay Place* (Austin: University of Texas Press, 1961). For a history of the radical political tradition in and around the University of Texas campus from the 1950s to the early 1970s, see Doug Rossinow, *The Politics of Authenticity: Liberalism, Christianity, and the New Left in America* (New York: Columbia University Press, 1998).

5. The Anglo category comprises those responding as White, non-Hispanic. The Other category includes Asian, Pacific Islander, some other race alone, or two or more races, all non-Hispanic. The Other category is predominantly Asian in Texas.

6. For comparative reasons I have reclassified one county included by the census bureau in the Dallas MSA and placed it in the Small Town category. That county is Delta, located far to the east of Dallas, with a total population of 5,231 in 2010, a decline from the 5,327 counted in 2000 and the 5,860 residents fifty years ago.

7. While the city of Dallas is mostly in Dallas County and El Paso is in El Paso County, Texas has a number of cities not located in the county of the same name, including Houston, Austin, Sherman, Caldwell, and Jefferson. I will endeavor to specify city when I refer to such locations, but throughout this work the major geographical point of reference will be the county.

8. Les Christie, "The Richest (and Poorest) Places in the U.S.," *Money*, August 28, 2007.

9. As of 2011, Grayson County (Sherman and Denison) was the only Other Metro county without commercial air service. Midland and Ector share an airport, as do Potter and Randall Counties.

10. Only six counties with less than 2,500 in 1960 increased in population over the fifty-year period: Glasscock, Hartley, Irion, Jeff Davis, Oldham, and Real.

11. Poll tax receipts and an explanation of the requirements for voting are from the *Texas Almanac, 1961–1962*, 476–477.

Chapter 3: A Century of One-Party Politics

1. Sean P. Cunningham, *Cowboy Conservatism: Texas and the Rise of the Modern Right* (Lexington: University Press of Kentucky, 2010), 14. See also Michael

Lind, *Made in Texas: George W. Bush and the Southern Takeover of American Politics* (New York: Basic Books, 2003), 1–50.

2. One candidate for governor (W. B. Ochiltree) received 25.4 percent of the vote as the Whig candidate in 1853, while D. C. Dickson obtained 37.9 percent running on the American (Know-Nothing) ticket in 1855. Sam Houston lost as the American Party candidate in 1857 and was elected as an "Independent Democrat" two years later. The most comprehensive source for historical election data is *Congressional Quarterly's Guide to U.S. Elections* (Washington: Congressional Quarterly, 1975). It provides most of the election statistics for statewide and federal elections cited here. The Elections Division of the Texas Secretary of State maintains primary and general election returns from 1992 to the present; some earlier data is available from the Lorenzo de Zavala State Archives and Library. A valuable printed source for some election returns by county is Kingston, Attlesey, and Crawford, eds., *The Texas Almanac's Political History of Texas*.

3. Paul D. Casdorph, *A History of the Republican Party in Texas: 1865–1965* (Austin: Pemberton Press, 1965), 4. As in most other Southern states, Republicans became divided into what were described as "lily white" and "Black and Tan" factions, each battling for control of the party and federal patronage up to 1932. For the political situation leading up to the formation of the party in Texas see James A. Baggett, "Birth of the Texas Republican Party," *Southwestern Historical Quarterly* 77, no. 1 (July 1974): 1–20.

4. Carl H. Moneyhon, *Republicanism in Reconstruction Texas* (Austin: University of Texas Press, 1980), 103. The Union League, originally formed in the North to rally support for the Union cause, became an organizing force for newly enfranchised Blacks during Reconstruction. Carl H. Moneyhon, "Union League," *Handbook of Texas Online*, published by the Texas State Historical Association, http://www.tshaonline.org/handbook/online/articles/wau01, accessed May 10, 2012.

5. Waller County was founded in 1873 and thus its votes were counted separately beginning with the 1876 presidential election.

6. Moneyhon, *Republicanism in Reconstruction Texas*, 123.

7. Casdorph, *History*, 15. Both J. W. Flanagan and Morgan C. Hamilton began their terms in March 1870, with Flanagan serving in the senate until 1875 and Hamilton until 1877.

8. Paul D. Casdorph, *Republicans, Negroes, and Progressives in the South, 1912–1916* (University: University of Alabama Press, 1981), 1. Casdorph here is quoting from W. J. Cash, *The Mind of the South* (New York: Alfred A. Knopf, 1944), 129.

9. Roscoe Martin, *The People's Party in Texas* (Austin: University of Texas Press, 1970). Reprint of bulletin first published in 1933, 16.

10. The wavering support for Reconstruction policies by the national Republican Party is covered in Charles W. Calhoun, *Conceiving a New Republic: The Republican Party and the Southern Question, 1869–1900* (Lawrence: University Press of Kansas, 2006).

11. www.texasgop.org/overview-and-history, accessed September 23, 2011.

12. Hanes Walton Jr., *Black Republicans: The Politics of the Black and Tans* (Metuchen, NJ: Scarecrow, 1975), 63.

13. Casdorph, *History*, 46. A valuable profile of Davis can be found in Carl H.

Moneyhon, *Edmund J. Davis: Civil War General, Republican Leader, Reconstruction Governor* (Fort Worth: Texas Christian University Press, 2010).

14. Walton, *Black Republicans*, 64.

15. From 1860 to 1912, Republicans controlled the White House for all but the two nonconsecutive terms of President Grover Cleveland (1885–1889; 1893–1897).

16. Martin, *People's Party*, 265. As Martin states, "The writer distinctly remembers the day not many years ago when, in a county in East Texas, his grandfather pointed out to him a citizen who looked like other men but who was set apart by virtue of his political beliefs. He was a Republican, the only white one in that part of the county."

17. Chandler Davidson, *Race and Class in Texas Politics* (Princeton, NJ: Princeton University Press, 1990), 18–23.

18. Martin, *People's Party*, 22–23.

19. Ibid., 210–211.

20. Walton, *Black Republicans*, 66. See also Richard B. Sherman, *The Republican Party and Black America: From McKinley to Hoover, 1896–1933* (Charlottesville: University Press of Virginia, 1973).

21. Davidson, *Race and Class in Texas Politics*, 21.

22. Moneyhon, *Republicanism in Reconstruction Texas*, 194.

23. *Smith v. Allwright*, 321 U.S. 649 (1944). When the Supreme Court first ruled the White primary unconstitutional in *Nixon v. Herndon*, 273 U.S. 536 (1927), the Texas legislature enacted a law ceding control of primary elections to the political parties. For further discussion of the various tactics used to exclude Blacks from the Democratic primary, see Key, *Southern Politics in State and Nation*, 619–624.

24. While their ability to influence public policy was not much greater, Mexican Americans frequently did vote, especially in South Texas counties under the direction of a *patrón*, or boss. See Anders, *Boss Rule*.

25. In the Texas legislature only a handful of non-Democratic or Republican candidates served, all but one serving only one term. One Populist was elected in 1902, one "no party" in 1914, four American Party candidates in 1920, and two independents in 1933, including Homer L. Leonard of McAllen, who served three terms. The Socialist Party also ran unsuccessful candidates in the early part of the twentieth century.

26. Casdorph, *History, 122*. Vote totals for the Black and Tan electors from *Congressional Quarterly's Guide to U.S. Elections*, 303.

27. Kevin P. Phillips, *The Emerging Republican Majority* (New Rochelle, NY: Arlington House, 1969), 271.

28. Technically one other Republican briefly represented a district centered on the city of Amarillo. Ben H. Guill won a special election in May 1950 but was then defeated in the November 1950 general election.

29. According to Paul Casdorph, "The party was generally pleased with Wurzbach's election even if Creager and the regular organization were not. The latter feared that Wurzbach, by exercising congressional courtesy, would interfere with their control of the patronage" (Casdorph, *History*, 123).

30. Creager's candidate won, 11,215 to 4,047 (ibid., 132).

31. According to historian T. R. Fehrenbach, "There was probably no injustice involved. As in most close races in Texas, Johnson men had not defrauded Stevenson, but successfully outfrauded him" (Fehrenbach, *Lone Star*, 659). See also Campbell, *Gone to Texas*, 413–414; Robert Dallek, *Lone Star Rising: Lyndon Johnson and His Times, 1908–1960* (New York: Oxford University Press, 1991), 330–348.

32. Julius Real of Kerr County was elected to the senate in 1908 and 1912 and then served again from 1925 to 1929. His district comprised much of the historically German areas of Bexar, Bandera, Kendall, Kerr, and Gillespie Counties.

33. www.texasgop.org/overview-and-history, accessed September 23, 2011. In each of these situations, only a handful of counties actually conducted a Republican primary; in most Texas counties, no volunteers could be found willing to identify as Republicans and conduct a primary election. When the party's candidate exceeded the hundred-thousand-vote level in 1944, Republicans convinced the legislature to increase the required minimum to two hundred thousand. See O. Douglas Weeks, "Texas: Land of Conservative Expansiveness," in *The Changing Politics of the South*, ed. William C. Havard (Baton Rouge: Louisiana State University Press, 1972), 209.

34. Casdorph, *History*, cites a 1930 Republican primary attracting 9,777 voters and a 1934 primary with 1,554 votes cast, followed by primaries in 1954 and 1958 involving some 11,000 and 16,000 participants, respectively. Of the roughly 16,000 votes in 1958, 11,000 were cast in Dallas County, where GOP Congressman Bruce Alger was challenged by Grover Cantrell, local leader of the Communications Workers Union. Cantrell's objective was to keep conservatives from taking part in the Democratic primary and precinct caucuses by pushing many of them into the Republican primary to protect Alger. Hawkins Henley Menefee Jr., "The Two-Party Democrats, the Study of a Political Faction," master's thesis, University of Texas, 1970, 34.

35. Weeks, "Texas: Land of Conservative Expansiveness," 211.

36. Presidential election years saw more voters in the general election only in 1940, 1944, 1952, and 1956. Even in the heated presidential election of 1948 involving President Truman, Thomas Dewey, Henry Wallace, and J. Strom Thurmond, more Texans voted in the Democratic primary.

37. Roger Olien, *From Token to Triumph* (Dallas: Southern Methodist University Press, 1982), 9.

38. Ibid., 24.

39. Davidson, *Race and Class in Texas Politics*, 198. The quote originally appeared in Jan Jarboe, "Lord of the Valley," *Texas Monthly* 14 (January 1986), 232.

40. Patronage and control of the party were major factors in the longstanding (1920–1931) feud between Creager and Congressman Harry Wurzbach, one of the very few Republicans in elective office during this time. For the debilitating effect of this conflict on the party, see Olien, *From Token to Triumph*, 30–57.

41. Ibid., 64.

42. Davidson, *Race and Class in Texas Politics*, 25. Davidson's comments echo those of V. O. Key, who in his classic work of 1949 maintained that "in Texas the vague outlines of a politics are emerging in which irrelevancies are pushed into the background and people divide broadly along liberal and conservatives lines,"

which he described as "terms of common usage in political discourse in the state" (*Southern Politics in State and Nation*, 255).

43. Key, *Southern Politics in State and Nation*, 259. Writing thirty years after Key and speaking of Democratic Party factionalism from the 1940s up to the late 1970s, Malcolm E. Jewell and David M. Olson noted that "labels such as 'liberal' and 'conservative' are inevitably vague and imperfect, but they are used more frequently in Texas than in most states by both candidates and observers of the political scene. Democratic factionalism in Texas is based less on individual personalities and dynasties than on ideology and socioeconomic interests" (*American State Political Parties and Elections* [Homewood, IL: Dorsey, 1978], 172).

44. George Norris Green, *The Establishment in Texas Politics: The Primitive Years, 1938–1957* (Westport, CT: Greenwood, 1979), 29–30. The vote at the Democratic State Convention was overwhelming, with 1,796 votes for the Garner delegation to 217 for the national convention delegates pledged to Roosevelt. At the Democratic National Convention of 1940 Garner received forty-six delegate votes from Texas but Roosevelt overwhelmingly won renomination. O. Douglas Weeks, *Texas Presidential Politics in 1952* (Austin: Institute of Public Affairs, University of Texas, 1953), 6.

45. Green, *Establishment in Texas Politics*, 30.

46. Cunningham, *Cowboy Conservatism*, 25.

47. According to Walter Hall, a wealthy liberal banker, "That was the beginning of the modern Texas liberal movement." Davidson, *Race and Class in Texas Politics*, 159.

48. Kari Frederickson, *The Dixiecrat Revolt and the End of the Solid South, 1932–1968* (Chapel Hill: University of North Carolina Press, 2001), 157–158.

49. As discussed later, Shivers and Daniel entered the 1952 election as the nominees of both the Democratic and Republican Parties, the only instance in which a candidate was on the ballot twice since the 1896 Democratic-Populist presidential campaign of William Jennings Bryan.

50. For a discussion of conservative Democratic areas of support for gubernatorial and senatorial nominations and within the Texas legislature during the 1950s, see Soukup, McCleskey, and Holloway, *Party and Factional Division in Texas*, 67–89.

51. Davidson, *Race and Class in Texas Politics*, 158.

52. For a discussion of the liberal success in 1976, see ibid., 180–197.

53. Alexander P. Lamis, *The Two-Party South*, 2nd ed. (New York: Oxford University Press, 1990), 193–201. Thure Barnett Cannon, "The Texas Political System: Shifting Dynamics in Political Party Power," master's thesis, University of Texas at Austin, 1998, 8–10.

54. Numan V. Bartley and Hugh D. Graham, *Southern Politics and the Second Reconstruction* (Baltimore, MD: Johns Hopkins University Press, 1975), 83.

55. James V. Allred served as governor from 1935 to 1939 and was a strong supporter of the New Deal. Allred led the pro-FDR forces against the Texas Regulars in 1944 and served as a federal district and court of appeals judge as well as a candidate against Senator W. Lee "Pappy" O'Daniel in 1942. The Allred campaigns, however, were not seen by most observers and voters as clear-cut liberal-conservative conflicts.

56. Cunningham, *Cowboy Conservatism*, 28. For an overview of liberal Democratic areas of strength, see Soukup, McCleskey, and Holloway, *Party and Factional Division in Texas*, 90–139.

57. Davidson, *Race and Class in Texas Politics*, 46. Rainey obtained 362,655 votes versus the 701,018 cast for Jester in the runoff.

58. Yarborough received 364,838 votes to 290,869 for Dies and 219,591 for Hutcheson in an election without any party designation, with other candidates receiving a scattering of votes. Yarborough's plurality victory led conservative Democrats to change the election law for future special elections to require a runoff when no candidate received a majority of the vote. For a discussion of the various liberal-conservative contests from 1946 to 1958, see Bartley and Graham, *Southern Politics and the Second Reconstruction*, 40–44.

59. Patrick L. Cox, *Ralph W. Yarborough: The People's Senator* (Austin: University of Texas Press, 2009).

60. Bartley and Graham, *Southern Politics and the Second Reconstruction*, 43.

61. Cannon, "The Texas Political System," 14.

62. Davidson, *Race and Class in Texas Politics*, 155–158. Texas citizens do not register by party. Thus, a voter can choose whether to participate in either party primary or none. However, casting a vote in one party's primary prohibits voting in the other party's runoff or convention process during that year. Conservatives who voted in a Republican primary could not then serve as delegates to a Democratic convention or vote in a runoff primary that year.

63. Creager's battles for control and influence within the party are discussed in Olien, *From Token to Triumph*, 58–101. As Olien sums up this period, "From 1932 to 1948, general elections were an insignificant aspect of the history of the Republican party in Texas" (64).

64. Michael Bowen, "The First Southern Strategy—The Taft and the Dewey/Eisenhower Factions in the GOP," in *Painting Dixie Red*, ed. Glenn Feldman (Gainesville: University Press of Florida, 2011), 223.

65. The internal battles between the Taft forces as represented by Creager and the Dewey forces encouraged by Brownell are discussed in Olien, *From Token to Triumph*, 87–101.

66. "H. J. Porter, Key Republican in Texas in 50s, Is Dead at 90," *New York Times*, December 10, 1986.

67. Olien, *From Token to Triumph*, 104.

68. Ibid., 105.

69. Casdorph, *History*, 174.

70. Olien, *From Token to Triumph*, 113.

71. For a more thorough discussion of the 1952 presidential nominating contest, see Michael Bowen, *The Roots of Modern Conservatism: Dewey, Taft, and the Battle for the Soul of the Republican Party* (Chapel Hill: University of North Carolina Press, 2011), especially 124–129. Other valuable sources are George H. Mayer, *The Republican Party, 1854–1966* (New York: Oxford University Press, 1967), 487–491; John Robert Greene, *The Crusade: The Presidential Election of 1952* (Lanham, MD: University Press of America, 1985), 91–94, 102–119; and Olien, *From Token to Triumph*, 112–138. The Texas conventions and election are covered thoroughly in Weeks, *Texas Presidential Politics in 1952*.

72. Those attending a Republican precinct convention were required to sign a statement maintaining that "I am a Republican, and desire to participate in Republican Party activities in the year 1952." This nonbinding statement did not prevent them, however, from subsequently voting in the Democratic primary later that year.

73. After the Porter delegation was recognized Texas cast thirty-three votes for Eisenhower and five for Taft before all thirty-eight shifted to Eisenhower following the first ballot results. "A Summary Statement on Behalf of the Porter Slate of Delegates, Chicago, July 9, 1952," pamphlet available at the Perry-Castañeda Library, University of Texas at Austin (JK2358 T4 R4685 19852).

74. Olien, *From Token to Triumph*, 169.

75. Cunningham, *Cowboy Conservatism*, 29.

76. For a detailed discussion of Shivers and his role in 1950s Texas politics, see Ricky F. Dobbs, *Yellow Dogs and Republicans: Allan Shivers and Texas Two-Party Politics* (College Station: Texas A&M University Press, 2005).

77. Privately printed document, a copy of which is available in the Perry-Castañeda Library, University of Texas at Austin (E816T78).

78. The resolution adopted by the Democratic State Convention on September 9, 1952, urged "every Democrat in Texas vote and work for the election of Dwight D. Eisenhower for President and Richard Nixon for Vice President." Weeks, *Texas Presidential Politics in 1952*, 88.

79. Cunningham, *Cowboy Conservatism*, 29–30.

80. Olien, *From Token to Triumph*, 134–136. The lone exception was agriculture commissioner John C. White, who would serve as secretary of agriculture and chairman of the Democratic National Committee during the Carter administration.

81. Jack Brooks won in the second district with 79 percent of the vote against Republican nominee R. C. Reed.

82. Casdorph, *History*, 198.

83. Donald S. Strong, *The 1952 Presidential Election in the South* (University: Bureau of Public Administration, University of Alabama, 1955), 384.

84. Fehrenbach, *Lone Star*, 660.

85. Campbell, *Gone to Texas*, 417.

86. Cunningham, *Cowboy Conservatism*, 31; Cannon, "The Texas Political System," 8. While remaining a Democrat, Shivers continued to endorse Republican candidates during his career, backing Ike again in 1956 and Nixon in 1960 as well as John Tower, Bill Clements, and Ronald Reagan in subsequent campaigns.

87. Writing in 1955, Donald S. Strong predicted that "the greatest stimulus to a grass-roots Republican party in any southern state would be a long series of victories by liberal candidates for state office in the Democratic primaries" (Strong, *The 1952 Presidential Election in the South*, 385). It would take several years before this would occur.

88. Cunningham, *Cowboy Conservatism*, 31.

89. Olien, *From Token to Triumph*, 152.

90. O. Douglas Weeks, "Republicanism and Conservatism in the South," *Southwestern Social Science Quarterly* 36 (December 1955): 252.

91. Olien, *From Token to Triumph*, 169.

92. Ibid., 158.

93. Clifton McCleskey, *The Government and Politics of Texas* (Boston: Little, Brown, 1963), 91. This point is also made in Alexander Heard, *A Two-Party South?* (Chapel Hill: University of North Carolina Press, 1952), especially chapter 5.

94. As quoted in Menefee, "The Two-Party Democrats," 4.

95. David M. Olson, "Towards a Typology of County Party Organizations," *Southwestern Social Science Quarterly* 48 (1968): 564.

96. O. Douglas Weeks, *Texas One-Party Politics in 1956* (Austin: Institute of Public Affairs, University of Texas, 1957), 5.

97. Ibid., 7.

98. Olien, *From Token to Triumph*, 140.

99. Unnamed leader quoted by Menefee, "The Two-Party Democrats," 26.

100. Weeks, *Texas One-Party Politics in 1956*, 49.

101. *Congressional Quarterly's Guide to U.S. Elections*, 505.

102. Olien, *From Token to Triumph*, 149–150.

103. As quoted in Meg McKain Grier, *Grassroots Women* (Boerne, TX: Wingscope, 2001), ix.

104. Casdorph, *History*, 210–212.

105. Campbell, *Gone to Texas*, 434–435.

106. The 1952 data are from Stefan D. Haag, Gary A. Keith, and Rex C. Peebles, *Texas Politics and Government*, 3rd ed. (New York: Longman, 2003), 121. Data for 1962 are from the *Houston Post*, December 23, 1962. Poll numbers vary within a small range. One 1952 survey showed 7 percent Republican and only 59 percent Democratic, while a 1964 survey indicated the GOP percentage had slipped to 8 percent and the Democratic self-identifiers constituted 65 percent of the Texas electorate. For the 1964 data, see James A. Dyer, Arnold Vedlitz, and David B. Hill, "New Voters, Switchers, and Political Party Realignment in Texas," *Western Political Quarterly* 41 (March 1988): 156.

Chapter 4: Stirrings and Small Cracks

1. James W. Lamare, J. L. Polinard, James Wenzel, and Robert D. Wrinkle, "Texas: Lone Star (Wars) State," in *The New Politics of the Old South*, ed. Charles S. Bullock III and Mark J. Rozell, 3rd ed. (Lanham, MD: Rowman and Littlefield, 2007), 286.

2. Gilbert Garcia, *Reagan's Comeback* (San Antonio, TX: Trinity University Press, 2012), 87.

3. John G. Tower, *Consequences: A Personal and Political Memoir* (Boston: Little, Brown, 1991), 13. Tower is quoting here from English essayist and poet Samuel Johnson.

4. Chapter 2, "Dividing the State," provides a listing of the Big 6, Suburban, and Other Metro counties, along with a description of the 198 Small Town counties. These specific groupings of counties, as opposed to a more general use of the words, are used here and in future chapters.

5. David Richards, *Once upon a Time in Texas: A Liberal in the Lone Star State* (Austin: University of Texas Press, 2002), 222–223.

6. The endorsement of Tower was considered significant enough to be included in a compendium of memorable articles in the publication's history and can be found in Char Miller, ed., *Fifty Years of the "Texas Observer"* (San Antonio, TX: Trinity University Press, 2004), 161–163.

7. Quoted in Menefee: "The Two-Party Democrats," 32.

8. John Knaggs, *Two-Party Texas: The John Tower Era, 1961–1984* (Austin: Eakin Press, 1986), 15.

9. Richards, *Once upon a Time in Texas*, 224. Richards's former wife, Ann, would become governor of Texas in 1990, the last Democratic governor to date.

10. Knaggs, *Two-Party Texas*, 7.

11. Kenneth Bridges, *Twilight of the Texas Democrats* (College Station: Texas A&M University Press, 2008), 11.

12. The totals and percentages here and in table 4.1 do not include the 584,269 votes received by George Wallace in the 1968 election (19.0 percent of the Texas total).

13. In every nonpresidential year through 1958, more votes were cast in the Democratic primary than in the November general election. In 1958, more than 1.3 million voters took part in the primary while less than 800,000 votes were cast in the general election. From 1962 to the present, the reverse has been true.

14. The office of state treasurer was abolished in 1995, leaving twenty-nine statewide elected positions.

15. State Representative Maurice Angly Jr. of Austin was an exception in his unsuccessful 1972 race for state treasurer. Knaggs, *Two-Party Texas*, 175–176.

16. Running in the same election that would re-elect John Tower and put William P. Clements Jr. in the Governor's Mansion, James A. Baker III mounted a well-financed race for attorney general but garnered just short of the competitive measure (44.1%), losing to the future governor Mark White by 250,000 votes. It would not be until 1998 when a Republican would first be elected to this office.

17. Texas House members are elected for two-year terms. Texas senators serve four-year staggered terms except that all thirty-one senate seats are up for election after reapportionment, which impacted the elections of 1962 and 1972. Data on races contested by Republicans from Jewell and Olson, *American State Political Parties and Elections*, 217, 242.

18. Real was the only Republican to serve in the Texas Senate in the twentieth century until 1967. He served from 1909 to 1915 and again from 1925 to 1929 (Casdorph, *History*, 93–94, 130).

19. Wayne Thorburn, "The Growth of Republican Representation in the Texas Legislature: Coattails, Incumbency, Special Elections, and Urbanization," *Texas Journal of Political Studies* 11, no. 2 (1991): 16–28.

20. Gregory A. Caldeira and Samuel C. Patterson, "Bringing Home the Votes: Electoral Outcomes in State Legislative Races," *Political Behavior* 4 (1982): 63.

21. Data for 1946–1963 from Austin Ranney, "Parties in State Politics," in *Politics in the American States*, 1st ed., ed. Herbert Jacob and Kenneth N. Vines (Boston: Little, Brown, 1965), 63–65. Data for 1962–1973 from Ranney, "Parties in State Politics," in *Politics in the American States*, 3rd ed., ed. Herbert Jacob and Kenneth N. Vines (Boston: Little, Brown, 1976), 59–61. Data for 1974–1980 from John F. Bibby, Cornelius P. Cotter, James L. Gibson, and Robert J. Hucks-

horn, "Parties in State Politics," in *Politics in the American States*, 4th ed., ed. Virginia Gray, Herbert Jacob, and Kenneth N. Vines (Boston: Little, Brown, 1983), 65–69.

22. Malcolm E. Jewell and Sarah M. Morehouse, *Political Parties and Elections in American States*, 4th ed. (Washington, DC: Congressional Quarterly, 2000), 28–32.

23. Menefee, "The Two-Party Democrats," 5.

24. Charles P. Elliot, "Democratic and Republican County Party Chairmen in Texas," in *Texas: Readings in Politics, Government and Public Policy*, ed. Richard H. Kraemer and Philip W. Barnes (San Francisco: Chandler, 1971), 40–49.

25. McCleskey, *Government and Politics of Texas*, 112.

26. Now Barbara Culver Clack, she is quoted in Grier, *Grassroots Women*, 259.

27. Kenneth Thompson, "Texas: A One-Party State," *New Guard*, July 1965, 6.

28. Knaggs, *Two-Party Texas*, 107.

29. Data on the number of Republican county officials was compiled from a number of sources, including L. Tucker Gibson Jr. and Clay Robison, *Government and Politics in the Lone Star State: Theory and Practice*, 6th ed. (Upper Saddle River, NJ: Pearson Prentice Hall, 2008), 178; William E. Maxwell, Ernest Crain, and Adolfo Santos, *Texas Politics Today* (Boston: Wadsworth Cengage, 2010), 116; Jon Ford, "GOP Group Forming to Raise Party's Texas Office Holders," *Austin American-Statesman*, March 1, 1975; Gregory Scott Davidson, "Three Phases of Republican Development and Competition in Texas, 1865–1997," master's thesis, University of Texas at Austin, 1997, 112.

30. Paul Burka, "Ticket to Ride?" *Texas Monthly*, October 1978.

31. Angus Campbell, Philip E. Converse, Warren E. Miller, and Donald E. Stokes, *The American Voter: An Abridgement* (New York: John Wiley and Sons, 1964), 67.

32. Richard Murray, "The 1982 Texas Election in Perspective," *Texas Journal of Political Studies* 5 (Spring 1983): 51.

33. Report, January 1966, p. 12, box 4, John Knaggs Papers, Southwestern University Special Collections, Georgetown, TX.

34. Thomas M. Carsey and Geoffrey C. Layman, "Changing Sides or Changing Minds? Party Identification and Policy Preferences in the American Electorate," *American Journal of Political Science* 50, no. 2 (April 2006): 467.

35. Cunningham, *Cowboy Conservatism*, 5.

36. Bridges, *Twilight of the Texas Democrats*, 19.

37. Data for 1952 from Haag, Keith, and Peebles, *Texas Politics and Government*, 121; 1962 from Belden Poll, November 1962, as reported in the *Houston Post*, December 23, 1962; 1964 and 1974 from Gibson and Robison, *Government and Politics in the Lone Star State*, 179; 1966 from Opinion Research Corporation, September 1966, copy in John G. Tower Papers; 1972 from Olien, *From Token to Triumph*, 227; 1978 from Texas Poll, August 1978, in Murray, "The 1982 Texas Election in Perspective," 51. Some surveys are of registered voters while others are of likely voters. Additionally, some of the surveys ask independents whether they lean toward one party or the other; those who do may be included as identifying with the Democratic or Republican Party or remain classified as indepen-

dent. This may account for the range of 10 percent to 37 percent in those classified as independent.

38. Jewell and Olson, *American State Political Parties and Elections*, 21.

39. Key, *Southern Politics in State and Nation*, 278.

40. O. Douglas Weeks, "Texas: Land of Conservative Expansiveness," in *The Changing Politics of the South*, ed. William C. Havard, 211.

41. Olson, "Toward a Typology of County Party Organizations," 564.

42. Cannon, "Texas Political System," 8.

43. Malcolm E. Jewell, "Participation in Southern Primaries," in *Party Politics in the South*, ed. Robert P. Steed, Lawrence W. Moreland, and Tod A. Baker (New York: Praeger, 1980), 20.

44. Bridges, *Twilight of the Texas Democrats*, 14.

45. Monroe Lee Billington, *The Political South in the Twentieth Century* (New York: Charles Scribner's Sons, 1975), 170–171. The same conclusion was reached by Lamis, *The Two-Party South*, 196.

46. Davidson, "Three Phases of Republican Development and Competition in Texas," 242.

47. Ibid., 202.

48. Olien, *From Token to Triumph*, 197.

49. Ibid., 83.

Chapter 5: Toward a Two-Party Texas

1. James Q. Wilson, *The Amateur Democrat: Club Politics in Three Cities* (Chicago: University of Chicago Press, 1962), 3.

2. "Texas: Rallying to Resign," *Time*, October 27, 1961; Knaggs, *Two-Party Texas*, 4.

3. While Barry Goldwater's *The Conscience of a Conservative* (Shepherdsville, KY: Victor, 1960) and William F. Buckley Jr.'s *Up from Liberalism* (New York: Hillman Books, 1961) are widely credited with activating many young people in the early 1960s, Senator Tower's own paperback, *A Program for Conservatives* (New York: A Macfadden Capitol Hill Book, 1962), was important in creating a national following for him, especially among younger Americans.

4. The involvement of these individuals is discussed in greater detail throughout Knaggs, *Two-Party Texas*.

5. Ibid., 7.

6. Wayne Thorburn, *A Generation Awakes: Young Americans for Freedom and the Creation of the Conservative Movement* (Ottawa, IL: Jameson Books, 2010), 78.

7. Ibid., 122.

8. Olien, *From Token to Triumph*, 61, 110, 111.

9. Quoted in Grier, *Grassroots Women*, 198.

10. Thorburn, *A Generation Awakes*, 55–56.

11. Billington, *The Political South in the Twentieth Century*, 170. The significant differences between the early 1960s and the latter part of the decade are outlined in Thorburn, *A Generation Awakes*, 39–42.

12. Quoted in Garcia, *Reagan's Comeback*, 40–41.

13. Interview with Ernest Angelo Jr., Midland, Texas, March 21, 2012.

14. Thomas W. Pauken, *The Thirty Years War: The Politics of the Sixties Generation* (Ottawa, IL: Jameson Books, 1995), 26.

15. Folder on Texas Young Republican Federation activity, James C. Oberwetter Papers, Southwestern University Special Collections, Georgetown, TX.

16. Quoted in Grier, *Grassroots Women*, 195.

17. Angelo interview, March 21, 2012.

18. Quoted in Grier, *Grassroots Women*, 197.

19. Grier, *Grassroots Women*, 194–195.

20. Karl Rove, *Courage and Consequence: My Life as a Conservative in the Fight* (New York: Threshold Editions, 2010), 32–33.

21. http://www.texasmonthly.com/blogs/burkablog/?p=1846, accessed July 20, 2012.

22. The initial invitation letter and related material can be found in the Camp Wannameetagop folder, Cyndi Taylor Krier Papers, 1963–1972, University of Texas at San Antonio Libraries Special Collections.

23. Doug Harlan, "A Summer Camp for Some 'Youngish' Republicans," *San Antonio Express-News*, August 1, 1982.

24. Jonathan Gurwitz, "Have Things Gone Sour in Sugar Land?" *Wall Street Journal*, March 24, 2005.

25. Doug Harlan, "Camp Wannameetagopers Believe That Hance Has a Chance," *San Antonio Light*, August 12, 1985.

26. http://www.texasmonthly.com/blogs/burkablog/?p=1846.

27. Ibid., 4.

28. Olien, *From Token to Triumph*, 143.

29. Cyndi Taylor, "Beryl Milburn: The Making of a Conservative," *Austin People Today*, April 1974, 20, 22. Copy located in Cyndi Taylor Krier Papers.

30. Grier, *Grassroots Women*, 211.

31. Ibid., 214.

32. Quotes from Ibid., 51, 55, 56.

33. Olien, *From Token to Triumph*, 202. The 2012 totals are from www.tfrw.org, accessed July 20, 2012.

34. Grier, *Grassroots Women*, 399.

35. Cunningham, *Cowboy Conservatism*, 207–208.

36. Grier, *Grassroots Women*, 207.

37. www.artexas.org/history, accessed July 20, 2012.

38. Knaggs, *Two-Party Texas*, 189.

39. Ibid., 241.

40. George Seay, "ART's Texas Success Is a Blueprint for Conservatives Everywhere," *Texas Insider*, January 12, 2011, http://www.texasinsider.org/?s=sEAY&submit.x=13&submit.y=9, accessed September 1, 2013.

41. www.artexas.org/hispanic-voter-network, accessed July 21, 2012.

42. John G. Tower, *Consequences*, discusses his 1989 nomination and rejection by the Senate.

43. See chapter 3. For a historical perspective on Texas liberalism, see David

O'Donald Cullen and Kyle G. Wilkison, eds., *The Texas Left: The Radical Roots of Lone Star Liberalism* (College Station: Texas A&M University Press, 2010).

44. For a fascinating fictional description of liberal Austin during the post–World War II period, see Brammer, *The Gay Place*, and the nonfiction history presented in Doug Rossinow, *The Politics of Authenticity*. Indicative of Austin's continuing liberalism was a statewide vote on marriage. When Texas voters amended the state constitution in 2005 to declare marriage as consisting only of the union of one man and one woman, 76 percent of the state's voters approved and it carried in 253 of the state's 254 counties; the exception was Travis County, whose largest city is Austin.

45. Patrick Cox, *Ralph W. Yarborough: The People's Senator* (Austin: University of Texas Press, 2009).

46. Davidson, *Race and Class in Texas Politics*, 159–160, 164–165; Michael T. Kaufman, "Maury Maverick Jr, 82, Champion of the Unpopular," *New York Times*, February 3, 2003; Richards, *Once upon a Time in Texas*, 226; Mike Shropshire and Frank Schaefer, *The Thorny Rose of Texas* (New York: Birch Lane, 1994), 66–97.

47. Davidson, *Race and Class in Texas Politics*, 155–179, discusses these efforts in detail. Copies of various printed materials from the Democrats of Texas organization from 1957 to 1960 can be found in the Allen Duckworth Papers, Dolph Briscoe Center for American History, University of Texas at Austin.

48. Campbell, *Gone to Texas*, 419.

49. Ronnie Dugger, "Randolph, Frankie Carter," *Handbook of Texas Online*, http://www.tshaonline.org/handbook/online/articles/fra34, accessed July 23, 2012.

50. Ann Fears Crawford, *Frankie: Mrs. R. D. Randolph and Texas Liberal Politics* (Austin: Eakin Press, 2000). Randolph, Democratic national committeewoman at the time, sponsored the initial organizing meeting for the Democrats of Texas group in May 1957. Dawson Duncan, "Liberal-Loyalists Organize, Declare War on Conservatives," *Dallas Morning News*, May 18, 1957.

51. Katharine Q. Seelye, "Molly Ivins, Columnist, Dies at 62," *New York Times*, February 1, 2007.

52. Knaggs, *Two-Party Texas*, 10.

53. Quoted in Davidson, *Race and Class in Texas Politics*, 157.

54. Cunningham, *Cowboy Conservatism*, 53.

55. Menefee, "The Two-Party Democrats," 10.

56. Ibid., 24.

57. Paul Burka, "Don Yarborough's Texas," *Texas Monthly*, October 2009.

58. Menefee, "The Two-Party Democrats," 53–54.

59. Joe Holley, "His Challenge to Party Brought Kennedy to Texas in '63," *Washington Post*, September 24, 2009.

60. William Grimes, "Don Yarborough Dies at 83: Stirred Texas Politics," *New York Times*, September 24, 2009.

61. Menefee, "The Two-Party Democrats," 56.

62. Knaggs, *Two-Party Texas*, 87.

63. Kemper Diehl, "Sen. Tower Predicts M-A EEOC Appointment," *San Antonio Express-News*, October 26, 1966. Copy in John G. Tower Papers.

64. Sam Kinch, "Liberals in Bexar Supporting Tower," *Fort Worth Star-Telegram*, October 23, 1966. Copy in John G. Tower Papers.

65. Olien, *From Token to Triumph* 216.

66. Menefee, "The Two-Party Democrats," 81.

67. Knaggs, *Two-Party Texas*, 129.

68. Note from Dave Shapiro to Marvin Collins and John Knaggs, June 2, 1968, John Knaggs Papers.

69. Cunningham, *Cowboy Conservatism*, 95.

70. In the seven elections between 1962 and the 1976 presidential primary, Republicans averaged 100,000 voters in each of their primaries; the Democratic average was 1,619,776 voters each time.

71. Knaggs, *Two-Party Texas*, 152.

72. Cunningham, *Cowboy Conservatism*, 134.

73. Knaggs, *Two-Party Texas*, 179.

74. Rove, *Courage and Consequence*, 47.

75. Cunningham, *Cowboy Conservatism*, 137.

76. Cannon, "Texas Political System," 34.

77. The only previous Republican presidential primary was a nonbinding "beauty contest" won by Barry Goldwater in 1964.

78. Davidson, *Race and Class in Texas Politics*, 176; the battle in 1976 for liberal control of the party organization is covered on pp. 180–197.

79. Davidson, "Three Phases of Republican Development and Competition in Texas," 52.

80. Cannon, "Texas Political System," 63.

81. Bridges, *Twilight of the Texas Democrats*, 116. Bridges provides a valuable overview of the 1978 campaign for governor and its lasting impact on Texas politics.

82. As quoted in *The Texas Way*, 4, published by the Republican Party of Texas, October 1982. In author's possession.

83. Davidson, *Race and Class in Texas Politics*, 242.

84. Cannon, "The Texas Political System," 40.

85. Ibid., 24.

86. Knaggs, *Two-Party Texas*, 120–121.

87. Carolyn Barta, *Bill Clements: Texian to His Toenails* (Austin: Eakin Press, 1996), 8–9, 114, 117.

88. Ibid., 161.

89. Knaggs, *Two-Party Texas*, 206.

90. Quoted in Barta, *Bill Clements*, xv.

91. Quoted in ibid., 11.

92. Barta, *Bill Clements*, 193–194.

93. Quoted in ibid., 195.

94. Grier, *Grassroots Women*, 304–305.

95. Olien, *From Token to Triumph*, 253.

96. Ibid., 255–256.

97. Barta, *Bill Clements*, 203.

98. Olien, *From Token to Triumph* 256.

99. Kent L. Tedin and Richard W. Murray, "The Dynamics of Candidate Choice in a State Election," *Journal of Politics* 31 (May 1981).

100. Kent L. Tedin, "The Transition of Electoral Politics in Texas: Voting for Governor in 1978–1986," in *Perspectives on American and Texas Politics*, ed. Donald S. Lutz and Kent L. Tedin (Dubuque, IA: Kendall/Hunt, 1987), 244.

101. Bridges, *Twilight of the Texas Democrats*, 67.

102. Cunningham, *Cowboy Conservatism*, 198.

103. Quoted in Barta, *Bill Clements*, 410.

104. George Kuempel, "Clements Challenge before Him," *Dallas Morning News*, January 8, 1979.

105. David T. Wilkie, *The Emergence of Two Party Competition in Texas, 1952–1982*, bachelor of arts thesis, Princeton University, 1984, 7.

106. Karl Rove, "William Perry Clements: Lone-Star Giant," *Wall Street Journal*, June 2, 2011.

107. Carolyn Barta, "Why Bill Clements Mattered," *Texas Tribune*, May 30, 2011, www.texastribune.org, accessed September 14, 2011.

108. Ronald Reagan, *An American Life* (New York: Simon and Schuster, 1990), 143.

109. Reagan's initial campaign for governor is covered in Matthew Dallek, *The Right Moment* (New York: Free Press, 2000). The reporter Lou Cannon covered Reagan throughout his entire career and authored a number of works on him. One particularly valuable source on Reagan's early political career is Lou Cannon, *Governor Reagan: His Rise to Power* (New York: Public Affairs, 2003).

110. Cunningham, *Cowboy Conservatism*, 90.

111. Ibid., 91.

112. Theodore H. White, *The Making of the President, 1968* (New York: Atheneum, 1969), 52. O'Donnell was manager for Bruce Alger's successful congressional re-election campaign in 1958, Dallas County GOP chairman in 1959, and state chairman in 1962. His Texas activities are discussed in Knaggs, *Two-Party Texas*. His efforts with the Draft Goldwater Committee are described throughout F. Clifton White, *Suite 3505: The Story of the Draft Goldwater Movement* (New Rochelle, NY: Arlington House, 1967).

113. Lewis Chester, Godfrey Hodgson, and Bruce Page, *An American Melodrama: The Presidential Campaign of 1968* (New York: Dell, 1969), 495.

114. Due to her boisterous advocacy of conservative politics, Palm was frequently referred to as "NaPalm." Commenting a few years later on Nancy Palm and her influence, one reporter noted, "No other area of the state can even compare with the successful election of Republican candidates from this area: There is a Republican congressman, a state senator, six state representatives and a county commissioner, all despite Democratic efforts to dilute GOP strength through redistricting" (Gayle McNutt, "The Texas GOP: A Rocky Road of Its Own Making in '72," *Houston Chronicle*, February 20, 1972).

115. Cunningham, *Cowboy Conservatism*, 90.

116. Steven F. Hayward, *The Age of Reagan: The Fall of the Old Liberal Order* (Roseville, CA: Forum, 2001), 208.

117. Knaggs, *Two-Party Texas*, 124. Haley was the author of several histori-

cal works on West Texas themes but is perhaps best known for *A Texan Looks at Lyndon* (Canyon, TX: Palo Duro, 1964), a diatribe against President Johnson widely distributed during the 1964 presidential campaign.

118. Chester, Hodgson, and Page, *American Melodrama*, 229.

119. Ibid., 496.

120. Interview with Ronald B. Dear, Houston, Texas, May 17, 2012.

121. Knaggs, *Two-Party Texas*, 185.

122. Angelo interview, March 21, 2012.

123. Olien, *From Token to Triumph*, 237. It is interesting to note the impact of Texas Democratic candidates seeking the presidential nomination. With Johnson's decision to seek both the vice presidency and re-election to the Senate, John Tower ended up becoming senator. Lloyd Bentsen's move to have a presidential primary ended up giving new life to the Reagan nomination effort and a lasting influence on Texas partisan loyalties.

124. For a discussion of the Bentsen campaign and its aftermath see Davidson, *Race and Class in Texas Politics*, 182–190.

125. Quoted in Garcia, *Reagan's Comeback*, 31.

126. Billy Hathorn, "Mayor Ernest Angelo, Jr., of Midland and the 96–0 Reagan Sweep of Texas, May 1, 1976," *West Texas Historical Association Year Book* 86 (2010): 81–82.

127. Garcia, *Reagan's Comeback*, 38.

128. Paul Burka, "Right Place, Right Time," *Texas Monthly*, February 2010.

129. "Republicans: Reagan's Startling Texas Landslide," *Time*, May 10, 1976.

130. Garcia, *Reagan's Comeback*, 110.

131. Craig Shirley, *Reagan's Revolution: The Untold Story of the Campaign That Started It All* (Nashville, TN: Nelson Current, 2005), 192.

132. Olien, *From Token to Triumph*, 238. Angelo interview, March 21, 2012.

133. Hathorn, "Mayor Ernest Angelo, Jr.," 80.

134. Cunningham, *Cowboy Conservatism*, 174–175.

135. Garcia, *Reagan's Comeback*, 171–172.

136. Quoted in Richard S. Dunham, "Reagan Revolution Changed the Course of Texas Politics," *Houston Chronicle*, February 6, 2011.

137. Craig Shirley, *Rendezvous with Destiny: Ronald Reagan and the Campaign That Changed America* (Wilmington, DE: ISI Books, 2009), 267.

138. Rhodes Cook, *United States Presidential Primary Elections: 1968–1996* (Washington, DC: Congressional Quarterly, 2000), 710–715.

139. Jeanie R. Stanley, "Party Realignment in Texas," in *Party Realignment and State Politics*, ed. Maureen Moakley (Columbus: Ohio State University Press, 1992), 82 (with data updated through 2012).

140. Woodard, *New Southern Politics*.

141. James W. Lamare, J. L. Polinard, James Wenzel, and Robert D. Wrinkle, "Texas: Lone Star (Wars) State," in *The New Politics of the Old South*, ed. Charles S. Bullock III and Mark J. Rozell, 287.

142. Dunham, "Reagan Revolution," 2.

143. Robert Mason, *The Republican Party and American Politics from Hoover to Reagan* (Cambridge, U.K.: Cambridge University Press, 2012), 269.

Chapter 6: The Two-Party Interlude

1. James A. Dyer, "Implications of a Two-Party Texas," *Texas Poll Report* 6, no. 4 (Fall 1989): 11.

2. Texas is one of fourteen states that allows a voter to cast a single vote for a party's entire slate of candidates.

3. Clements's strong personality and the national economic downturn, combined with Congressman Jim Collins's campaign against Lloyd Bentsen, were viewed as rallying Democratic support against his re-election. See Knaggs, *Two-Party Texas*, 268–274; and Barta, *Bill Clements*, 270–296.

4. That candidate, Virgil Mulanax, ran in the 1984 Reagan landslide year, obtaining 49.0 percent of the vote.

5. The record from 1978 to 1994 stands at seven candidates elected, six candidates losing with at least 45 percent of the vote, and seven candidates falling short of the competitiveness mark. John L. Bates receives the award for determination in pursuit of an unfulfilled objective. He was the GOP candidate for the supreme court in 1982, 1984, and 1986, garnering 46.9 percent of the vote in his last campaign. Bates's baton was taken up by Charles Ben Howell, a former lower court judge for ten years, who ran five times unsuccessfully for the supreme court beginning in 1986.

6. Interestingly, the one noncompetitive race was run by David L. Berchelmann, who had been appointed to the court of criminal appeals by Governor Clements and was seeking election for the first time.

7. Tower was re-elected with 50.3 percent of the two-party vote in 1978 and Gramm was re-elected in 1996 with 54.8 percent. Bentsen's re-elections in 1982 (59.1%) and 1988 (59.7%) as well as Gramm's performance in 1984 (58.6%) and 1990 (61.7%) were beyond the range of competitiveness, as were Hutchison's special election runoff victory of 1993 (67.3%) and general election win of 1994 (60.8%).

8. From 1960 to 1976 the GOP ran candidates in 58.9 percent of the possible congressional contests but only 22 percent of these individuals were able to obtain at least 45 percent of the vote on election day.

9. Senate terms are four years except in the election year immediately following redistricting. Thus, in 1978 only sixteen of the thirty-one districts were up for election. Due to court-ordered redistricting, all thirty-one senate seats were on the ballot in 1994.

10. Two additional Republicans won special elections, bringing the total number of Republican state representatives to twenty-four prior to the 1980 general election.

11. Redistricting after each census impacted the number of districts contained in each of the four categories of counties. While the Big 6 counties and the Other Metro counties each gained one more district (from 71 to 72 and from 30 to 31, respectively) after the 1990 census, the greatest growth took place in the Suburban grouping of counties, which went from sixteen to twenty-two house districts. Thus, the Small Town counties lost eight districts (from a high of thirty-three down to twenty-five as of the 1992 election).

12. It is instructive that the *Texas State Directory* (Austin: Texas State Directory, various years) did not list party affiliation for court of appeals justices during this period of time, while it did include the party for supreme court and court of criminal appeals justices.

13. While there are eighty justices, each elected for six-year terms, unexpired terms account for twenty additional contests during this period.

14. This contrasts with the more recent period, when not a single Democratic candidate for the court of appeals ran unopposed in either 2010 or 2012; only two did so in 2008. As of 2013, Republicans held sixty-five of the eighty positions.

15. Data from the Republican Party of Texas as reported in L. Tucker Gibson Jr. and Clay Robison, *Government and Politics in the Lone Star State: Theory and Practice*, 6th ed. (Upper Saddle River, NJ: Pearson Prentice Hall, 2008), 178.

16. Brian D. Posler and Daniel S. Ward, "Texas," in *State Party Profiles*, ed. Andrew M. Appleton and Daniel S. Ward (Washington, DC: Congressional Quarterly, 1997), 309. See also Olson, "Toward a Typology of County Party Organizations," for a discussion of Democratic county chairmen perceiving their role as more civic contribution than partisan advocacy.

17. J. Scott Lucas, *Political Attitudes of Suburban Texans*, master of business administration paper, University of Texas at Austin, 1984. The survey focused on voters in precincts with significant growth, where 67 percent or more had voted for Ronald Reagan in 1980. The eight counties studied were Harris, Dallas, Tarrant, and Bexar as well as the suburban counties of Collin, Denton, Fort Bend, and Montgomery.

18. Ibid., 63. Since the author was focusing on strongly Republican precincts it is not surprising that his sample consisted of 59.5 percent Republican, 24.0 percent independent, and only 15.7 percent Democratic self-identifiers. Indicative of the influx of new residents to the state's metropolitan areas, 30.2 percent of the respondents had lived in Texas less than ten years, 35.9 percent more than ten, and only 33.8 percent were native-born Texans.

19. Ibid., 65.

20. Gibson and Robison, *Government and Politics in the Lone Star State*, 6th ed., 178.

21. Jeanie R. Stanley, "Party Realignment in Texas," in *Party Realignment and State Politics*, ed. Maureen Moakley, 83.

22. Cindy Rugeley, "GOP Takes Tarrant as Stronghold: More Democrats Switching Parties," *Houston Chronicle*, February 4, 1990, 1.

23. Sam Howe Verhovek, "Texas Democrats, Especially Richards, View an Alarming Landscape," *New York Times*, June 8, 1993, A12.

24. Appleton and Ward, *State Party Profiles*, 313.

25. Wilkie, *Emergence of Two Party Competition in Texas*, 83.

26. This point was made by Jeanie R. Stanley, "Party Realignment in Texas," in *Party Realignment and State Politics*, ed. Maureen Moakley, 85.

27. Data for 1978, 1980, 1984, and 1986 were collected by the Center for Public Policy at the University of Houston, as reported in Kent L. Tedin, "The Transition of Electoral Politics: Voting for Governor in 1978–1986," in *Perspectives on American and Texas Politics: A Collection of Essays*, ed. Donald S. Lutz and Kent L. Tedin (Dubuque, IA: Kendall/Hunt, 1987), 236; data for 1982 is from the Center

for Public Policy at the University of Houston as reported in Murray, "The 1982 Texas Election in Perspective," 51; data for 1988 from the *Texas Poll Report* 5, no. 3 (1988). The 1991 and 1994 results appear in Haag, Keith, and Peebles, *Texas Politics and Government*, 121. The 1996 data are from Gibson and Robison, *Government and Politics in the Lone Star State*, 3rd ed., 179.

28. The classification "independent" can vary widely depending on how a pollster categorizes leaners (those who "lean" Republican or Democratic but do not describe themselves as partisans).

29. Jewell and Morehouse, *Political Parties and Elections in American States*, 42.

30. *Texas Poll Report* 2, no. 3 (1985): 10–11.

31. As cited in Dyer, Vedlitz, and Hill, "New Voters," 160.

32. Tedin, "Transition of Electoral Politics," 237.

33. James A. Dyer, Jan E. Leighley, and Arnold Vedlitz, "Party Identification and Public Opinion in Texas, 1984–1994: Establishing a Competitive Two-Party System," in *Texas Politics: A Reader*, ed. Anthony Champagne and Edward J. Harpham, 2nd ed. (New York: W. W. Norton, 1998), 108.

34. Dyer, Vedlitz, and Hill, "New Voters," 160.

35. Dyer, Leighley, and Vedlitz, "Party Identification and Public Opinion in Texas," in *Texas Politics*, ed. Anthony Champagne and Edward J. Harpham, 109.

36. Ibid., 116.

37. Danny Hayes and Seth C. McKee, "Toward a One-Party South?" *American Politics Research* 36, no. 1 (2008): 8.

38. Harold W. Stanley, "Southern Partisan Changes: Dealignment, Realignment or Both?" *Journal of Politics* 50 (1988): 84.

39. Aggregation of surveys in 1985 as reported in Tedin and Murray, "The Dynamics of Candidate Choice in a State Election," 238.

40. Gibson and Robison, *Government and Politics in the Lone Star State*, 6th ed., 174–175.

41. Tedin and Murray, "The Dynamics of Candidate Choice in a State Election," 238. Similar results for 1986 were reported in Arnold Vedlitz, James A. Dyer, and David B. Hill, "The Changing Texas Voter," in *The South's New Politics: Realignment and Dealignment*, ed. Robert H. Swansbrough and David M. Brodsky (Columbia: University of South Carolina Press, 1988), 45.

42. Stanley, "Southern Partisan Changes," 80; Texas Poll Report 2, no. 3 (October 1985); Texas Poll Report 3, no. 4 (Fall 1986); Texas Poll Report 8, no. 3 (Fall 1991); "Texans Getting Younger, More Educated, Poll Says," Austin American-Statesman, September 3, 1989; Dyer, Vedlitz, and Hill, "New Voters," 45.

43. *Texas Poll Report* 2, no. 3 (October 1985): 1.

44. According to Stanley, "In 1984, the composition of the Republican coalition was 22 percent newcomers (10 years or less in Texas); 25 percent new voters (under 30 years old); 28 percent switchers (23% former Democrats and 5% former Independents); and 25 percent loyal Republicans" ("Southern Partisan Changes," 78).

45. Tod A. Baker, *Political Parties in the Southern States: Party Activists in Partisan Coalitions* (New York: Praeger, 1990), 180.

46. Dorothy Davidson Nesbit, "Changing Partisanship among Southern Party Activists," *Journal of Politics* 50, no. 2 (1988): 331.

47. Charles D. Hadley and Lewis Bowman, eds., *Southern State Party Organizations and Activists* (Westport, CT: Praeger, 1995), 79.

48. John M. Bruce, "Texas: A Success Story, at Least for Now," in *God at the Grass Roots, 1996*, ed. Mark J. Rozell and Clyde Wilcox (Lanham, MD: Rowman and Littlefield, 1997), 35. By the 1990s the Texas Republican Party had attracted and activated a large number of evangelical Christians, whose focus tended to be on a range of social issues. It has been estimated that 60 to 65 percent of the delegates to the 1994 convention were evangelical Christians. According to Natasha Nicole Self, "The trend throughout the decade is towards an increase in the connections between party officers and the Religious Right" ("The Religious Right and the Texas Republican Party," honors thesis, University of Texas at Austin, 2002, 33). See also R. G. Ratcliffe, "Conservatives to Take Reins at GOP State Convention," *Houston Chronicle*, June 6, 1994; Kimberly H. Conger, *The Christian Right in Republican State Politics* (New York: Palgrave Macmillan, 2009); James W. Larmare, Jerry L. Polinard, and Robert D. Wrinkle, "Texas: Religion and Politics in God's Country," in *The Christian Right in American Politics*, ed. John C. Green, Mark J. Rozell, and Clyde Wilcox (Washington, DC: Georgetown University Press, 2003), 59–78.

49. John P. Frendreis, "Migration as a Source of Changing Party Strength," *Social Science Quarterly* 70, no. 1 (March 1989): 218–219.

50. Vedlitz, Dyer, and Hill, "The Changing Texas Voter," in *The South's New Politics: Realignment and Dealignment*, ed. Robert H. Swansbrough and David M. Brodsky, 46.

51. Dyer, Leighley, and Vedlitz, "Party Identification and Public Opinion in Texas, 1984–1994," in *Texas Politics*, ed. Anthony Champagne and Edward J. Harpham, 115.

52. *Texas Poll Report* 3, no. 1 (Winter 1986): 1. Data are from the January/February 1986 Texas Poll. Similar results were found in surveys taken in 1987 and 1989 measuring ratings of the Reagan presidency.

53. Seth C. McKee, *Republican Ascendancy in Southern U.S. House Elections* (Boulder, CO: Westview, 2010), 60.

54. Hayes and McKee, "Toward a One-Party South?" 9–10.

55. McKee, *Republican Ascendancy*, 56.

56. Hayes and McKee, "Toward a One-Party South?" 4.

57. Data from the 1984 and 1994 Texas Poll presented in *Texas Poll Report* 11, no. 3 (Fall 1994): 5. Data for 1991 from *Texas Poll Report* 8, no. 3 (Fall 1991): 4.

58. "Undercurrents and Future Winds: A Decade of Changing Texas Political Parties," *Texas Poll Report* 11, no. 3 (Fall 1994): 5.

59. Survey of 1,430 Texas party activists as reported in Hadley and Bowman, *Southern State Party Organizations and Activists*, 79.

60. Malcolm E. Jewell, "Participation in Southern Primaries," in *Party Politics in the South*, ed. Robert P. Steed, Lawrence W. Moreland, and Tod A. Baker, 31.

61. This trend would not continue into the next century, however. Democrats cast more primary votes in 2002, 2004, and 2008, with more Republican votes cast in the other five subsequent primaries. The historic high in turnout was the 2,874,986 votes cast in the 2008 Democratic primary involving Barack Obama and Hillary Clinton.

62. Big 6 counties contributed only 29.7 percent of all Democratic primary voters in 1996 even though they contained some 45 percent of all registered voters. The Other Metro category of counties produced 20.7 percent of the Democratic primary electorate while those in the Suburban grouping constituted only 9.6 percent of statewide participation. Both Other Metro and Suburban counties each held around 18 percent of all registered voters.

63. Interview with William "Peck" Young, Austin Community College Center for Public Policy and Political Studies, Austin, Texas, August 7, 2012. The Center for Public Policy and Political Studies has issued valuable reports on straight-ticket voting in Texas since 1998, but their reports do not cover the period under discussion in this chapter.

64. Unfortunately, the Elections Division of the Texas Secretary of State does not capture the number of straight-ticket votes cast, and few counties make this information available on a historical basis. Only for elections in the twenty-first century can one locate accurate information on straight-ticket voting from most of the state's larger counties.

65. According to Carolyn Barta, in the 1982 election "forty-one percent of Democrats voted a straight ticket, and straight ticket voting was particularly high in Harris County, where 60 percent of Democratic voters pulled a single lever" (Barta, *Bill Clements*, 291).

66. Collin increased from 20.2 percent straight-ticket votes in 1992 to 32.1 percent in 1994 and 39.3 percent in 1996. Tarrant's share grew from 43.9 percent in 1994 to 49.8 percent in 1996. Straight-ticket voters in both counties had Republican majorities.

67. El Paso is unique among the Big 6 counties in that it is located in the mountain standard time zone and has no suburban counties in Texas surrounding it. Absent the straight-ticket Democratic votes from El Paso, the Republican vote advantage from the three Suburban counties listed surpassed the Democratic margin in the other five Big 6 counties by 13,180 votes.

68. The Supreme Court's 2013 decision in *Shelby County v. Holder*, ruling that Section 4 of the Voting Rights Act is unconstitutional, may limit federal oversight of Texas election law, although its impact on redistricting remains to be seen.

Chapter 7: The Era of Republican Dominance

1. University of Texas–Austin/*Texas Tribune* Texas Statewide Survey, October 2008. The Democratic Party was viewed as "middle of the road" by 12 percent and as conservative by 8 percent of those surveyed. Only 9 percent viewed the GOP as liberal and 12 percent described it as in the middle. Poll data from 2008 to 2013 is available at http://texaspolitics.laits.utexas.edu/11_1_0.html, accessed September 1, 2013.

2. The Libertarian Party of Texas fielded eighty-four candidates in statewide contests during this same time period.

3. The 1998 candidate for comptroller was Paul Hobby, son of long-serving lieutenant governor William P. Hobby Jr. and grandson of Governor William P. Hobby Sr. Also running a competitive race that year was incumbent comptroller

John Sharp, who obtained 48.2 percent of the vote and lost by 68,731 votes to agriculture commissioner Rick Perry in the contest for lieutenant governor.

4. Haag, Keith, and Peebles, *Texas Politics and Government*, 198.

5. From 1960 to 1976, during the period of two-tiered politics, the Republican presidential candidate always performed below his national percentage. Even when Eisenhower carried the state, his Texas percentage was more than 2 percent below his national average. The Reagan election of 1980 started a trend of better performance in Texas than nationally. Brian Arbour and Mark Jonathan McKenzie, "Texas: After the Bush Era," in *A Paler Shade of Red: The 2008 Presidential Election in the South*, ed. Bronwell DuBose Kapeluck, Lawrence W. Moreland, and Robert P. Steed (Fayetteville: University of Arkansas Press, 2009), 203.

6. While Johnson carried the Big 6 counties in that election, he received his lowest percentage of the two-party vote (60.6%) in these counties.

7. It should be noted, however, that Barack Obama carried Harris County in 2012 by 971 votes out of nearly 1.2 million cast.

8. According to the 2010 census, the population of Nueces County is 60.6 percent Hispanic, 3.6 percent African American, 32.9 percent Anglo, and 3.0 percent other. Ector County, with a Hispanic majority of 52.7 percent, has voted Republican in every presidential election since 1952. http://www.census.gov/, accessed September 3, 2013.

9. Of the 198 counties in the Small Town category, twenty-five had less than one thousand voters, with as few as sixty-four voters (Loving County) participating in the 2012 presidential election. The other 116 ranged from one thousand to slightly over seven thousand votes cast.

10. Just as the GOP retained its historical base in the counties of Cooke, Gillespie, Hutchinson, Kerr, and Washington, so too the Democrats have continued to hold onto strong majorities in Jim Wells, Maverick, and Starr Counties in the Rio Grande Valley. It is in the other forty-nine counties analyzed where the transition of political support has taken place.

11. Sue Tolleson-Rinehart and Jeanie R. Stanley, *Claytie and the Lady: Ann Richards, Gender, and Politics in Texas* (Austin: University of Texas Press, 1994), 141.

12. Peter Schweizer and Rochelle Schweizer, *The Bushes: Portrait of a Dynasty* (New York: Doubleday, 2004), 421.

13. Christopher Andersen, *George and Laura: Portrait of an American Marriage* (New York: William Morrow, 2002), 122.

14. George W. Bush, *A Charge to Keep* (New York: William Morrow, 1999), 26.

15. Jan Reid, *Let the People In: The Life and Times of Ann Richards* (Austin: University of Texas Press, 2012), 387.

16. Rove, *Courage and Consequence*, 89. Espinosa was a Hispanic Baptist from East Texas who said he was running for religious reasons and in 2008 announced for president but did not appear on any state ballots. "Bush's Son Wins Gov Nod," *Philadelphia Daily News*, March 9, 1994. Espinosa's 2008 effort is cited at http://votesmart.org/candidate/biography/82923/lou-gary-espinosa#.UZJamaI3v2s, accessed May 14, 2013.

17. Shropshire and Schaefer, *Thorny Rose of Texas*, 235.

18. Reid, *Let the People In*, 405.

19. Cameron gave a slight plurality to Perry in 2006 while Jefferson did the same in 2010.

20. Gibson and Robison, *Government and Politics in the Lone Star State*, 139.

21. A winter 1998 survey of likely voters showed that Sharp had 41 percent, Perry 35 percent, and 19 percent undecided. Two later surveys, in spring and summer, had the percentage of undecided at 32 percent and 26 percent, respectively, with Perry slightly ahead both times. *Texas Poll Report* (Winter 1998), 7; *Texas Poll Report* (Spring 1998) 7; Texas Poll Report (Summer 1998), 7.

22. Rove, *Courage and Consequence*, 117.

23. Wayne Slater and Sam Attlesey, "Latest Poll Finds Bush Headed for a Landslide: Sharp, Perry Appear Tied for Texas' No. 2 Job," *Dallas Morning News*, October 22, 1998.

24. Rove, *Courage and Consequence*, 121.

25. The Democrats' statewide candidates, referred to by some as their "dream team," included Ron Kirk, an African American attorney who had built an impressive record as mayor of Dallas, for U.S. senator; banker Tony Sanchez of Laredo for governor; Sharp for lieutenant governor; former Austin mayor Kirk Watson for attorney general; and Senator David Bernsen of Beaumont for land commissioner.

26. Clay Robison, "Former Comptroller Sharp to Seek U.S. Senate Seat," *Houston Chronicle*, December 8, 2008.

27. Sharp once again carried the Big 6 counties by more than 20,000 votes but lost the 2002 election to David Dewhurst by 259,594 votes. His statewide running mates all lost by at least 500,000 votes, with land commissioner candidate Bernsen coming closest, but still 512,335 votes shy of victory.

28. The first quote is from Seth C. McKee and Daron R. Shaw, "Redistricting in Texas: Institutionalizing Republican Ascendancy," in *Redistricting in the New Millennium*, ed. Peter F. Galderisi (Lanham, MD: Lexington Books, 2005), 282. The second quote is from Michael Barone and Grant Ujifusa, *The Almanac of American Politics, 1994* (Washington, DC: National Journal, 1993), 1209.

29. Earl Black and Merle Black, *The Rise of Southern Republicans* (Cambridge, MA: Belknap, 2002), 344–345.

30. A three-judge federal court redrew the boundaries of thirteen districts in 1996 and ordered that an open primary be held. If no candidate received a majority of the votes, then a runoff between the top two candidates would be held in December. In Congressional District 9, Congressman Steve Stockman had a 4,389-vote lead over Democrat Nick Lampson but was short of a majority. Stockman then lost the runoff to Lampson. Ten years later, another federal court ordered the redrawing of five districts and the holding of an open primary. This time, Congressman Henry Bonilla was 1,725 votes short of a majority in Congressional District 23 and subsequently lost the runoff to Democrat Ciro Rodriguez.

31. Steve Bickerstaff, *Lines in the Sand* (Austin: University of Texas Press, 2007), 110.

32. McKee and Shaw, "Redistricting in Texas," in *Redistricting in the New Millennium*, ed. Peter F. Galderisi, 293.

33. Bickerstaff, *Lines in the Sand*, 86.

34. For a detailed discussion of the various strategies and tactics used in the redistricting battle see Bickerstaff, *Lines in the Sand*, 121–257, and McKee, *Republican Ascendency in Southern U.S. House Elections*, 96–109.

35. McKee, *Republican Ascendency in Southern U.S. House Elections*, 111.

36. McKee and Shaw, "Redistricting in Texas," in *Redistricting in the New Millennium*, ed. Peter F. Galderisi, 297.

37. The three Anglo Democrats were Chet Edwards, Gene Green, and Lloyd Doggett. Both Edwards and Doggett overcame GOP efforts to defeat them in the Democratic primary and the general election.

38. "Court Allows Texas Redistricting Maps to Be Used for 2014 Elections," www.oag.state.tx.us/oagnews/release.php?id=4519, accessed September 11, 2013. See also www.txredistricting.org for commentary on the redistricting dispute.

39. Sherri Greenberg, "The New Art and Science of Texas Redistricting: What about Public Policy?" *LBJ Journal of Public Affairs* 17, no. 1 (Fall 2004): 11.

40. Ibid., 12.

41. Brian K. Arbour and Seth C. McKee, "Cracking Back: The Effectiveness of Partisan Redistricting in the Texas House of Representatives," *American Review of Politics* 26 (Winter 2005–2006): 387.

42. Richard H. Kraemer, Charldean Newell, and David F. Prindle, *Essentials of Texas Politics*, 9th ed. (Belmont, CA: Wadsworth, 2004), 106.

43. Arbour and McKee, "Cracking Back," 385.

44. Ibid., 397.

45. Haag, Keith, and Peebles, *Texas Politics and Government*, 245.

46. Arbour and McKee, "Cracking Back," 396.

47. Greenberg, "The New Art and Science of Texas Redistricting," 13.

48. Chris Tomlinson, "Texas Elections Show Redistricting Was Destiny," *Waco Tribune*, November 11, 2012.

49. In Senate District 10 (Tarrant County), Senator Wendy Davis defeated Representative Mark Shelton by a vote of 147,103 (51.1%) to 140,656 (48.9%).

50. During twelve years as governor, Rick Perry appointed 224 attorneys to fill vacancies on Texas courts or to newly created district courts. Ross Ramsey, "Perry a Judgemaker, but He Can't Control Them," *Austin American-Statesman*, December 9, 2012.

51. Arbour and McKenzie, "Texas: After the Bush Era," in *A Paler Shade of Red*, ed. Bronwell DuBose Kapeluck, Lawrence W. Moreland, and Robert P. Steed, 208.

52. Lyle C. Brown, Joyce A. Langenegger, Sonia R. Garcia, Ted A. Lewis, and Robert E. Biles, *Practicing Texas Politics*, 13th ed. (Boston: Wadsworth, 2010), 149.

53. Gary A. Keith and Stefan D. Haag with L. Tucker Gibson Jr. and Clay Robison, *Texas Politics and Government*, 4th ed. (Glenview, IL: Longman, 2012), 73.

54. Republican Party of Texas, "It's Official, Texas GOP Sets a New Record!" December 5, 2012. According to the Republican state chairman the total number of all Republican county officeholders in 2013 had reached 3,195 after party

switches, comprising some 60 percent of the total in the state (interview with Steve Ministeri, Austin, Texas, February 19, 2013).

55. David Lublin, *The Republican South* (Princeton, NJ: Princeton University Press, 2004), 57.

56. Ibid., 19–20.

57. Young interview, August 7, 2012. This generational impact is not limited to rural Texas. Nelson Wolff is a former state legislator and San Antonio mayor now serving as the Democratic county judge of Bexar County. His oldest son, Kevin, is a former San Antonio city councilman now serving as the Republican county commissioner in Bexar County.

58. Lublin, *The Republican South*, 72.

59. Ibid., 95.

60. Young interview, August 7, 2012.

61. Lublin, *The Republican South*, 7.

62. "One Texas County Evolves from Democratic Majority into GOP Stronghold," *San Antonio Express-News*, April 11, 2000.

63. In 2012, Hansford was joined by twelve other predominantly rural counties that could find no one willing to administer a Democratic primary election.

64. Glenn Evans, "Sabine County Switch Sustains GOP Tide in East Texas, Rural Parts of State," *Longview News-Journal*, June 26, 2011. News release, Republican Party of Texas, September 6, 2013.

65. Ibid.

66. Rodger G. McLane, "Political Change Comes to Panola County," *Panola Watchman*, November 25, 2011.

67. "Coke County Elected Officials Switch to the Texas GOP," release from Republican Party of Texas, Austin, Texas, May 1, 2012.

68. "County Makes Switch to Republican Party," *Austin American-Statesman*, May 11, 2012.

69. R. G. Ratcliffe, "Texas Yellow Dog Democrats Get a Rural Whipping," *Houston Chronicle*, December 6, 2010.

70. This total does not include the county judges who switched parties after the 2010 election or filled a vacancy in the 2012 election.

71. It should be noted that among these 141 smaller counties are five cited previously where officials left the Democratic Party as well as six additional counties failing to conduct a Democratic primary in either 2010 or 2012 and four others that did not do so in 2012. Without a Democratic primary no candidates can be nominated for county office on that party's ticket.

72. Jeffrey M. Jones, "More States Move to GOP in 2011," Gallup Politics, February 2, 2012, http://www.gallup.com/poll/152438/states-move-gop-2011.aspx, accessed January 4, 2013.

73. It should be noted that I have excluded any "exit poll" data collected from individuals leaving a polling place on election day. Such data is reflective only of those who chose to participate in a specific election. The discussion here is of the entire eligible electorate, including those who may or may not have voted in any one election. Among the sources for party identification data from 1996 to 2012 are Haag, Keith, and Peebles, *Texas Politics and Government*, 121; Gibson and

Robison, *Government and Politics in the Lone Star State*, 6th ed., 179, 183; Gallup Poll, "State of the States Snapshot: Party ID," January 28, 2009, http://www.gal lup.com/poll/114016/State-States-Political-Party-Affiliation.aspx, accessed September 3, 2013; Bullock and Rozell, eds., *New Politics of the Old South*, 288; University of Texas–Austin/*Texas Tribune* Texas Statewide Survey, http://texaspolitics .laits.utexas.edu/11_1_0.html, accessed September 1, 2013.

74. Ross Ramsey, "No Voter Turnout in Some Counties," *Austin American-Statesman*, June 24, 2012.

75. Maverick County, population 54,258, did not conduct a GOP primary in 2006 or 2008.

76. According to the *Republican Party of Texas 1980 Yearbook*, Kerr County had a Republican county judge and two commissioners as well as three other elected officials; Llano County had a GOP county judge and six others holding county elective office; Nacogdoches County had one county commissioner; both Hardin and Van Zandt Counties had a Republican serving as constable. No other counties among the fifty-seven mostly rural counties surveyed had a Republican in any elective office in 1980.

77. The data for 1998 to 2010 is from "Studies of Political Statistics: Straight Ticket Voting in Texas 1998–2012," Report no. 8, December 2012, Center for Public Policy and Political Studies, Austin Community College, Austin, TX. My thanks to William "Peck" Young for providing this data. The number of counties covered in each election ranges from thirty to forty-six, containing from 73 to 83 percent of all votes cast in that election. Further data on past elections can be found in Reports 1, 3, and 6 from the Center for Public Policy and Political Studies. The data for 2012 was collected by the author and covers 112 counties with 95.2 percent of all votes cast in the 2012 election. The 2012 data reflects only those straight-ticket votes cast for the Democratic or the Republican Party. The center's data shows an even higher level of straight-ticket voting in 2012 (64.2%) since it covers only the forty-nine most heavily voting counties, accounting for 84 percent of all votes cast, and also includes the small number of Libertarian and Green Party straight-ticket votes.

78. The counties were Johnson, Parker, and Rockwall outside Dallas-Fort Worth; Chambers and Montgomery surrounding Houston; and Bandera, Comal, and Kendall Counties near San Antonio. In Kendall County, 87.0 percent of all straight-ticket votes were Republican.

79. Nevertheless, these counties differed dramatically. In Bee and Uvalde, only 30.5 and 40.7 percent, respectively, voted straight ticket. The Democratic percentage was 55.7 percent in Bee and 57.9 percent in Uvalde. The percentage of voters casting a straight-ticket ballot was 73.4 percent in Starr and 55.0 percent in Maverick—both above the average for the 56 Small Town counties from which data was obtained. Of these straight-ticket votes, 92 percent were Democratic in Starr County and 83.8 percent were Democratic in Maverick County.

80. Quoted in Reeve Hamilton, "In November, Straight Ticket Votes Decide Winner," *The Texas Tribune*, March 2, 2010, 1–2.

81. Young interview, August 7, 2012.

82. Quoted in Hamilton, "In November, Straight Ticket Votes Decide Winner," 2.

Chapter 8: The Future of Texas Politics

1. Grieder, *Big, Hot, Cheap, and Right*, 198. According to Grieder, "Forty years ago, for the reasons described, Texas voters started to give Republicans a chance, and thus far, they haven't been disappointed enough to do anything about it. For decades, Republicans have had the edge in structure, in organization, in money, and in candidates, whereas Democrats are still trying to recover their footing" (158).

2. Voters aged sixty and over comprised the only group with more Democratic than Republican identifiers. Those aged forty to forty-nine stood at 41 percent Republican, with those thirty to thirty-nine and fifty to fifty-nine both at 38 percent Republican. Results are from four Scripps Howard Texas Polls taken in 2003–2004 with four thousand respondents. Reported in Gibson and Robison, *Government and Politics in the Lone Star State*, 6th ed., 182.

3. University of Texas–Austin/*Texas Tribune* Texas Statewide Survey, May 2011. The Reuters/IPSOS 2012 exit poll showed voters aged eighteen to thirty-four to be the only cohort to identify more closely with the Democratic Party, while voters aged fifty-five or greater were the most likely to be Republican (American Mosaic Polling Explorer, elections.reuters.com/#poll, accessed March 6, 2013).

4. Some examples of this potential conflict can be seen in Brad Watson, "Source: AG Abbott Tells Donors He'll Run for Governor," *WFAA*, January 10, 2013, http://www.wfaa.com/news/local/Source-AG-Abbott-tells-donors-he'll-run-for -governor-186385771.html#, accessed January 12, 2013; Patricia Kilday Hart, "Abbott War Chest Dwarfs Perry's, Fueling Speculation of Challenge," *Houston Chronicle*, January 17, 2013; Wayne Slater, "GOP Stalwart Tom Pauken to Run for Governor, Says Texas Needs 'a Different Style of Leadership,'" *Dallas Morning News*, March 21, 2013; Gromer Jeffers Jr., "Texas Land Commissioner Jerry Patterson Says He's on Track to Beat David Dewhurst for Lieutenant Governor," *Dallas Morning News*, January 12, 2013.

5. This, of course, was exactly the situation that produced the Republican gubernatorial victory in 1978.

6. Self, "The Religious Right and the Texas Republican Party"; John M. Bruce, "Texas: A Success Story, at Least for Now," in *God at the Grassroots, 1996*, ed. Mark J. Rozell and Clyde Wilcox; Theda Skocpol and Rebecca Williamson, *The Tea Party and the Remaking of Republican Conservatism* (New York: Oxford University Press, 2012); Ronald P. Formisano, *The Tea Party: A Brief History* (Baltimore, MD: Johns Hopkins University Press, 2012).

7. Jason Stanford, "Texas Democrats' Conservatism Widespread Outside of Austin," *Austin American-Statesman*, July 28, 2011.

8. Alexander Burns, "Democrats Launch Plan to Turn Texas Blue," *Politico*, January 24, 2013; Jonathan Tilove, "'Blue' Group Turns to Texas," *Austin American-Statesman*, February 27, 2013. Since 2005, the political consultant Matt Angle has maintained the "Lone Star Project" as an effort from DC to challenge GOP dominance in Texas, operating as a federal political action committee. See www.lonestarproject.net, accessed March 6, 2013.

9. Ross Ramsey, "Democrats Did Not Do All That Badly on Election Day," *New York Times*, November 24, 2012.

10. Jason Stanford, "Texas Democrats Still Wandering in the Wilderness," *Austin American-Statesman*, December 2, 2012.

11. M. V. Hood III, Quentin Kidd, and Irwin I. Morris, *The Rational Southerner: Black Mobilization, Republican Growth, and the Partisan Transformation of the American South* (New York: Oxford University Press, 2012), 67.

12. Among examples of this commentary are Matthew Yglesias, "The GOP's Hispanic Nightmare," *Slate*, November 7, 2012, www.Slate.com/articles/business /moneybox/2012/11/latino_vote_2012, accessed January 8, 2013; Markos Moulitsas, "GOP Needs Latino Vote," *The Hill*, November 27, 2012; Seth Mandel, "What's behind the GOP's Continuing Trouble Wooing Latino Voters," *Commentary*, November 6, 2012; Kathleen Parker, "GOP Needs to Speak Spanish if It Wants to Win at Ballot Box," *Austin American-Statesman*, January 12, 2013. See also Maggie Haberman and Jonathan Martin, "RNC Launches Official Review on 2012 Election," *Politico*, December 10, 2012.

13. Roughly consistent results were found in Hispanic support for Romney in the May 2012 and October 2012 surveys conducted by the University of Texas–Austin/*Texas Tribune*. The second poll cited comprises Texas responses to the ImpreMedia/Latino Decisions 2012 Latino Election Eve Poll, www.latinovote2012 .com/app/#all-Tx-all, accessed January 8, 2013. The 26 percent Hispanic Republican figure is from Paul Burka, "The Party Never Ends!" *Texas Monthly*, June 2012. This percentage is consistent with the Reuters/IPSOS exit poll indicating that 27.2 percent of Texas Hispanic voters self-identified as Republican (www.elec tions.reuters.com/#poll, accessed March 6, 2013).

14. Munisteri interview, February 19, 2013. Romney's support among Texas Hispanics was greater than what he obtained in any other state, including Florida, where 35 percent reported voting for Romney in the Reuters/IPSOS exit poll.

15. Burka, "The Party Never Ends!" Not all GOP activists share this concern, however. See Tim Eaton, "State GOP Split on Hispanic Outreach," *Austin American-Statesman*, November 11, 2012.

16. Quoted in Jason Margolis, "Could Latino Voters Turn Deep-Red Texas Democratic by 2020?" *Atlantic*, May 2012, www.theatlantic.com/politics/archive /2012/05/could-latino-voters-turn-deep-red-texas-democratic-by-2020/257738, accessed January 8, 2013.

17. Quoted in Christy Hoppe and Holly K. Hacker, "Hispanic Population Boom Will Reshape Texas Politics, but Question Is When," *Dallas Morning News*, November 11, 2012. Peña's advice was taken by GOP activist Brad Bailey, who called for a program of "Gringo Inreach" on the immigration question at a program of the Texas Public Policy Foundation prior to the opening of the 2013 legislative session (Jordan Fabian, "Texas Conservatives Try 'Gringo Inreach' on Immigration," ABC Univision, January 10, 2013, http://abcnews.go.com /ABC_Univision/Politics/texas-conservatives-gringo-inreach-immigration /story?id=18184846&utm_source, accessed January 12, 2013).

18. Quoted in Lisa Falkenberg, "Hispanic Vote Should Be a Clue for Texas Republicans," *Houston Chronicle*, November 7, 2012.

19. Quoted in Ruben Navarrette, "Texas Rock Star Cruz Will Have Democrats Shaking in Boots," *Austin American-Statesman*, January 11, 2013.

20. Stephen Dinan, "Data Show Hispanics More Likely to Relate to Democrats," *Washington Times*, November 27, 2012.

21. Quoted in ibid., 2012.

22. R. Michael Alvarez and Lisa Garcia Bedolla, "The Foundations of Latino Voter Partisanship: Evidence from the 2000 Election," *Journal of Politics* 65, no. 1 (February 2003): 44.

23. Abrajano and Alvarez found that 37.4 percent of self-identified Democrats and 36.7 percent of independents responded either "don't think of self in these terms" or "don't know" (Marisa A. Abrajano and R. Michael Alvarez, "Hispanic Public Opinion and Participation in America," *Political Science Quarterly* 126, no. 2 [Summer 2011]: 280).

24. Ibid., 281. This was not true of the small percentage of Hispanic Republicans, 46 percent of whom considered themselves conservative.

25. Ibid., 282. For further discussion, see Marisa A. Abrajano and R. Michael Alvarez, *New Faces, New Voices: The Hispanic Electorate in America* (Princeton, NJ: Princeton University Press, 2010).

26. Seth Motel and Eileen Patten, "Latinos in the 2012 Election: Texas," October 1, 2012, released by Pew Research Hispanic Center, http://www.pewhispanic.org/2012/10/01/latinos-in-the-2012-election-texas/, accessed January 11, 2013.

27. Joe Holley, "Idea of Hispanic Voter Surge Fading This Year," *Houston Chronicle*, April 1, 2012. Data on Hispanic voter registration and turnout are imprecise. An attempt to clarify the situation was made by PolitiFact Texas in response to a claim by Battleground Texas that 54 percent of Hispanics were registered but only 35 percent voted in the 2008 election. PolitiFact concluded that "our own estimates starting from Texas studies suggest a larger share of voting-age Latino citizens registered and a smaller share of them voted" *Austin American-Statesman*, March 22, 2013, http://www.politifact.com/texas/statements/2013/mar/22/battleground-texas/battleground-texas-says-54-percent-texas-latinos-r/, accessed March 25, 2013.

28. Ross Ramsey, "George P. Bush: The TT Interview," *Texas Tribune*, January 15, 2013.

29. Quoted in Melody C. Mendoza, "Experts Discuss Latino Vote, Impact on Texas," *San Antonio Express-News*, December 9, 2012.

30. "U.S. Census Bureau, Current Population Survey, November 2012," www.census.gov/hhes/www/socdemo/voting/publilcations/p20/2012/tables.html, accessed May 10, 2013. The census bureau allows a number of race and ethnicity options for respondents, including reporting more than one race. Those responding Hispanic may be of any race. In the discussion above we have used data for "White non-Hispanic alone" rather than for the more inclusive categories of "White alone" or "White alone or in combination."

31. Stanford, "Texas Democrats Still Wandering in the Wilderness."

32. In the application of national data and conclusions to Texas it is helpful to keep in mind the observations of Michael Barone, co-founder of *The Almanac of American Politics* and political commentator: "My observation in travel over the years is that Hispanics are treated very differently by Anglos in Texas than in California. In Texas, white Anglos see people with Hispanic features as fellow Tex-

ans. They smile and say howdy. They know, because they have to take Texas history in high school, that Hispanics have been living in Texas for more than 200 years and that some fought for Texas independence against Mexico. In California, white Anglos, liberal or conservative, treat people with Hispanic features as landscape workers or parking valet attendants. They look past them without speaking or hand them their car keys" (Michael Barone, "Republicans Must Show Support for Hispanic Dreams," *Real Clear Politics*, March 21, 2013, http://www.real clearpolitics.com/articles/2013/03/21/republicans_must_show_support_for_his panic_dreams_117549.html, accessed March 25, 2013).

33. W. Gardner Selby, "Es verdad: GOP in Texas Gets 40% of Latino Votes," *Austin American-Statesman*, June 9, 2013.

34. Through both retirement and defeat the GOP lost five Hispanic state representatives and one congressman in the 2012 election, all from majority-Hispanic districts.

35. Elise Foley, "Texas Democratic Party Chairman Gilberto Hinojosa: Republicans Will Block Immigration Reform," *Huffington Post Politics*, November 28, 2012, http://www.huffingtonpost.com/2012/11/28/texas-democratic-party -gilberto-hinojosa_n_2206559.html, accessed January 12, 2013.

36. "Democrats Desperately Seeking Senate Candidate after Sanchez Quits Race," *Houston Chronicle*, December 19, 2011. When the Democrats first nominated a Hispanic candidate for governor in 2002, Tony Sanchez received 40.9 percent of the two-party vote as contrasted with Chris Bell's 43.3 percent in 2006, and the 43.5 percent cast for Bill White in 2010.

37. Nate Cohn, "A Blue Texas? Keep Dreaming," *New Republic*, November 19, 2012. Located in north central Texas, Comanche County had a population of 13,974 in the 2010 census.

38. Data from Reuters/IPSOS exit poll of 2,403 Texans casting ballots in the 2012 election, www.elections.reuters.com/#poll, accessed March 6, 2013.

39. Grieder, *Big, Hot, Cheap, and Right*, 196.

40. Will Weissert, "GOP Seeks Favor with South Texas Hispanics," *Austin American-Statesman*, November 3, 2012.

41. Melissa Del Bosque, "Meet the Middle Man," *Texas Observer*, May 6, 2011, 8.

42. Will Weissert, "AP Interview: George P. Bush Weighing Run in Texas," *Waco Tribune*, January 12, 2013.

43. Quoted in Kate Glueck, "Texas GOP Touts Its Hispanic Model," *Politico*, November 30, 2012.

44. Quoted in Glueck, "Texas GOP Touts Its Hispanic Model." In a survey by Public Policy Polling conducted on June 4–5, 2013, Texas residents were asked, "Do you support or oppose an immigration reform plan that ensures undocumented immigrants currently living in the U.S. pay a penalty, learn English, pass a criminal background check, pay taxes, and wait a minimum of thirteen years before they can be eligible for citizenship?" Overall, 46 percent strongly supported the position; among Republicans, 55 percent strongly supported with an additional 25 percent responding "somewhat support." Among Democrats, 43 percent strongly supported the proposal and 21 percent somewhat supported

it (e-mailed report from Tom Jensen, Public Policy Polling, to author, June 14, 2013).

45. Recently there has been discussion as to "symbolic ideology" versus "operational ideology" and the distinction between self-identification and policy preferences. In this context, the above discussion focuses on symbolic ideology, or the ways in which voters describe their political orientation. For more on this distinction, see Paul Brace, Kevin Arceneaux, Martin Johnson, and Stacy G. Ulbig, "Does State Political Ideology Change over Time?" *Political Research Quarterly* 57, no. 4 (December 2004); and William D. Berry, Evan J. Ringquist, Richard C. Fording, and Russell L. Hanson, "The Measurement and Stability of State Citizen Ideology," *State Politics and Policy Quarterly* 7, no. 2 (June 2007): 111–132.

46. John D. Holm and John P. Robinson, "Ideological Identification and the American Voter," *Public Opinion Quarterly* 42, no. 2 (1978): 235–246.

47. William G. Jacoby, "Ideology and Vote Choice in the 2004 Election," paper prepared for delivery at the Shambaugh Conference, "The American Voter: Change or Continuity over the Last Fifty Years," Department of Political Science, University of Iowa, May 8–10, 2008, http://myweb.uiowa.edu/bhlai/voter/paper/jacoby.pdf, accessed January 8, 2013.

48. Alan I. Abramowitz and Kyle L. Saunders, "Exploring the Bases of Partisanship in the American Electorate: Social Identity vs. Ideology," *Political Research Quarterly* 59, no. 2 (June 2006): 185.

49. Ibid., 177.

50. Eric M. Wilk, "Party and Ideological Polarization in the American Electorate," paper posted at www.thepresidency.org/storage/documents/Vater/wilk.pdf, accessed January 8, 2013.

51. Cunningham, *Cowboy Conservatism*, 5.

52. Ibid.

53. Ibid., 51.

54. University of Texas–Austin/*Texas Tribune* Texas Statewide Survey, May 2011.

55. Data from all fourteen surveys can be found at http://texaspolitics.laits.utexas.edu/11_1_0.html, accessed January 9, 2013.

56. In a 2008 exit poll, 46 percent identified as conservative, 15 percent liberal, and 39 percent moderate, as reported in Arbour and McKenzie, "Texas: After the Bush Era," in *A Paler Shade of Red*, ed. Bronwell DuBose Kapeluck, Lawrence W. Moreland, and Robert P. Steed.

57. Survey released by the University of Texas–Austin/*Texas Tribune* in October 2012, http://texaspolitics.laits.utexas.edu/11_1_0.html, accessed January 9, 2013.

58. Abramowitz and Saunders, "Exploring the Bases of Partisanship in the American Electorate," 184.

59. Susan Welch and Lee Sigelman, "The Politics of Hispanic Americans: Insights from National Surveys, 1980–1988," *Social Science Quarterly* 74, no. 1 (March 1993): 76.

60. Paul Taylor, Mark Hugo Lopez, Jessica Hamar Martinez, and Gabriel Velasco, "When Labels Don't Fit: Hispanics and Their Views of Identity," Pew

Hispanic Center, Washington, DC, www.pewhispanic.org/files/2012/04/PHC
-Hispanic-Identity.pdf, accessed January 9, 2013.

61. As cited in Jay Root, "Against the Grain, G.O.P. Dominated on Election
Day," *New York Times*, November 8, 2012. A post-election survey of Hispanic
voters found 44 percent who identified as conservative and 18 percent as liberal
(Munisteri interview, February 19, 2013). According to a recent review of mi-
nority opinions, "As one group in a state becomes more Republican (or Demo-
cratic), the other groups have a tendency to move in the same direction," and "in
Texas, Latino ideology has a conservative slant" (Barbara Norrander and Sylvia
Manzano, "Minority Group Opinion in the U.S. States," *State Politics and Policy
Quarterly* 10, no. 4 [Winter 2010]).

62. Stanford, "Texas Democrats' Conservatism Widespread Outside of
Austin."

Bibliography

Archival Sources

Allen Duckworth Papers. Dolph Briscoe Center for American History, University of Texas at Austin.

Cyndi Taylor Krier Papers, 1963–1972. University of Texas at San Antonio Libraries Special Collections.

Eugene Nolte Family Papers, 1886–1964. University of Texas at San Antonio Libraries Special Collections.

Frankie Carter Randolph Papers, 1913–1983. Fondren Library, Rice University, Houston, TX.

Harry McLeary Wurzbach Papers, 1853–1984. Dolph Briscoe Center for American History, University of Texas at Austin.

James C. Oberwetter Papers, 1963–1972. Southwestern University Special Collections, Georgetown, TX.

John G. Tower Papers. Southwestern University Special Collections, Georgetown, TX.

John Knaggs Papers. Southwestern University Special Collections, Georgetown, TX.

Mexican American Democrats of Texas Records, 1962–1987. University of Texas at San Antonio Libraries Special Collections.

Miscellaneous Primary and General Election Returns, 1960–1990. Lorenzo de Zavala State Archives and Library, Austin, TX.

Miscellaneous Primary and General Election Returns, 1992–2012. Elections Division, Secretary of State, Austin, TX. Accessed at www.sos.state.tx.us /elections/.

Norman D. Brown Collection, 1921–1933. Dolph Briscoe Center for American History, University of Texas at Austin.

Newspapers

Austin American-Statesman	*Philadelphia Daily News*
Dallas Morning News	*San Antonio Express-News*
Fort Worth Star-Telegram	*San Antonio Light*
Houston Chronicle	*Waco Tribune*
Houston Post	*Wall Street Journal*
Longview News-Journal	*Washington Post*
New York Times	*Washington Times*
Panola Watchman	

Books, Periodicals, Papers, and Interviews

Abrajano, Marisa A., and R. Michael Alvarez. "Hispanic Public Opinion and Participation in America." *Political Science Quarterly* 126, no. 2 (Summer 2011): 255–285.

———. *New Faces, New Voices: The Hispanic Electorate in America*. Princeton, NJ: Princeton University Press, 2010.

Abramowitz, Alan I., and Kyle L. Saunders. "Exploring the Bases of Partisanship in the American Electorate: Social Identity vs. Ideology." *Political Research Quarterly* 59, no. 2 (June 2006): 175–187.

Alvarez, R. Michael, and Lisa Garcia Bedolla. "The Foundations of Latino Voter Partisanship: Evidence from the 2000 Election." *Journal of Politics* 65, no. 1 (February 2003): 31–49.

Anders, Evan. *Boss Rule in South Texas*. Austin: University of Texas Press, 1982.

Anderson, Christopher. *George and Laura: Portrait of an American Marriage*. New York: William Morrow, 2002.

Angelo, Ernest, Jr. Interview. Midland, Texas, March 21, 2012.

Appleton, Andrew M., and Daniel S. Ward, eds. *State Party Profiles*. Washington, DC: Congressional Quarterly, 1997.

Arbour, Brian K., and Seth C. McKee. "Cracking Back: The Effectiveness of Partisan Redistricting in the Texas House of Representatives." *American Review of Politics* 26 (Winter 2005–2006): 385–404.

Atwood, E. Digby. *The Regional Vocabulary of Texas*. Austin: University of Texas Press, 1962.

Baggett, James A. "Birth of the Texas Republican Party." *Southwestern Historical Quarterly* 77, no. 1 (July 1974): 1–20.

Bainbridge, John. *The Super-Americans*. New York: Doubleday, 1961.

Baker, T. Lindsay. *The First Polish Americans: Silesian Settlements in Texas*. College Station: Texas A&M University Press, 1979.

Baker, Tod A. *Political Parties in the Southern States: Party Activists in Partisan Coalitions*. New York: Praeger, 1990.

Barone, Michael, and Grant Ujifusa. *The Almanac of American Politics, 1994*. Washington, DC: National Journal, 1993.

Barta, Carolyn. *Bill Clements: Texian to His Toenails*. Austin: Eakin Press, 1996.

Bartley, Numan V., and Hugh D. Graham. *Southern Politics and the Second Reconstruction*. Baltimore, MD: Johns Hopkins University Press, 1975.

Benjamin, Patricia. *The Perot Legacy: A New Political Path*. Lincoln, NE: iUniverse, 2007.

Berry, William D., Evan J. Ringquist, Richard C. Fording, and Russell L. Hanson. "The Measurement and Stability of State Citizen Ideology." *State Politics and Policy Quarterly* 7, no. 2 (June 2007): 111–132.

Bickerstaff, Steve. *Lines in the Sand*. Austin: University of Texas Press, 2007.

Billington, Monroe Lee. *The Political South in the Twentieth Century*. New York: Charles Scribner's Sons, 1975.

Black, Earl, and Merle Black. *The Rise of Southern Republicans*. Cambridge, MA: Belknap, 2002.

———. *The Vital South: How Presidents Are Elected*. Cambridge, MA: Harvard University Press, 1992.

Bowen, Michael. *The Roots of Modern Conservatism: Dewey, Taft, and the Battle for the Soul of the Republican Party*. Chapel Hill: University of North Carolina Press, 2011.

Brace, Paul, Kevin Arceneaux, Martin Johnson, and Stacy G. Ulbig. "Does State Political Ideology Change over Time?" *Political Research Quarterly* 57, no. 4 (December 2004): 529–540.

Brammer, Billy Lee. *The Gay Place*. Austin: University of Texas Press, 1961.

Bridges, Kenneth. *Twilight of the Texas Democrats*. College Station: Texas A&M University Press, 2008.

Brown, Lyle C., Joyce A. Langenegger, Sonia R. Garcia, Ted A. Lewis, and Robert E. Biles. *Practicing Texas Politics*. 13th ed. Boston: Wadsworth, 2010.

Buckley, William F., Jr. *Up from Liberalism*. New York: Hillman Books, 1961.

Buenger, Walter, and Arnoldo De Leon, eds. *Beyond Texas through Time: Breaking Away from Past Interpretations*. College Station: Texas A&M University Press, 2011.

Bullock, Charles S., III, and Mark J. Rozell, eds. *The New Politics of the Old South*. 3rd ed. Lanham, MD: Rowman and Littlefield, 2007.

Burka, Paul. "Don Yarborough's Texas." *Texas Monthly*, October 2009.

———. "The Party Never Ends!" *Texas Monthly*, June 2012.

———. "Right Place, Right Time." *Texas Monthly*, February 2010.

———. "Ticket to Ride?" *Texas Monthly*, October 1978.

Burns, Alexander. "Democrats Launch Plan to Turn Texas Blue." *Politico*, January 24, 2013.

Bush, George W. *A Charge to Keep*. New York: William Morrow, 1999.

"Business: Mad Eddie," *Time*, May 26, 1980.

Caldeira, Gregory A., and Samuel C. Patterson. "Bringing Home the Votes: Electoral Outcomes in State Legislative Races." *Political Behavior* 4 (1982): 33–67.

Calhoun, Charles W. *Conceiving a New Republic: The Republican Party and the Southern Question, 1869–1900*. Lawrence: University Press of Kansas, 2006.

Campbell, Angus, Philip E. Converse, Warren E. Miller, and Donald E. Stokes. *The American Voter: An Abridgement*. New York: John Wiley and Sons, 1964.

Campbell, Randolph B. *Gone to Texas*. New York: Oxford University Press, 2012.

————. *Sam Houston and the American Southwest*. New York: HarperCollins College, 1993.

Cannon, Lou. *Governor Reagan: His Rise to Power*. New York: Public Affairs, 2003.

Cannon, Thure Barnett. "The Texas Political System: Shifting Dynamics in Political Party Power." Master's thesis, University of Texas at Austin, 1998.

Carsey, Thomas M., and Geoffrey C. Layman. "Changing Sides or Changing Minds? Party Identification and Policy Preferences in the American Electorate." *American Journal of Political Science* 50, no. 2 (April 2006): 464–477.

Casdorph, Paul D. *A History of the Republican Party in Texas: 1865–1965*. Austin: Pemberton Press, 1965.

————. *Republicans, Negroes, and Progressives in the South, 1912–1916*. University: University of Alabama Press, 1981.

————. "Texas Delegations to Republican National Conventions, 1860–1896." Master's thesis, University of Texas, 1961.

Cash, W. J. *The Mind of the South*. New York: Alfred A. Knopf, 1944.

Champagne, Anthony, and Edward J. Harpham, eds. *Texas Politics: A Reader*. 2nd ed. New York: W. W. Norton, 1998.

Chester, Lewis, Godfrey Hodgson, and Bruce Page. *An American Melodrama: The Presidential Campaign of 1968*. New York: Dell, 1969.

Christie, Les. "The Richest (and Poorest) Places in the U.S." *Money*, August 28, 2007.

Clark, John A., and Charles L. Prysby. *Southern Political Activists: Patterns of Conflict and Change, 1991–2001*. Lexington: University Press of Kentucky, 2004.

Cohn, Nate. "A Blue Texas? Keep Dreaming." *New Republic*, November 19, 2012.

Collins, Gail. *As Texas Goes: How the Lone Star State Hijacked the American Agenda*. New York: Liveright, 2012.

Cook, Rhodes. *United States Presidential Primary Elections: 1968–1996*. Washington, DC: Congressional Quarterly, 2000.

Conger, Kimberly H. *The Christian Right in Republican State Politics*. New York: Palgrave Macmillan, 2009.

Congressional Quarterly's Guide to U.S. Elections. Washington, DC: Congressional Quarterly, 1975.

Cox, Patrick L. *Ralph W. Yarborough: The People's Senator*. Austin: University of Texas Press, 2009.

Crawford, Ann Fears. *Frankie: Mrs. R. D. Randolph and Texas Liberal Politics*. Austin: Eakin Press, 2000.

Cullen, David O'Donald, and Kyle G. Wilkison, eds. *The Texas Left: The Radical Roots of Lone Star Liberalism*. College Station: Texas A&M University Press, 2010.

Cunningham, Sean P. *Cowboy Conservatism: Texas and the Rise of the Modern Right*. Lexington: University Press of Kentucky, 2010.

Dallek, Matthew. *The Right Moment*. New York: Free Press, 2000.

Dallek, Robert. *Lone Star Rising: Lyndon Johnson and His Times, 1908–1960*. New York: Oxford University Press, 1991.

David, Paul T. *Party Strength in the United States, 1872–1970*. Charlottesville: University Press of Virginia, 1972.

Davidson, Chandler. *Race and Class in Texas Politics*. Princeton, NJ: Princeton University Press, 1990.

Davidson, Gregory Scott. "Three Phases of Republican Development and Competition in Texas, 1865–1997." Master's thesis, University of Texas at Austin, 1997.

Dear, Ronald B. Interview. Houston, Texas, May 17, 2012.

Del Bosque, Melissa. "Meet the Middle Man." *Texas Observer*, May 6, 2011.

De Leon, Arnoldo. *They Called Them Greasers*. Austin: University of Texas Press, 1983.

Dobbs, Ricky F. *Yellow Dogs and Republicans: Allan Shivers and Texas Two-Party Politics*. College Station: Texas A&M University Press, 2005.

Dyer, James A. "Implications of a Two-Party Texas." *Texas Poll Report* 6, no. 4 (Fall 1989).

Dyer, James A., Arnold Vedlitz, and David B. Hill. "New Voters, Switchers, and Political Party Realignment in Texas." *Western Political Quarterly* 41, no. 1 (March 1988): 155–167.

Eichholz, Alice, ed. *Red Book: American State, County and Town Sources*. Provo, UT: Ancestry, 2004.

Elazar, Daniel. *American Federalism: A View from the States*. New York: Thomas Y. Crowell, 1966.

Fauntroy, Michael K. *Republicans and the Black vote*. Boulder, CO: Lynne Rienner, 2007.

Fehrenbach, T. R. *Lone Star: A History of Texas and the Texans*. New York: Macmillan, 1968.

———. *Seven Keys to Texas*. El Paso: Texas Western Press, 1986.

Feldman, Glenn, ed. *Painting Dixie Red*. Gainesville: University Press of Florida, 2011.

Foley, Douglas E. *From Peonies to Politicos: Class and Ethnicity in a South Texas Town, 1900–1987*. Austin: University of Texas Press, 1988.

Foner, Eric. *Free Soil, Free Labor, Free Men: The Ideology of the Republican Party before the Civil War*. New York: Oxford University Press, 1970.

Formisano, Ronald P. *The Tea Party: A Brief History*. Baltimore, MD: Johns Hopkins University Press, 2012.

Frederickson, Kari. *The Dixiecrat Revolt and the End of the Solid South, 1932–1968*. Chapel Hill: University of North Carolina Press, 2001.

Frendreis, John P. "Migration as a Source of Changing Party Strength." *Social Science Quarterly* 70, no. 1 (March 1989): 211–220.

Galderisi, Peter F., ed. *Redistricting in the New Millennium*. Lanham, MD: Lexington Books, 2005.

Garcia, Gilbert. *Reagan's Comeback*. San Antonio, TX: Trinity University Press, 2012.

Gibson, L. Tucker, Jr., and Clay Robison. *Government and Politics in the Lone Star State: Theory and Practice*. 1st ed. Englewood Cliffs, NJ: Prentice Hall, 1993.

———. *Government and Politics in the Lone Star State: Theory and Practice*. 2nd ed. Englewood Cliffs, NJ: Prentice Hall, 1995.

———. *Government and Politics in the Lone Star State: Theory and Practice*. 3rd ed. Englewood Cliffs, NJ: Prentice Hall, 1999.

————. *Government and Politics in the Lone Star State: Theory and Practice*. 6th ed. Upper Saddle River, NJ: Pearson Prentice Hall, 2008.

Gimpel, James G., and Jason E. Schuknecht. "Interstate Migration and Electoral Politics." *Journal of Politics* 63 (February 2001), 207–231.

Glueck, Kate. "Texas GOP Touts Its Hispanic Model." *Politico*, November 30, 2012.

Goldwater, Barry M. *The Conscience of a Conservative*. Shepherdsville, KY: Victor, 1960.

Gray, Virginia, Herbert Jacob, and Kenneth N. Vines. *Politics in the American States*. 4th ed. Boston: Little, Brown, 1983.

Green, George Norris. *The Establishment in Texas Politics: The Primitive Years, 1938–1957*. Westport, CT: Greenwood, 1979.

Green, John C., Mark J. Rozell, and Clyde Wilcox, eds. *The Christian Right in American Politics*. Washington, DC: Georgetown University Press, 2003.

Greenberg, Sherri. "The New Art and Science of Texas Redistricting: What about Public Policy?" *LBJ Journal of Public Affairs* 17, no. 1 (Fall 2004): 11–16.

Greene, John Robert. *The Crusade: The Presidential Election of 1952*. Lanham, MD: University Press of America, 1985.

Grieder, Erica. *Big, Hot, Cheap, and Right: What America Can Learn from the Strange Genius of Texas*. New York: Public Affairs, 2013.

Grier, Meg McKain. *Grassroots Women*. Boerne, TX: Wingscope, 2001.

Haag, Stefan D., Gary A. Keith, and Rex C. Peebles. *Texas Politics and Government*. 3rd ed. New York: Longman, 2003.

Haberman, Maggie, and Jonathan Martin. "RNC Launches Official Review on 2012 Election." *Politico*, December 10, 2012.

Hadley, Charles D., and Lewis Bowman, eds. *Southern State Party Organizations and Activists*. Westport, CT: Praeger, 1995.

Haley, J. Evetts. *A Texan Looks at Lyndon*. Canyon, TX: Palo Duro, 1964.

Hathorn, Billy. "Mayor Ernest Angelo, Jr., of Midland and the 96–0 Reagan Sweep of Texas, May 1, 1976." *West Texas Historical Association Year Book* 86 (2010): 77–91.

Havard, William C., ed. *The Changing Politics of the South*. Baton Rouge: Louisiana State University Press, 1972.

Hayes, Danny, and Seth C. McKee. "Toward a One-Party South?" *American Politics Research* 36, no. 1 (2008): 3–32.

Hayward, Steven F. *The Age of Reagan: The Fall of the Old Liberal Order*. Roseville, CA: Forum, 2001.

Heard, Alexander. *A Two-Party South?* Chapel Hill: University of North Carolina Press, 1952.

Hogan, William Ransom. *The Texas Republic: A Social and Economic History*. Austin: University of Texas Press, 1969.

Holm, John D., and John P. Robinson. "Ideological Identification and the American Voter." *Public Opinion Quarterly* 42, no. 2 (1978): 235–246.

Hood, M. V., III, Quentin Kidd, and Irwin I. Morris. *The Rational Southerner: Black Mobilization, Republican Growth, and the Partisan Transformation of the American South*. New York: Oxford University Press, 2012.

Jacob, Herbert, and Kenneth N. Vines, eds. *Politics in the American States*. 1st ed. Boston: Little, Brown, 1965.

———. *Politics in the American States*, 3rd ed. Boston: Little, Brown, 1976.

Jacoby, William G. "Ideology and Vote Choice in the 2004 Election." Paper prepared for the Shambaugh Conference, "The American Voter: Change or Continuity over the Last Fifty Years," Department of Political Science, University of Iowa, May 8–10, 2008.

Jarboe, Jan. "Lord of the Valley." *Texas Monthly* (January 1986).

Jewell, Malcolm E., and Sarah M. Morehouse. *Political Parties and Elections in American States*. 4th ed. Washington, DC: Congressional Quarterly, 2000.

Jewell, Malcolm E., and David M. Olson. *American State Political Parties and Elections*. Homewood, IL: Dorsey, 1978.

Jordan, Terry G. "A Century and a Half of Ethnic Change in Texas: 1836–1986." *Southwestern Historical Quarterly* 89, no. 4 (1986): 389–421.

———. *Texas: A Geography*. Boulder, CO: Westview, 1984.

Kapeluck, Bronwell DuBose, Lawrence W. Moreland, and Robert P. Steed, eds. *A Paler Shade of Red: The 2008 Presidential Election in the South*. Fayetteville: University of Arkansas Press, 2009.

Keillor, Garrison. *Lake Wobegon Days*. New York: Viking Penguin, 1985.

Keith, Gary A., and Stefan D. Haag with L. Tucker Gibson Jr. and Clay Robison. *Texas Politics and Government*. 4th ed. Glenview, IL: Longman, 2012.

Key, V. O., Jr. *Southern Politics in State and Nation*. New York: Alfred A. Knopf, 1949.

Kingston, Mike, Sam Attlesey, and Mary G. Crawford, eds. *The Texas Almanac's Political History of Texas*. Austin: Eakin Press, 1992.

Knaggs, John R. *Two-Party Texas: The John Tower Era, 1961–1984*. Austin: Eakin Press, 1986.

Kotkin, Joel. "The Next Big Boom Towns in the U.S." *Forbes*, July 6, 2011.

Kraemer, Richard H., and Philip W. Barnes, eds. *Texas: Readings in Politics, Government and Public Policy*. San Francisco: Chandler, 1971.

Kraemer, Richard H., Charldean Newell, and David F. Prindle. *Essentials of Texas Politics*. 9th ed. Belmont, CA: Wadsworth, 2004.

Lamis, Alexander P. *The Two-Party South*. 2nd ed. New York: Oxford University Press, 1990.

Lind, Michael. *Made in Texas: George W. Bush and the Southern Takeover of American Politics*. New York: Basic Books, 2003.

Lublin, David. *The Republican South*. Princeton, NJ: Princeton University Press, 2004.

Lucas, J. Scott. "Political Attitudes of Suburban Texans." Master of business administration paper, University of Texas at Austin, 1984.

Lutz, Donald S., and Kent L. Tedin, eds. *Perspectives on American and Texas Politics: A Collection of Essays*. Dubuque, IA: Kendall/Hunt, 1987.

Lynch, Dudley. *Duke of Duval*. Waco: Texian Press, 1978.

Malcolm, Andrew H. *The Canadians*. New York: St. Martin's Griffin, 1991.

Mandel, Seth. "What's behind the GOP's Continuing Trouble Wooing Latino Voters?" *Commentary*, November 6, 2012.

Martin, Roscoe. *The People's Party in Texas*. Austin: University of Texas Press, 1970.

Mason, Robert. *The Republican Party and American Politics from Hoover to Reagan*. Cambridge, U.K.: Cambridge University Press, 2012.

Maxwell, William E., Ernest Crain, and Adolfo Santos. *Texas Politics Today*. Boston: Wadsworth Cengage, 2010.

Mayer, George H. *The Republican Party, 1854–1966*. New York: Oxford University Press, 1967.

Mazmanian, Daniel A. *Third Parties in Presidential Elections*. Washington, DC: Brookings Institution, 1974.

McCleskey, Clifton. *The Government and Politics of Texas*. Boston: Little, Brown, 1963.

McClure, Frederick. Interview. Miller Center, University of Virginia, September 20, 2001. http://millercenter.org/president/bush/oralhistory/frederick-mc clure. Accessed July 13, 2012.

McKee, Seth C. *Republican Ascendancy in Southern U.S. House Elections*. Boulder, CO: Westview, 2010.

Meinig, D. W. *Imperial Texas: An Interpretive Essay in Cultural Geography*. Austin: University of Texas Press, 1985.

Menefee, Hawkins Henley, Jr. "The Two-Party Democrats, the Study of a Political Faction." Master's thesis, University of Texas at Austin, 1970.

Miller, Char, ed. *Fifty Years of the "Texas Observer."* San Antonio, TX: Trinity University Press, 2004.

Moakley, Maureen, ed. *Party Realignment and State Politics*. Columbus: Ohio State University Press, 1992.

Moneyhon, Carl H. *Edmund J. Davis: Civil War General, Republican Leader, Reconstruction Governor*. Fort Worth: Texas Christian University Press, 2010.

———. *Republicanism in Reconstruction Texas*. Austin: University of Texas Press, 1980.

Montejano, David. *Anglos and Mexicans in the Making of Texas, 1836–1986*. Austin: University of Texas Press, 1987.

Moulitsas, Markos. "GOP Needs Latino Vote." *The Hill*, November 27, 2012.

Munisteri, Steve. Interview. Austin, Texas, February 19, 2013.

Murray, Richard. "The 1982 Texas Election in Perspective." *Texas Journal of Political Studies* 5 (Spring 1983): 49–54.

Nesbit, Dorothy Davidson. "Changing Partisanship among Southern Party Activists." *Journal of Politics* 50, no. 2 (1988): 322–334.

Norrander, Barbara, and Sylvia Manzano. "Minority Group Opinion in the U.S. States." *State Politics and Policy Quarterly* 10, no. 4 (Winter 2010): 446–483.

O'Connor, Stephen. *Orphan Trains*. Chicago: University of Chicago Press, 2004.

Olien, Roger. *From Token to Triumph*. Dallas: Southern Methodist University Press, 1982.

Olson, David M. "Towards a Typology of County Party Organizations." *Southwestern Social Science Quarterly* 48 (1968): 558–572.

Pauken, Thomas W. *The Thirty Years War: The Politics of the Sixties Generation*. Ottawa, IL: Jameson Books, 1995.

Phillips, Kevin P. *The Emerging Republican Majority*. New Rochelle, NY: Arlington House, 1969.

Pitre, Merline. *Through Many Dangers, Toils and Snares: Black Leadership in Texas, 1868–1900*. Austin: Eakin Press, 1985.

Pool, William C. *An Historical Atlas of Texas*. Austin: Encino, 1975.

Posner, Gerald. *Citizen Perot: His Life and Times*. New York: Random House, 1996.

Reagan, Ronald. *An American Life*. New York: Simon and Schuster, 1990.

Reid, Jan. *Let the People In: The Life and Times of Ann Richards*. Austin: University of Texas Press, 2012.

"Republicans: Reagan's Startling Texas Landslide." *Time*, May 10, 1976.

Rhodes, Terrel L. *Republicans in the South: Voting for the State House, Voting for the White House*. Westport, CT: Praeger, 2000.

Richards, David. *Once upon a Time in Texas: A Liberal in the Lone Star State*. Austin: University of Texas Press, 2002.

Riding, Alan. *Distant Neighbors*. New York: Vantage Books, 2000.

Rosenstone, Steven J., Roy L. Behr, and Edward H. Lazarus. *Third Parties in America*. Princeton, NJ: Princeton University Press, 1984.

Rossinow, Doug. *The Politics of Authenticity: Liberalism, Christianity, and the New Left in America*. New York: Columbia University Press, 1998.

Rove, Karl. *Courage and Consequence: My Life as a Conservative in the Fight*. New York: Threshold Editions, 2010.

Rozell, Mark J., and Clyde Wilcox, eds. *God at the Grass Roots, 1996*. Lanham, MD: Rowman and Littlefield, 1997.

Sabato, Larry J. *Pendulum Swing*. Boston: Longman, 2011.

Sanford, William Reynolds. "History of the Republican Party in the State of Texas." Master's thesis, University of Texas at Austin, 1954.

Schweizer, Peter, and Rochelle Schweizer. *The Bushes: Portrait of a Dynasty*. New York: Doubleday, 2004.

Seagull, Louis M. *Southern Republicanism*. New York: Schenkman, 1975.

Self, Natasha Nicole. "The Religious Right and the Texas Republican Party." Honors thesis, University of Texas at Austin, 2002.

Sherman, Richard B. *The Republican Party and Black America: From McKinley to Hoover, 1896–1933*. Charlottesville: University Press of Virginia, 1973.

Shirley, Craig. *Reagan's Revolution: The Untold Story of the Campaign That Started It All*. Nashville: Nelson Current, 2005.

———. *Rendezvous with Destiny: Ronald Reagan and the Campaign That Changed America*. Wilmington, DE: ISI Books, 2009.

Shropshire, Mike, and Frank Schaefer. *The Thorny Rose of Texas*. New York: Birch Lane, 1994.

Skocpol, Theda, and Rebecca Williamson. *The Tea Party and the Remaking of Republican Conservatism*. New York: Oxford University Press, 2012.

Skrabanek, Robert L. *We're Czechs*. College Station: Texas A&M University Press, 1989.

Soukup, James R., Clifton McCleskey, and Harry Holloway. *Party and Factional Division in Texas*. Austin: University of Texas Press, 1964.

Stanley, Harold W. "Southern Partisan Changes: Dealignment, Realignment or Both?" *Journal of Politics* 50 (1988): 64–88.

Steed, Robert P., Lawrence W. Moreland, and Tod A. Baker, eds. *Party Politics in the South*. New York: Praeger, 1980.

Stowers, Carlton. *Where Dreams Die Hard: A Small American Town and Its Six-Man Football Team*. Cambridge, MA: Da Capo, 2005.

Strickland, Kristi Throne. "The Significance and Impact of Women on the Rise of the Republican Party in Twentieth Century Texas." PhD diss., University of North Texas, August 2000.

Strong, Donald S. *The 1952 Presidential Election in the South*. University: Bureau of Public Administration, University of Alabama, 1955.

"Studies of Political Statistics: Straight Ticket Voting in Texas, 1998–2012." Report no. 8. Center for Public Policy and Political Studies, Austin Community College, Austin, TX. December 2012.

Swansbrough, Robert H., and David M. Brodsky, eds. *The South's New Politics: Realignment and Dealignment*. Columbia: University of South Carolina Press, 1988.

Taylor, Paul, Mark Hugo Lopez, Jessica Hamar Martinez, and Gabriel Velasco. "When Labels Don't Fit: Hispanics and Their Views of Identity." Pew Hispanic Center, Washington, DC. www.pewhispanic.org/files/2012/04/PHC.

Tedin, Kent L., and Richard W. Murray. "The Dynamics of Candidate Choice in a State Election." *Journal of Politics* 31 (May 1981): 435–455.

Texas Almanac, 1961–1962 (Dallas: A. H. Belo Company, 1961).

Texas Almanac, 1992–93 (Dallas: Dallas Morning News, 1991).

Texas Almanac, 2000–2001 (Dallas: Dallas Morning News, 1999).

Texas Almanac, 2004–2005 (Dallas: Dallas Morning News, 2003).

"Texas: Rallying to Resign." *Time*, October 27, 1961.

Thompson, Kenneth. "Texas: A One-Party State." *New Guard*, July 1965.

Thorburn, Wayne. *A Generation Awakes: Young Americans for Freedom and the Creation of the Conservative Movement*. Ottawa, IL: Jameson Books, 2010.

———. "The Growth of Republican Representation in the Texas Legislature: Coattails, Incumbency, Special Elections, and Urbanization." *Texas Journal of Political Studies* 11, no. 2 (1991): 16–28.

Tolleson-Rinehart, Sue, and Jeanie R. Stanley. *Claytie and the Lady: Ann Richards, Gender, and Politics in Texas*. Austin: University of Texas Press, 1994.

Tower, John G. *Consequences: A Personal and Political Memoir*. Boston: Little, Brown, 1991.

———. *A Program for Conservatives*. New York: A Macfadden Capitol Hill Book, 1962.

Untermeyer, Chase. Interview. Miller Center, University of Virginia, July 27–28, 2000. http://millercenter.org/president/bush/oralhistory/chase-untermeyer. Accessed June 9, 2013.

Walton, Hanes, Jr. *Black Republicans: The Politics of the Black and Tans*. Metuchen, NJ: Scarecrow, 1975.

Weeks, O. Douglas. "Republicanism and Conservatism in the South." *Southwestern Social Science Quarterly* 36 (December 1955): 248–256.

———. *Texas One-Party Politics in 1956*. Austin: Institute of Public Affairs, University of Texas, 1957.

———. *Texas Presidential Politics in 1952*. Austin: Institute of Public Affairs, University of Texas, 1953.

Welch, Susan, and Lee Sigelman. "The Politics of Hispanic Americans: Insights from National Surveys, 1980–1988." *Social Science Quarterly* 74, no. 1 (March 1993): 76–94.

White, F. Clifton. *Suite 3505: The Story of the Draft Goldwater Movement*. New Rochelle, NY: Arlington House, 1967.

White, Theodore H. *The Making of the President, 1968*. New York: Atheneum, 1969.

Wilk, Eric M. "Party and Ideological Polarization in the American Electorate." Paper posted at www.thepresidency.org/storage/documents/Vater/wilk.pdf. Accessed January 8, 2013.

Wilkie, David T. "The Emergence of Two Party Competition in Texas, 1952–1982." Bachelor of arts thesis, Princeton University, 1984.

Wilson, James Q. *The Amateur Democrat: Club Politics in Three Cities*. Chicago: University of Chicago Press, 1962.

Wood, Virginia B. "We Gotcha Kolache." *Texas Monthly*, November 1998.

Woodard, J. David. *The New Southern Politics*. Boulder: Lynne Rienner, 2006.

Wyly, Sam, and Andrew Wyly. *Texas Got It Right*. New York: Melcher Media, 2012.

Young, William "Peck." Interview. Austin Community College Center for Public Policy and Political Studies, Austin, Texas, August 7, 2012.

Index

presidential election: of 1912, 48, 49, 50; of 1920, 48, 49, 52; of 1928, 42, 47, 48, 49; of 1932, 49, 52, 53; of 1936, 48, 49; of 1940, 49, 50, 53, 54, 61, 110, 242n36, 243n44; of 1944, 49, 57, 61, 242n36; of 1948, 49, 54, 57, 58, 59, 61, 90, 110, 242n36; of 1952, 42, 48, 55, 60–65, 90, 98, 106, 110–111, 114, 116, 242n36, 243n44, 244n71, 245n78, 246n106, 248n37; of 1956, 55, 63, 67, 90, 116, 242n36; of 1960, vii, viii, 63, 65, 71, 72, 73, 75, 76, 90, 91, 136, 137, 168, 245n86, 260n5; of 1964, 56, 76, 93, 102, 127, 137; of 1968, 76, 91, 101, 103, 126–129, 137, 247n12; of 1972, 75, 76, 91, 115, 116, 133, 136–138; of 1976, 75, 76, 91, 92, 101, 106, 116–121, 129–131, 136–137, 169–170, 230; of 1980, 131–132, 136–139, 149, 168; of 1984, 132, 133, 139; of 1988, 133, 139, 227; of 1992, 9, 139, 168; of 1996, 9, 139, 159, 167–171; of 2000, 169–171, 220; of 2004, 136, 170–171; of 2008, 169–171, 189, 218, 222; of 2012, 169–171, 189, 211, 218, 221–223, 231
"Presidential Republicans," 93
Price, Bob, 80, 84
pride and patriotism (of Texan), 1–3
primary participation: in 1960–1978, 90–96; in 1978–1996, 158–162; in 1996–2012, 197–207
Project 230, 123, 124
Pryor, Molly, 100

Quirk, Tom, 103
Quist, Terry, 101

Radical Republicans, 43, 44, 235n4
Railroad Commission of Texas, 18, 141
Rainey, Homer, 55, 56, 110, 244n57
Rains County, 132
Ramsey, Ross, 216

Rand, Ayn, 74
Randall County, 34, 35, 138, 161, 191, 204, 210, 239n9
Randolph, R. D. "Frankie," 63, 74, 111, 112, 251n50
Ranney, Austin, 81, 83, 247n21
Rayburn, Sam, 58
Reagan, Ronald: and Clements campaign, 121, 124; and conservatism, 230; generational impact of, 149, 153, 155, 192, 214; and 1968 campaign, 126–129; and 1976 campaign, 93, 116, 119, 124, 129–132, 254n123; and 1980 campaign, 132–134, 145, 149, 260n5
Reagan County, 224
Real, Julius, 80, 242n32
Reconstruction, the, viii, 6, 18, 42, 43, 45, 46, 47, 74, 240nn4,10
redistricting, 178–185, 187, 216, 255n9, 259n68, 262nn34,38
Reid, Jan, 172
Religious Right, the, 133, 214, 258n48, 265n6
Republican, Mr., 57–61
Republican National Convention: 1920, 52; 1928, 47; 1948, 58; 1952, 64; 1968, 127
Republican women, 106–108
resignation rallies, 99
Reuters/IPSOS exit poll, 219, 227, 265n3, 266nn13,14, 268n38
Richards, Ann, 40, 111, 117, 119, 142, 171, 172, 182, 227
Richards, David, 73, 74
Richardson, Texas, 27
Rio Grande Valley, 2, 10, 20, 35, 190, 210, 224, 260n10
Robertson County, 43
Rockefeller, Nelson, 127, 129
Rockwall County, 29, 32, 161, 201, 202, 239n1, 264n78
Rodham, Hillary, 116
Roman Catholic Church, 5, 6, 19, 42, 71
Romney, Mitt: conservatives and, 231; and Hispanic vote, 218–219,